A Radical Manifesto for the Control of Crime, Lawlessness and Disorder

Local, Regional, International Documents in Words and Pictures

By

Andy A. Burkett

authorHOUSE

AuthorHouse™
1663 Liberty Drive
Bloomington, IN 47403
www.authorhouse.com
Phone: 833-262-8899

Published by AuthorHouse 03/24/2023

ISBN: 978-1-4184-7768-4 (sc)
ISBN: 978-1-4184-9208-3 (e)

Print information available on the last page.

Any people depicted in stock imagery provided by Getty Images are models, and such images are being used for illustrative purposes only. Certain stock imagery © Getty Images.

This book is printed on acid-free paper.

THIS BOOK IS DEDICATED TO ALL THE VICTIMS OF CRIME, ESPECIALLY THOSE MAIMED, MURDERED, OR RAPED BY THOSE WHO WITH CRIMINAL PREDATORY INSTINCT.

TO ALL THOSE LAW-ABIDING WHO KEEP OUR SOCIETY FREE FROM CRIMINAL ANARCHY, LAWLESSNESS AND INDISCIPLINE.

TO THE LAWENFORCEMENT AGENCIES DEDICATED BY VIRTUE OF THEIR OFFICE TO FIGHT THE SCOURGE OF CRIME.

INCLUDING THE FORENSIC SCIENTISTS, CORONER, CRIMINOLOGISTS RESEARCHERS WHO HAVE INVENTED, DEVELOPED INDEFATIGABLY CRIME METHODS AND TOOLS TO APPREHEND THE CRIMINAL.

UNLIKE SPORTS AND ENTERTAINMENT, YOU HAVE NO ADMIRABLE,CHEERING FANS; BUT YOU LIKE OTHER SCIENTISTS WHO HAVE IMPROVED THE CONDITIONS OF HUMAN LIFE, ARE THE UNRECOGNISED HEROES OF OUR SOCIETIES.

ANDY A. BURKETT

2003

ABOUT THE AUTHOR

Andy A. Burkett attended Shorter College, Wilberforce University and Atlanta University, U.S.A.

He has been in the filed of research at: the US Government and Business Division, Cincinnati/Hamilton County Library, Ohio, Trinidad Public Library, in the government service Ministry of Petroleum and Mines, Ministry of External Affair, Ministry of Foreign Affairs, Court of Appeal, Research Officer, Regional Council, Community Police, North Eastern Division.

He has done a number of research papers on crime which include:
"The relationship between alcohol and crime" 31 pages, March 1996,
"The high cost of crime to taxpayers" 20 pages, January 1998,
"SPEED-The automobile as a killing machine" 20 pages, 15 pages, 1998,
"Policing the nation of Trinidad and Tobago" 31 pages, January 2000,
"Proposal for a law to deal with delinquent parents of juvenile delinquents in matters of crime" 24 pages, October 2000.

He has completed a 296 pages documented in words and pictures manuscript titled "Manifesto for the control of crime, lawlessness and disorder" to be submitted for publishing.

On race relations he has published in 2003 a 225 pages book documented in words and pictures titled "The Christian church: racial discrimination, gender discrimination against women, financial discrimination, ecclesiastical grants government funding of the churches" and he has completed a 104 pages documented in words and pictures manuscript titled "Racism against peoples of Indian origin from India, Pakistan, Bangladesh, West Indies, Caribbean, South America living in Canada, England, South Africa and U.S.A."(Part one) and "Who were the first known native people of India as stated by Indian scholars in India and the government of India? (Part two)" to be submitted for publishing.

TABLE OF CONTENTS

PREFACE

STATEMENT OF THE PROBLEM:

Crime is one of the biggest debacle of iniquity to strike a country. Let me expand on that-"high levels of crime"- since crime exist everywhere humans abode, but the level of crime differ relatively.

It is like a tornado, a hurricane of cataclysmic proportions-it is destructive,it not only destroys life but it can wreck the economy of a country, it is of a consequence that criminals will strike down anything that stand in their pursuit of lawless dominance.

Because of modern technology, rapid modes of transportation and communication allows for trans-border criminal transfer of activities. Criminal activities have become increasingly sophisticated as they seek to use every imaginative, intelligent method to defy and cover-up their nefarious deeds. Criminals are far more organized in their pursuits than those who abide by laws.

Obversely crime fighters have had to develop countervailing ingenious methods to curtail the attacking onslaught of perverted demonic minds. This is an ongoing effort of passionate dedication of sleuth-hounds known as detectives and forensic scientists, the crime pathologists and criminologists. May they prevail in this "war against crime."

RATIONALE:

There have been many initiatives undertaken by governments around the world as has police agencies worldwide, joint efforts have criss-cross international boundaries in effortless inter-communications- such as Interpol the International Police Criminal Commision and Europol.

Police services have had to form new squads, units and task forces as new methods of crime have grown by leaps and bounds. High tech cyber crimes,internet viruses, cell phone encryption, money laundering, industrial espionage, stock brokers insider-trading are but some of the new police units formed to counter these problematic menaces.

All of these efforts of lawful combatants cost money, because it must be spent if the law-abiding are to survive. But it is a double edge sword since the criminals affect the growth of legitimate revenue of governments, businesses and families.

The fear of crime run tourists away from ports of call, businesses close down and move to safer haven countries with less crime and so too do families of financial means to do so and the rebound is increase taxation, government budgets increase to fight crime and it is the taxpayers that stand the measures by having to pay for law enforcement amenities.Windows and doors are doubled with iron encasement and businesses employ security guards adding financial burdens.

Violence at high schools have grown and some labelled"high risk," walls around schools have been built with security guards and added budgetary cost.   e

To comprehend the magnitude of these problems is what has occupied my thoughts for a long time. Much has been said by many about the causes of crime, the sociology of crime, and many have looked at it from different angles.

I have wished to contribute, to making a dent that would in some way ameliorate, better the conditions under which crime thrives and for this reason therefore it is necessary for me to bring the subject of crime to the forefront, knowing full well that it is a transboundry problem that requires transnational co-operation. Hence my effort to convey my opinions by publishing this book.

METHODICAL PROCEDURES:

I have developed over the years my own personal collection of resource materials local,regional and international on a number of subjects which I perceive are factors that engender criminal behaviour.

I have looked at incarceration prison figures annually and have noted the heavy expense that the state which is really the taxpayers have to pay to maintain the prison system. I have noted that the ratio of women imprisoned are so few in comparison to the huge volume of predominantly men that make up the prison population. I have noted the increase of youthful offenders.

Others may wish to provide answers other than that which is in this book, I have chosen these subjects in the table of contents and have amplified on them from different perspectives. What is even valuable to the readers of this book, is that for whatever opinions I have deduced, I have supplied documents which I have assessed, and culminate with recommendation

CONCLUSION:

The embodiment of all that has preceded before in statements made and documents supplied are condensed synpotically into a numerical engrossment of ideas as solutions and classed as recommendations.

Andy A. Burkett
2003

CHAPTER 1. GOVERNMENTS CHANGE BUT UNCONTROLLED CRIME REMAIN.

I wish to present the readers of this" manifesto on the control of crime lawlessness and disorder" with a brief chronology of stakeholders' efforts to provide solutions effective of a visible drastic reduction of crime 1994 to 2002.

Such stakeholders are: The Government, Police,U.W.I University Center for Criminology, Media, Downtown Merchants Association(D.O.M.A), political parties, Businessmen Association and the Chambers of Commerce. There may be others, but these are the most prominent(supporting documents included).

1994
TRINDAD & TOBAGO CHAMBER OF COMMERCE

"Invites you to searching for solutions on crime. A public meeting on the growing crime crisis in Trinidad & Tobago. Change T & T on Monday March 21, from 9.00am to 5.00pm at Queens Hall."

1995
PEOPLES NATIONAL MOVEMENT(P.N.M PARTY)
GENERAL ELECTIONS POSTER NOVEMBER 6,1995

"We share a desire of all citizens for a greater security for themselves, their families,their properties. The PNM Government aware of the scourge of drug trafficking and the unacceptable high incidences of crime, will ensure that the police are afforded improved surveillance and detection capability. In the 1995 PNM Manifesto, the measures the PNM Government has put in place to increase the police and the administration of justice are:

- An ambitious police station rebuilding programme.
- More than 650 new police vehicles.
- One way mirrors for ID parades.
- Increase community police patrols in conjunction with neighbourhood watch groups.
- Tougher dangerous drugs and firearms legislation.
- Introduction of night courts

MONDAY NOVEMBER 6, 1995 VOTE P.N.M

1995
UNITED NATIONAL CONGRESS(U.N.C PARTY)
GENERAL ELECTIONS POSTER UNC CANDIDATE

For Barataria/San Juan, November 6,1995,FIGHT CRIME VOTE UNC, DR FUAD KHAN. Give yourselves a chance.

1995
UNITED NATIONAL CONGRESS(U.N.C) poster letter For general elections Monday November 6, 1995
"THE UNC CRIME & DRUGS SOLUTION

Dear Neighbour,

I will work to get tough on crime and drugs, provide training and equipment for police and make sure if bandits and murderers do crime, they will do time.

On November 6 please vote U.N.C to give yourself a chance."

Dr. Fuad Khan

THE U.N.C PLAN

- Outfit the police with the equipment necessary to fight violent crime.
- Provide basic training for the police to:
  Control systematic investigations
  Break up suspicious activities before crimes are committed.
- Give swift punishment to criminals who break the law through more
- Judges and expanding the court system.

DO YOU FEEL SAFER NOW THAN YOU DID FOUR YEARS AGO?
IF THE ANSWER IS NO PNM MUST GO."

1995
" WORKING GROUP IN CARIBBEAN CRIMINOLOGY
UNIVERSITY OF THE WEST INDIES
ST AUGUSTINE CAMPUS
TRINIDAD

NATIONAL ACTION PLAN AGAINST CRIME
DECEMBER 11, 1995
PAGE 14. GOVERNMENT—U.W.I TALKS ON CRIME

Presentation of the 12 point national action plan against crime

1996

Presented to the government on January 27,1996, pages 18-25, 12 Point National Action Plan Against Crime(N.A.P.A.C), Causes, Pevention, Management and Training(two year target).Pages 26-27: 30 Conclusion and Implementation Plan submitted to government on behalf of the Working Group in Caribbean Criminology.

Ramesh Deosaran.,Ph.D
Deputy Dean(Research & Publications)
Chairman,Working Group Caribbean Criminology."

1997

"Inferential Leap" INDEPENDENT NEWSPAPER, Tuesday December 9,1997, page 8. Editorial by the editor.

"The address to the nation delivered by Prime Minister Basdeo Panday code named 'Operation Leap' (LAW ENFORCEMENT ACTION PLAN).

The initiative mobilizes all personnel and other resources of the police, army and other national security services in a zero tolerance onslaught against the criminal coalitions and the desperate criminal elements.

The plan calls for combined police, military roadblock at strategic points and a dedicated phone lines(624-LEAP) through which citizens can contact the police 24 hours a day. All of this follows on OTHER INITIATIVES of the government has taken two years ago…

DESPITE ALL OF THIS THE CRIME SITUATION HAS CONTINUED UNABATED AND IN SOME RESPECTS HAVE GROWN WORST since Mr Panday's government came into power. **CLEARLY IT WILLTAKE MORE THAN GREATER POLICING TO ARREST THE DETERIORATION."**

1999

"Public Enemy No 1" EXPRESS NEWSAPER Monday January 4, 1999. Editorial by the editor.

"When the government of the United National Congress(UNC) then in coalition with the National Alliance for Reconstruction(NAR) came to power just over three years ago, A MAJOR PLANK IN ITS ELECTION PLATFORM WAS THE PROMISE TO DEAL WITH CRIME.

It is a promise given great emphasis both by Prime Minister Basdeo Panday and Attorney General Ramesh Lawrence Maharaj… and IF THREE YEARS AGO THE UNC IDENTIFIED CRIME AS PUBLIC ENEMY NO 1, IT IS NO LESS SO TODAY.

It is not that we doubt the sincerity of the government's promise or intent. But the evidence is mounting that nothing that the government has done to date has really had any serious impact on the ease with which people continue to be murdered, raped and robbed.

THE GOVERNMENT IT IS CLEAR NEEDS TO TAKE A SECOND LOOK AT ITS ANTI-CRIME PLAN…BUT THE LAW-ABIDING CITIZENS OF THIS COUNTRY ARE FACING YET ANOTHER GRAVE THREAT TO THEIR PERSONAL SECURITY. We are yet to be convinced that the threat is being adequately dealt with."

2000

" Fiddiling with crime" NEWSDAY NEWSPAPER Sunday July 30, 2000, page 10. Editorial by the editor.

"It is silly for any politician to think that quoting statistics about the level of extent of criminal activity during the P.N.M or U.N.C administration, will in any way EASE THE ANXIETY OF T & T's LAW-ABIDING POPULATION.

While leaders of the U.N.C and the P.N.M in their pre-election battle shooot each other with statistics about the levels during their respective administration, THE SOCIETY REMAINS UNDER SEIGE. What do they plan to do about it? "

2001

(Full Page Advertisement of the P.N.M) EXPRESS NEWSPAPER FRIdAY November 30, 2001, page 39

"Performance? What performance? Real crime under the U.N.C:
Shootings and robberies increased 12%, murder, fraud increased 28.4%
Number of cases solved declined from 33% to 27%, Tobago saw crime increased 19.2 %, this UNC government increased its spending on National Security by 7.9%.
SAVE T & T VOTE PNM."

2001

(Full page advertisement of the P.N.M Party) NEWSDAY NEWSPAPER Friday November 30, 2001, page 4, Section 1

"Performance What Performance?
THE TRUE CRIME REPORT IN T & T
In 1995, the UNC said Trinidad and Tobago was not safe…and asked for your vote because 'the nation is in crisis'
ARE YOU SAFER NOW?! CRIME INCREASED IN EVERY YEAR SINCE 1995 THE COUNTRY IS NOW IN THE HANDS OF LAW-BREAKERS SAVE T & T VOTE PNM,PEOPLES NATIONAL MOVENENT"

2002

"Minister declares prolonged WAR ON CRIME" by Ria Taitt NEWSDAY NEWSPAPER Tuesday February 26, 2002, page 3

"DECLARING DESPERATE TIMES CALL FOR DESPERATE MEASURES, NATIONAL SECURITY MINISTER HOWARD CHIN LEE promised that in this prolonged war, government was prepared to do whatever it takes within the bounds of the law including limited curfews in high crime hot spot areas.

He didn't identify the areas, although 'OPERATION ANACONDA ' which is one element of the plan has been targeting Laventille and the Beetham.

Speaking at the formal launch of his WAR ON CRIME AT THE HILTON HOTE, Chin Lee presented the most aggressive assault ever on crime in this country... some of the features the plan have been borrowed from the USA/USA criminal expert , Dr Robin Engel had stated earlier that US Criminologist had developed the 'broken window' theory in which they argued that small social disorders such as ABANDONED BUILDINGS, LITTER, TRASH,PUBLIC INTOXICATION, VAGRANCY,LOITERING OF JUVENILES eventually led to a spiral of disorder and decline in neighbourhoods."

In this chapter I have provided a record of statements of efforts made by diverse stakeholders in the fight against the crime menace which has become a national plague. These diverse efforts are A CHRONOLOGY OF AN EIGHT YEAR SPAN 1994—2002.

From 2002, now we have entered the year 2003, and around the world countries are bombarded by criminal acts some to a greater or lesser extent. However law and order in societies are under attack. Who are the protagonists? what are the causes? what can be done to protect the rule of law.?

Crime can be described as a "tumor" which is requiring constant incisions to delay its growth; it is surgery for a sick society and the yearly prognosis is bad indeed. Civil society is under threat of anarchy and all of us have been called-that is the law-abiding have been call to close ranks against this menace. We are led down a road where we self-destruct, some elements of society spur on no rules of conduct of civility and they have an abhorrence for anything orderly. Even entertainers subtly use words in songs "get on bad," "misbehave," "mash up the place."

Their choice of words encourage rude boys, rude girls,ragamuffins and vagabonds who strive on the permissiveness and laxity of society and provide a ground for slackness. Checks and balances must always be put in place and maintained as the meridian guide of containment and stability.

On January 14,2000 I provided a research paper "POLICING THE NATION OF TRINIDAD AND TOBAGO" I suggested and with documentations the need for a law that will allow the police via the courts to be allowed to intercept mail and tap/bug phones/cell phone eavesdropping of suspected and known criminals as part of police intelligence gathering and information surveillance co-ordination(pages 1,2,11 and 12).

In police communications/observance systems I suggested the use of thermal imaging zoom cameras used in the under-belly of surveillance aircrafts,heat scanning devices with heat sensing equipment(pages 3,6,13,15)

Vehicular traffic video cameras scanners on selected streets and police cars; and station close circuit television monitors of selected streets(pages 5,6,16,18).

In police identification systems, I suggested the use of integrated multifunction computers fitting of police cars with computer consoles capable of bringing-up the photo or mug-shot and criminal record of legal name and address of owner or anyone stopped by the police.

Look up car number plates stolen or otherwise, voice activated allowing police officers to speak into computers without having to drive back to the station precincts, and hooked up also to Transport Licensing Department.

Computer database on fingerprints, with cross-checking, criminal records history, missing persons,illegal aliens and deported persons,stolen firearms/firearms records and portable finger print equipment of a small reader on which a suspect's fingers are placed on a small reader while the computer automatically relay back to police station precinct from the police car(pages 4,5).

High density mapping of "crime hot spots and methods of control(pages 7,8,20,21,23).

9:00a.m. to 5:00p.m.
MONDAY MARCH 21ST
QUEEN'S HALL
AMONG PROBLEMS TO BE SOLVED:
• *The Narcotics Problem*
• *Illegal Firearms*
• *The Crime Detection Fund* ✔
• *Improving the Quality of Police Training*
• *Witness Protection*
• *Identification Parades*
• *Granting of Bail*

Whether it's the day or just an hour, you
must attend and make your contribution.
Remember, crime affects everyone.

Call the Chamber at **624-6082**

CHANGE T&T

The T&T Chamber of Industry and Commerce invites you to

Searching for Solutions on
CRIME

**A PUBLIC MEETING ON THE GROWING CRISIS
IN CRIME IN TRINIDAD & TOBAGO**

8
Crime
Prevention

We share the desire of all citizens for a greater feeling of security for themselves, their families and their property. The measures the PNM Government has put in place to increase Police effectiveness and improve the administration of justice are beginning to make a difference:

- an ambitious Police station rebuilding programme

- more than 650 new Police vehicles

- one-way mirrors for ID parades

- increased community Police patrols in conjunction with Neighbourhood Watch groups

- tougher dangerous drugs and firearms legislation

- introduction of night court

- more courts and judicial officers

- additional Coast Guard bases and faster patrol

"The PNM Government, aware of the scourge of drug trafficking and the unacceptably high incidence of crime, will ensure that the police are afforded improved surveillance and detection capability."

1995 PNM Man...

MON. 6TH NOVEMBER '95
VOTE
PNM

7

FIGHT CRIME
VOTE

DR. FUAD KHAN
San Juan/Barataria
"Give Yourself a Chance"

THE UNC CRIME & DRUGS
SOLUTION

Dear Neighbour,

I will work to get tough on crime and drugs, provide training and equipment for police, and make sure that if bandits and murderers do the crime, they will do the time.

Dr. Fuad Khan
San Juan / Barataria

On November 6, please vote UNC to give yourself a chance.

THE UNC PLAN

- Dr. Fuad Khan

> Outfit the police with the equipment necessary to combat violent crime.

> Provide better training for the police to:

- conduct systematic investigations

- break up suspicious activities before crimes are committed.

Give swift punishment to criminals who break the law appointment of more judges and expanding the courts system

Trinidad Guardian November 13,1995

THE WORKING GROUP IN CARIBBEAN CRIMINOLOGY

received a cheque from **Nationwide Insurance Co. Ltd.** and **Presidential Insurance Co. Ltd.** for $10,000. This donation was presented to The Faculty of Social Sciences on October 10th, 1995. The presentation was made at St. Augustine Campus at the Psychological Research Centre, the Working Group's Administrative Base.

Working Group members discuss crime prevention/management proposals. Seated from left to right are Mr. Kenneth Lalla, Professor Richard Bennett, Dr. Ramesh Deosaran and Dr. Patrick Watson.

MEMBERS

The Faculty of Social Sciences also wishes to acknowledge the professional support and assistance of the members of the Working Group in Caribbean Criminology which is chaired by Dr. Ramesh Deosaran: Professor Richard Bennett, Professor of Criminal Justice, The American University, USA; Mr. Kenneth Lalla, Chairman, Police & Public Service Commissions; Mr. Jules Bernard, Commissioner of Police; Supt. Mr. James Clarkson, Royal Grenada Police Force; Ms. Shirley Christian-Maharaj, Acting Senior Statistician, Central Statistical Office; Dr. Hamid Ghany, Political Scientist; Professor Jagan Lingamneni, Coordinator of Criminal Justice, Governors State University, USA; Mr. Frank Mouttet, Former President, Chamber of Industry and Commerce; Mr. Vasant Ramkissoon, Acting Asst. Chief Probation Officer and Mrs. Jennifer Sampson, Chief Technical Officer, Ministry of Social Development; Mr. Rawle Richardson, Director of School Supervision, Ministry of Education; Acting Supt. of Prisons, Mr. Verne Sylvester, Ministry of National Security and Mr. Gordon Deane, Chief Executive Officer, Algico Insurance Company Limited.

A PARTNERSHIP WORKING AGAINST CRIME

The Working Group headed by Dr. Ramesh Deosaran, Deputy Dean and Head, Department of Sociology (Social Work & Psychology) held its in inaugural meeting at the Holiday Inn, Port of Spain on September 30, 1995. This meeting was formally opened by Dr. Patrick Watson, Dean, Faculty of Social Sciences.

WORK PLAN

At the inaugural meeting, the Working Group agreed on its mandate to work alongside governmental agencies and the police to help develop a coordinated approach to deal with crime having among its priorities juvenile crimes, domestic violence, drug trafficking and the relationship between socio-economic conditions and deviance. The Group intends to use its expertise in social work, psychology, sociology and criminology to collaborate with the protective and prison services, judiciary and the other agencies in dealing with crime and justice in Trinidad and other parts of the Caribbean.

12–POINT NATIONAL ACTION PLAN AGAINST CRIME (NAPAC)

CAUSES, PREVENTION, MANAGEMENT AND TRAINING
(Two-Year Target)

1.0 BACKGROUND

1.1   At its inaugural meeting at the Holiday Inn on Saturday September 30, 1995, and through subsequent consultations, the Working Group in Caribbean Criminology established by the University of the West Indies agreed to develop a public policy and action plan package for submission to the Government. This document contains the National Action Plan Against Crime (NAPAC)

1.2   This National Action Plan Against Crime has also been scrutinised and strongly recommended by several international experts in crime prevention and crime management; some of them are members of our Working Group in Caribbean Criminology (for example, Professor Richard Bennett of the American University; Professor Daniel Maier-Katkin of Florida State University; Professor Jagan Lingamneni, Illinois State University).

Inferential LEAP

THE ADDRESS to the nation delivered by Prime Minister Basdeo Panday on Saturday evening is comforting mainly in one sense - it shows that Government is acutely aware of the great unease existing in the country over the continued escalation of crime and the apparent inability of the police to contain it.

But the measures announced by the Prime Minister do not inspire confidence.

Code-named Operation LEAP (Law Enforcement Action Plan), the initiative mobilizes all personnel and other resources of the police, army and other national security services in a "zero tolerance onslaught against the criminal coalitions and the disparate criminal elements."

The plan calls for combined police and military roadblocks at strategic points and a dedicated telephone line (624-LEAP) through which citizens can contact the police 24 hours a day.

All this follows on the other initiatives the Government has taken since coming to power two years ago. The fleet of vehicles available to the police has been significantly upgraded, and the police has implemented a community policing programme to ensure a better relationship between its service and the people it aims to protect and serve. The E-999 emergency service has also been welcomed in the North, South, and the East where it has been implemented.

Despite all this, however, the crime situation continues unabated and in some respects has grown worse since Mr Panday's Government came to power. Clearly it will take more than than just greater policing to arrest the deterioration.

The economic policies adopted by the two previous administrations and continued by Mr Panday's Government, have throughout the world, when successfully implemented, been accompanied by strong economic growth. But they also have their downside in great social dislocation breakdown in family life and unsustainable levels of unemployment - factors that contribute to high crime levels.

Our Opinion

Public enemy No 1

WHEN THE Government of the United National Congress (UNC), then in coalition with the National Alliance for Reconstruction (NAR), came to power just over three years ago, a major plank in its election platform was the promise to deal with crime.

It is a promise, in fact, given great emphasis both by Prime Minister Basdeo Panday and Attorney General Ramesh Lawrence Maharaj, even if the emphasis was on implementing the death penalty.

This was clearly the intent behind the Prime Minister's going on national television to announce the start of Operation Leap, in which both the police and the army would conduct regular roadblocks and other exercises aimed at keeping criminals at bay.

There is no doubt that Operation Leap has resulted in the arrest of dozens, if not hundreds, of people who might otherwise have escaped the scrutiny of the police.

And it is to be noted as well that recent statistics issued by the police suggest a decline in serious criminal activity. But this is not the public perception—and if three years ago the UNC identified crime as Public enemy No 1, it is no less so today.

It is not that we doubt the sincerity of the Government's original promise or indeed its intent. But the evidence is mounting that nothing that the Government has done to date has really had any serious impact on the apparent ease with which people continue to be murdered, raped and robbed.

If anything, in fact, the spilling of innocent blood has continued to alarm all law-abiding citizens to such an extent that people are close to taking their own measures to defend themselves.

The Government, it is clear, needs to take a second hard look at its anti-crime campaign. Legislation against money-laundering and a consistently stern attitude towards drug pushers are all well and good. But the law-abiding citizens of this country are facing yet another year of grave threats to their personal security. We are yet to be convinced that the threat is being adequately dealt with.

Newsday

Published by Daily News Ltd.

Fiddling with crime

THE Roman emperor Nero, the story goes, fiddled while Rome burnt. In Trinidad and Tobago, the political leaders argue tiresomely over the incidence of crime, while the criminals continue to rape, rob, plunder and murder. The crazy Roman dictator blamed the conflagration on the Christians; TT political leaders accuse their different Governments, the PNM and the UNC, of failing to keep the criminals at bay. Nero, who fancied himself an artist, cared little for the eternal city and its residents. We are now left to wonder how much the political leaders of our country care about the safety of its citizens if they are more concerned about scoring pre-election points over the problem of crime, than about taking effective action to curb the menace.

It is silly for any politician to think that quoting statistics about the levels or extent of criminal activity during the PNM or UNC Administration will in any way ease the anxiety of TT's law abiding population, or relieve their fear that at any time and any place, even in their homes or while walking along the street, they may become victims of a violent assault or robbery. It matters little or nothing to the country's citizenry whether or not there were less rapes, murders, robberies or violent attacks under the PNM or UNC Governments when, as a matter of every-day experience, these acts of lawlessness appear to be rampant.

On Wednesday, the police seized a cache of sophisticated weapons and 1,221 rounds of ammunication at a Santa Rosa Heights home, Arima. Shortly after midnight on Thursday, a bandit went on a shooting spree in downtown Port-of-Spain, robbing a bar and pumping bullets into three men and a female vagrant as he fled along Independence Square.

What, for example, are the Police and the Government doing about the apparently easy availability of guns in the country? It now seems that every petty bandit or criminal can get hold of a firearm to help him pursue his nasty business. Also, the seizure of the arms and ammunition cache at Santa Rosa Heigths last week tells us that the most sophisticated high-tech weapons are finding their way into the country undetected. How can this be?

Diego Martin West MP, Dr Keith Rowley comes up, at least, with a positive idea, calling for a separate law enforcement agency to deal with the proliferation of illegal guns and ammunition. The UNC Government may not want to go that far, but it must respond to the urgent need to stop the flow of illegal weapons into our country.

EXPRESS NOVEMBER 30,2001,page 29

You mean: PERFORM - ANTS

Real CRIME...

under the UNC

- murder and fraud (increased) by **28.4%**

- shootings and robberies (increased) by **12%**

- number of cases solved (declined) from **33%** to **27%**

- Tobago saw crime (increase) by **19.2%**

- this UNC Government (increased) its spending on national security by a mere **7.9%**

EXPRESS Friday, November 30, 2001 Page 39

SAVE T&T from these PERFORM-ANTS! VOTE PNM
PEOPLE'S NATIONAL MOVEMENT

PAID ADVERTISEMENT

15

NEWSDAY NOVEMBER 30,2001

THE TRUE CRIME REPORT IN T&T

In 1995, the UNC said Trinidad and Tobago was not safe... and asked for your vote because "the Nation is in a crisis".

ARE YOU SAFER NOW?!

They got some Jeep Cherokees from a Party financier.
...And some Motorola radios.

THAT WAS IT!

CRIME INCREASED
...in every year since 1995!

And they are still doing nothing!

Basdeo Panday, the *Prime Minister*, has been Minister of National Security for all of 2001. He has done nothing — except **TALK**.

And now he has bought two Mercedes Benz limos, with burglar alarms!
(Reports say they go off whenever he approaches the cars.)

The country is now in the hands of law-breakers!

Question: Are *you* SAFER now?!

Answer: Read tomorrow's newspapers and... hope not to see your name.

Page 4 NEWSDAY SECTION 1 Friday November 30, 2001

SAVE T&T! **VOTE PNM**
PEOPLE'S NATIONAL MOVEMENT

Minister declares war on crime

NEWSDAY Tuesday February 26, 2002 Page

NEWSDAY Tuesday February 26, 2002 Page 3

By RIA TAITT

DECLARING that "desperate times called for desperate measures", National Security Minister Howard Chin Lee yesterday promised that "in this prolonged war" government was prepared to do "whatever it takes, within the bounds of law," including imposing limited curfews in high crime — "hot spot" — areas.

He didn't identify the areas, although "Operation Anaconda," which is one element of the plan, has been targeting Laventille and the Beetham.

Speaking at the formal launch of his "War on Crime" at the Hilton yesterday, Chin Lee presented with all the vigour he could muster, "the most aggressive assault ever" on crime in this country, consisting of policing strategy as well as social measures. Some of the features of the plan have been borrowed from the United States.

Employing all the metaphors of combat, the Minister said his multifaceted package aimed ultimately at "flushing" out the criminals, "bent on destruction, murder and mayhem" from the "dens of activity". He

warned that the Government would also be "going after the big fish... the white collar criminals who hide behind the cloak of what appears to be legitimate businesses, but which are really money laundering operations".

Because the ambitious plan proposed a total community clean-up, Chin Lee warned that there would be a clampdown on 'minor' offences such as urinating, littering and spitting on the nation's streets. Zero tolerance on lawlessness at any level, he vowed.

Chin Lee also announced that a "smart policing" policy, would enable computer-generated statistics to be used to help the Police study, and identify the trends and patterns in criminal behaviours and to pinpoint "hot spots" communities.

The high tech 'war' on crime, Chin Lee stated, would be further enhanced by the addition of 114 new police vehicles as well as high tech, fast Coast Guard vessels and two sophisticated surveillance aircrafts. Digital maps to assist the E999 Rapid Response were on the way as well as an upgrading of the radar grid around Trinidad

through quickly; you cannot live without respect, law and order".

US criminal expert, Dr Robin Engel had stated earlier that US criminologists had developed the 'broken window' theory in which they argued that 'small' physical and social disorders such as, abandoned buildings, litter, trash, public intoxication, vagrancy, loitering of juveniles eventually led to a spiral of disorder and decline in a neighbourhood.

Chin Lee said the Ministry will move therefore to repair or tear down abandoned buildings, clean unkempt streets, remove graffiti as part of the move to nurture a new mentality.

Chin Lee said he consulted extensively in the formulation of the crime plan, talking with former Ministers of National Security, religious leaders of all faiths, current and former police chiefs, senior members of the armed forces and fire services, NGOs, technological experts in crime detection and "the finest minds in criminology both locally and overseas". He also talked with prisoners and victims of crime. "We are equipping ourselves with the technology, equipment and manpower to wage and win this war."

The audience seemed to think that the "War on Crime" plan appreciated the seriousness of the crime situation and was appropriately designed to "natch the severity of the crime wave.

$1B to fight crime

NEWSDAY Saturday December 13, 1997 Page 3

By NALINEE SEEPAUL

A BUDGET of one billion dollars to fight crime and upgrade facilities of those agencies which fall under the Ministry of National Security was announced yesterday by Finance Minister Brian Kuei Tung.

The allocation of funds represents a 150 million dollar increase.

In his Budget presentation, the Minister said that in keeping with the concerted effort being made to combat crime, as-sure stability and increase national security, resources amounting to 105.5 million have been allocated in 1998 to support capital programmes for the promotion of public order and safety.

Coupled with that, the Ministry of Na-tional Security will administer a pro-gramme of $58.9 million. Twenty-six mil-lion will be spent on upgrading and reha-bilitating the Defence Force's facilities and equipment.

Improvement works are to be carried out at Camp Ogden, Staubles Bay, Teteron Bay, Camp Omega and Camp Cumuto.

A further allocation of $12.0 million has been made for the refitting of vessels and purchase of new vessels for the Coast Guard.

In addition, new vehicles and equipment are to be purchased for the Regiment and Coast Guard.

Additionally, on-going programmes for the construction and refurbishment of po-lice and fire stations will be continued in 1998.

Provisions have been made for the fund-ing of construction of police stations in Arouca, El Socorro/Barataria, Roxborough and Gasparillo.

Four new stations have been included in the programme: Oropouche, Carenage, Mayaro and Matelot.

Refurbishment of the San Fernando Po-lice Station will be commenced during the year, while improvement works will also be carried out at various police stations throughout the country.

Additionally, $1.5 million will be spent on the establishment of police posts.

Also, $4 million of expenditure has been allocated for implementation of a new com-puter system for the police service; new vehicles and equipment will be purchased at a cost of $1.0 million.

Additional resources have been provided

Page 8, TRINIDAD GUARDIAN, Thursday, January 30, 1997

Trinidad Guardian

NATIONAL NEWSPAPER OF TRINIDAD AND TOBAGO

Established September 2, 1917

22-24 St. Vincent Street, Port of Spain.

Paradise lost?

DRUGS, greed and domestic violence seem to be at the heart of all the murders that are tearing this country apart. And it is ironic that a Government which came to power with the promise of curbing crime is being greatly embarrassed by the facts of an escalating crime rate.

All the new and proposed laws, all the new and refurbished stations, all the expensive and radio-equipped vehicles, all the increased police and army patrols, all the community public relations, all the intervention and cooperation by the Americans with fast boats and marijuana burnings, all of these things don't seem to be making any significant dent in crime.

And while the political opponents of the Government grab the opportunity to gloat at the failure of the promise to curb crime, there is this feeling in the population that something has gone morally wrong with the country.

It's not good enough to say that it is a worldwide problem that can't be avoided like globalisation. It's not good enough to blame the Panday administration and say it's their responsibility to keep the nation safe. We know that can't work and even if it did it would mean a police state. And we certainly don't want that.

The Real Solution

the survey done by the ANSA McAL Psychological Research Centre of the University of the West Indies on crime, justice and politics. Sixty-eight percent of those surveyed said that parents should be held responsible for the crimes of their children. The implications of this response, if taken seriously, can be very far-reaching.

Vices And Virtues

Old people had a saying that you can make a child, but you can't make its mind. We know from experience today how false that is. For most of the vices and virtues — justice, mercy, racism, kindness, love, hate — that children learn, come from the breasts of their mothers and fathers and those responsible for their upbringing. It's a fact: we make the criminals and we develop the exemplars — from our own habits and behaviour. It's as simple as that.

What this means is that adults — parents, bosses, teachers, politicians — have to take the blame for the mess the country is in today. We can't blame the children who are turning to violence at a younger age. And once we accept the fact that we must take most of the blame for the crimes of our children, we will then be forced to do something about the situation.

Once we bring children into the world, our responsibililty is to mould their minds,

19

NEWSDAY SEPTEMBER 30,2002,page 41

THE PNM CONFRONTS CRIME

The People's National Movement will:

- Construct 18 new police stations and refurbish 9 more

- Increase neighbourhood police patrols

- Purchase more police vehicles

- Construct a new E-999 Command Centre

- Purchase 4 fast-patrol craft for drug-interdiction

- Provide specialised training for the police in areas such as:
  - Narcotics and Money Laundering
  - Criminal Investigations
  - Fraud Investigations
  - Financial Crimes Investigations
  - Advanced Hostage Negotiations
  - Drug Law Enforcement
  - Computer and Information Technology Training

- Expand the Community Policing Programme to include anti-crime and anti-drug lectures in schools

- Strengthen the Neighbourhood Watch Programme

- Construct a new Medium Security Correctional Facility in Tobago

- Improve facilities at the Youth Training Centre

FIGHTING CRIME... A PNM PRIORITY!
We'll Deliver...
Because We Care! VOTE PNM

TRINIDAD GUARDIAN OCTOBER 1,2002

The UNC has an effective Crime Reduction Plan and the Right Man

In the first 45 days we will begin implementation of a crime reduction plan that includes these measures:

- Appoint as Minister of National Security a proven leader of acknowledged stature who will command the respect of the protective services and the national community
- Give the Commissioner of Police the genuine authority to manage the force that he leads

- Set up a Crime Reduction Task Force drawn from the widest community of experts. including strategic partners from overseas; with responsibility for formulating a comprehensive Crime Reduction programme by December 31, 2002

- Increase the penalty for rape, kidnapping and armed robbery to possible life imprisonment

- A Dedicated Highway Patrol Unit with an initial strength of 250 Motorcycle Cops and other mobile officers

- Equip the Police Service with state of the art technology, including closed circuit television systems at peak traffic points and in crime-risk commercial areas.

- Initiate implementation of the Sir Ellis Clarke report

- Enlist the media as allies in the fight against crime

- Establish Police/Citizens partnerships reduce crime

- Toughen gun laws

MORE COMPREHENSIVE DETAILS IN MANIFESTO

©2002 **Under T&T's Intellecutual Property Legislation, prior publication is proof of ownership and will be invoked against another political party plagiarising these pledges.**

Stong Leadership for a Safe T&T

UNC
UNITED NATIONAL CONGRESS

CHAPTER 2. TRINIDAD AND TOBAGO DO NOT NEED AN ARMY, ESTABLISH ONE NATIONAL SECURITY FORCE WITH POWERS OF ARREST.

Many views have been opinioned about the nature and solutions to crime. And if an analogy can be made of the criminal it would be that of termite pests as the leaf cutting ants bachac,which savage and strip trees of every leaf, destroying growth and harvests as do other insects such as locusts and grasshopper or like the tiny wood lice who set their nest in and on wood, living and eating away the wood flooring and wood rafters of houses, destroying those areas of the house made of wood and rendering them vulnerable.

But for the destruction of these pests, many insecticides have been developed to counteract or counter-attack their marauding spread and therefore bringing them under control. "CRIMINALS ARE PESTS."

There are those who are reformists and will believe that even recidivists or repeat offenders, prison and rehabilitation is the way. Even though in many instances this process has failed.

Some believe that religion is the way to solve crime.But in some christian and non=christian religions have had violent past,human rights violations, like the inquisitions, burning to death of heritics, even today there are visible events of religion and violence and war conquets and racial segregation in the churches.

So having said the above, opening sentences let me turn now to the subject of this chapter. The chapter relates to policing manpower and its relation to crime control. Many developing countries view it as a status symbol and a necessity to have military contingents. These countries may be poor, budgets are limited, yet they do not see it fit to comprehend that there is an internal war to be fought with crime. It is not a civil war or civil insurrection and the war with crime is not only on land where the police are hard-pressed, at sea where marine police and customs officers patrol to arrest contraband traders in commerce, firearms and drugs.

Let me say that the coast guards play valuable service in the enforcement of maritime interdiction too, maintaining especially territorial sea limits, fishing agreements with other countries. Police has to worry too about even the air space where planes drop drugs in remote areas or use illegally constructed strips to deliver arms and drugs. These are the air couriers of the illicit trade

The larger the population of a country, the greater the manpower of the protective services ratio – the police are called upon to match at a manageable level. What purpose is the military serving? Day to day the police show their indispensable service as a force. On land sea or air; developing countries are world powers. The more the population grows criminally defenseless, the more the call is made to increase the size of the police service. This is the case with many developed and developing countries. There are three factors for this:

(1) higher rate of crime   (2) low ratio of manpower   (3) efficiency.

There is a drawback to these demands for increases, for it means that government's budgets must increase in order to pay increase salaries for every additional new police recruit, but there maybe other budgetary increases.such as more police vehicles, and stations precincts built especially in high crime areas.,since these are zones of combat in the war against crime.

Let us look at one developing country and see how it has had to deal with this issue. I focus therefore on the country of Trinidad and Tobago adjacent ten miles off the South American main land proximity to Venezuela and in the Caribbean. With a population of about 1,300,000 and a police service of about 7,000Let us cover a chronology from 1996 to 2002:

1996

The Police Service advertised vacancies for male and female applicants. Upon enlistment in the police service as CONSTABLES, A SALARY RANGE 21 OF $25,000.00 A YEAR. MEAL ALLOWANCE OF $2100.00 A YEAR, HOUSE ALLOWANCE(SINGLE) OF $2100.00 A YEAR, HOUSE ALLOWANCE (MARRIED) OF $3300.00 A YEAR.
SOURCE: Trinidad Guardian September 20, 1996, page 27

1997

The police service advertised the names and addresses of 229 male and 45 female applicants and requested urgently any public information on the applicants character.
SOURCE: Express February 1, 1997, page 14

1998

The police service advertised the names and addresses of 446 male applicants and requested urgently and public information on the applicants character.
SOURCE: Newsday January 9,1998, pages 40-41

1999

The police service advertised the names and addresses of 417 applicants and requested urgently any public information on the applicants character.
SOURCE: Express January 20,1999, page 18.

2001

One hundred and fifty police recruits entered police training college for six months said Assistant Commissioner of Police(Training) Glenn Roach.
SOURCE: September 4, 2001, page 9

2002

In 2002 a further 250 police recruits were required
SOURCE: Trinidad Guardian April 30, 2002.

How many more police recruits needed? How much longer will the recruitment process be needed? Is there to be an annual affair of recruitment? what are the budgetary implications.?

I now move into a new phase on the subject of manpower and the police service by turning the attention to the military. What is the day to day itinerary of the Trinidad and Tobago Army? What do they do down at Tetron Barracks.? What will they do even if they will ever be dispersed all over the country? Except for the coast guard which indeed perform drug interdiction and watch over the Trinidad/Venezuela seabed boundaries.

It is my feeling that Trinidad and Tobago do not need an army, the role of the army is questionable, they should have the type of daily challenges as the police fighting a common enemy-the criminal element, enforcing law, arresting and charging law breakers, patrolling the streets throughout the country. But that is not the role of the army. That is the continued urgency –"enemy No.1-crime."

Manpower recruitment an ever expanding Service-that is how the police service is augmented. I wish to suggest that as a developing country, Trinidad and Tobago do not need a separate army/military personnel and a separate police personnel. Already we have seen in the

past that whenever there is a peak in crime, The Minister of National Security calls up the army to have joint army-police patrols- but the army does not have an delegated powers of arrest.

TIME TO DISBAND THE ARMY AND JOIN BOTH THE ARMY AND POLICE INTO ONE NATIONAL SECURITY FORCE WITH POWERS OF ARREST WHICH WILL DO THE POLICING AND BE READY FOR BOTH INTERNAL AND EXTERNAL AGGRESSION. THE SALARIED PERSONNEL OF THE ARMY WILL THEN BE INCORPORATED INTO ONE FORCE, DOUBLING THE STRENGTH OF THE POLICING FORCE AS UNIFIED WITHOUT THE NEED FOR ANY INCREASE RECRUITMENT IN THE NEAR FUTURE, AND SPARING THE TREASURY OF THE COUNTRY ANY FURTHER FINANCIAL EXPENDITURE.

If this is done, gone will be the days of call up of the army to work with the police in joint patrols often as short term measures lasting less than three months. Such popular names of the police and army combinations as the 1997 "INFERENTIAL LEAP" and the 2002 "OPERATION ANACONDA" will be THINGS OF THE PAST.

In the research paper on policing done in 2000 which I mentioned before, this suggestion was included in that paper.

I used as examples the countries of COSTA RICA (Central America) and the PRINCIPALITY OF LIECHTENSTEIN (Europe), both countries have no army which were abolished years ago and replaced by one single force that functions as a policing/military defense force. I used the following sources that give information on Costa Rica and Liechtenstein:

(1)
"INFORMATION PLEASE ALMANAC 1991"
HOUGHTON MIFFIN PUBLISHERS
NEW YORK, U.S.A
PAGES, 177,225—226

(2)
"STATEMAN YEARBOOK, A STATISTICAL AND
HISTORICAL OF STATES OF THE WORLD 1987-1988,
(124th EDITON)
JOHN PAXTON, editor
LONDON, ENGLAND
Page 382. COSTA RICA:
> **Defence—"The army was abolished in1948 and replaced by a CIVIL GUARD reported to be 6000 strong.**
> **Population—(census 1985) 2,655,000**
> **Area--- 51`100sq km(19,`730sq miles)**

Page 806. LICHTENSTEIN:
> **Police--- The principality has NO ARMY, the police force is 41,**
> **Auxiliary police is 31(1986).**
> **Population—(census 1980) 2525**
> **Area—160sq km (618 sq miles)."**

Remember in a previous paragraph I suggested the disbanding of the army in a research paper done in the year 2000, well there were two other persons who have held this same idea as myself and made it known in the newspapers. One was in Trinidad, the other in Jamaica and both of them did this in the year 2001. I quote briefly from each as follows(l) "We need a para-military police force" by Ellis Manigot/Trincity, Trinidad. NEWSDAY NEWSPAPER January 9,2001,page 24 "I think the time has come for us to make drastic changes in our national security system. I cannot see the need for us to maintain an army and a coast guard as a separate body to protect us from outside invasion. It will make more sense for us to disband the army and coast Guard and aligned them with the police altogether to establish a para-military national security police force united to protect us from insurrection from within and without and to control the present state of lawlessness.

The Republic of Costa Rica have disbanded their army and have established a strong and powerful military para-military police force to maintain security."

It is so interesting to see how people can have similar ideas which are rarely expressed -urging the country's authorities to break with tradition and conventional practice. However while Mr Maingot did mention Costa Rica, he did not mention Lichtenstein. While Mr Maingot is from Trinidad, the next writer with similar idea is from Jamaica, and she is a Jamaican politician.

(2) "Bennett proposes gun amnesty ,merge of army and police" DAILY OBSERVER NEWSPAPER (Jamaica) July 26,2001

"National Democratic Movement(N.D.M) President Hyacinth Bennett yesterday proposed that the government merge the army and the police in an effort to stem Jamaica's nagging crime problem. She said that the security forces were unable to deal with the crime problem because they were over stretched as the number of police personnel per capita was to low and needed to be increased.

NDM proposed that the JDF(Jamaica Defence Force) which has over the last three decades functioned more as a Constabulary than its original intended role. It need to merge with the Jamaica Constabulary Force(JCF) to increase the number of police personnel."

Here in Trinidad, we see once again the intent of using the army with the police when the Minster of National Security Howard Chin Lee announced as follows: "Chin Lee Creates Extract Crime Squad" by Ken Chee Hing NEWSDAY NEWSPAPER March 29,2002, page 47

"National Security Minister Chin Lee has announced the formation of a special Army/Police Unit called EXTRACT CRME SQUAD(ESC) to carry out increase surgical strikes against criminals and crime organisations in the country.

Chin Lee made the disclosure on Wednesday during a re-launch of the "Crime Stoppers Programme at Trinidad and Tobago Chamber of Commerce, Westmorrings."

Government's expenditures must always be studied with vigilance so as *to* show fiscal prudence and to me government's expenses to maintain an army as separate from the police does NOT carry valid weight. Let us look at part of this expenditure-remember I am supportive of the coast guard division but it should be a police marine unit. Here are some recent expenditures taken on by government in favour of the army:

> TRINIDAD AND TOBAGO DEFENCE FORCE REGIMENT CAREER OPPORTUNITY FOR COMMISSIONED OFFICERS Newsday Newspaper, February 23,2000, page 40 "The Trinidad and Tobago Regiment is inviting applications from suitable qualified nationals of Trinidad and Tobago to be considered for leadership positions in the Infantry Unit. COMPENSATION:
>
> J.Basic pay on entry $29,583.25 per annum, On completion of training between $65,134.25 and $66,922.75 per annum (2) Gratuity after 10 years(3) Gratuity and pension after 29 years service(3) When married housing, travelling and meal allowance as well as medical and dental services *to* the officers family."

"ARMY GETS NEW TRUCKS FOR WAR ON CRIME" Newsday Newspaper January 10,2003

"...the Trinidad and Tobago Defence Force(TTDF) will have the use of 16 new ISUZU trunks. Another 16 trucks are scheduled to arrive in the country next two weeks. Cost of the vehicles has been put at $10 million sources said. We had a major impediment during Operation Anaconda and these vehicles are going to be useful.

Sources told Newsday that in about two months time the Defence Force will have an additional 30 vehicles..."

"!!3 NEW COAST GUARD OFFICERS WELCOMED" Newsday Newspaper January 25,2003, page 2

"Minister of National Security Howard Chin Lee inspects the parade of 113 new Coast Guard officers..."

So we see that money is spent now on the army transport to fight crime.But money has been spent before on police transport in 1998 by government to purchase 100 Cherokee Jeeps at a cost of $17.6 million(Express Newspaper August 17,1998) and in 2002,54 Vauxhall police vehicles were purchased(Express August 21,2002, page 3).A sizable number of police motorcycles were also purchased.

Apart from the regular police personnel, there are the Special Reserve Police(SRP a small sector of police officers, and there are the small Municipal Police Service(MPS) who are part of the Municipalities of Port of Spain, San Fernando, Arima, Chaguanas and Point Fortin each run by a Mayor and Council.

Recently the Ministry of Local Government under which the munacipalities fall, sought to recruit 394 applicants to the MPS. This was reported as "Officers Start training for municipal police Service" NEWSDAY NEWSPAPER August 24, 2002, page 27.

We need para-military police force

THE EDITOR: I agree with the proposals of the Hugh Wooding Commission and Sir Ellis Clarke, constitutionalist, that the time is ripe for a change of our Constitution away from the Westminster system, which we have certainly outgrown.

With this in mind, I think the time is also ripe to make drastic changes in our National Security system. For instance, I cannot see the need for us to maintain an Army and Coast Guard as a separate body to protect us from outside invasion. Our military and naval forces certainly do not have the capacity or equipment to resist outright attack by air, sea or land forces. In fact, the greatest threat to our security over these past few years has come from within. And that has put a great deal of strain and pressure on our Police Service which is very much understaffed and ill-equipped.

It would make more sense to disband the Army and Coast Guard and amalgamate them altogether with our Police Service to establish a para-military National Security Police Force united to protect us from insurrection from within and without. And also to control the present state of lawlessness that prevails. The republic of Costa Rica has just gone that way. They have disbanded their army and established a strong and powerful para-military police force to maintain security.

As our world becomes more and more a global village, as evidenced by the formation of the European Economic Community, we find ourselves leaning more and more to the USA in terms of trade, but also as well in terms of protection of our sovereignty. It makes no sense, therefore, as a small island nation, for us to fool ourselves into believing that we can protect ourselves from outside attack. We have no airforce, we have no heavy artillery or army tanks. In fact nothing to resist even a mild attack. Only conventional weaponry. Of course, there are those who, following the philosophy of "Divide Et Impera", may well argue to have a Police Force quite separate from that of a Military Army force. It is felt in some quarters that that would provide a more comfortable balance to national security.

The grave question of leadership, however, comes in here. Whenever two "man crabs" (to use local dictum), live in the same hole, there is bound to be dissent, to put it mildly. It makes it easier for dissident elements to drive a shaft between the two forces. That's how revolution starts.

But last of all, from an economic point-of-view, it would make more sense to have one uniform and united National para-military Police Force instead.

ELLIS MAINGOT
Tri...

WRITE TO:
Newsday, Chacon Street, Port-of-Spain

Time to re-examine TT's constitution

Newsday July 7, 2001

THE EDITOR: I beg you to publish this: Your Newsday under the headline of "We need a Para-Military Police Force," published an article of mine on January 9. In this article I suggested that we should disband our Army and Coast Guard and establish a para-military Police Force strong enough to maintain law and order in the face of an increasing crime situation in this country.

Mr Andy Burkett, Research Officer, Regional Council, Community Police (NED) fully supported me in this. The republic of Costa Rica has already gone that way since 1949. They are in the same situation as we are today. The greatest threat to their security comes from within their borders rather than from the outside.

In our situation here, it is obvious why our Prime Minister prefers to hold on to the portfolio of Minister of National Security. It is purely an attempt to follow the philosophy of "Divide Et Impera."

As a nation, we are so divided ethnically and religiously, that he takes comfort in the fact that a division or dividing line between two forces - the Police and the Armed Forces - would best serve our country. The one serving as a watch-dog over the other.

That philosophy will never work. It would leave room for dissident forces and elements to drive a shaft between the two forces.

That is how revolution really starts. Like putting a wedge between two forces. Let us therefore re-examine our Constitution, and as intelligent people put in place a powerful Police Service recruited from the best qualified members of our society to do the job of national security.

And our Constitution should be so framed that it would leave our President of the Nation as commander-in-chief of our para-military Police Service.

ELLIS MAINGOT
Trincity

WRITE TO:
Newsday, Chacon Street, Port-of-Spain

DAILY OBSERVER JULY 26, 2001, JAMAICA

Bennett proposes gun amnesty, merger of army and police

Daily Observer (Jamaica)

NATIONAL Democratic Movement (NDM) president, Hyacinth Bennett, yesterday proposed that the government offer an amnesty on illegal guns and merge the army and police in an effort to stem Jamaica's nagging crime problem.

"A gun amnesty should be declared, after which the security forces must use a combination of intelligence and superior force, to destroy gang rule and restore proper policing to the affected communities," Bennett told journalists at the NDM headquarters in Kingston.

Bennett was reporting on her party's weekend retreat which, she said, dealt mostly with the island's crime dilemma.

She said that the security forces were unable to deal with the crime problem because they were overstretched, as the number of police personnel per capita was too low and needed to be increased.

Bennett also argued that the tools, training and other resources available to the security forces needed to be improved. However, she conceded that retooling would be limited because of the unavailability of new sources of money.

Said Bennett: "In light of the foregoing, the NDM proposes (that) the JDF (Jamaica Defence Force), which has, over the last three decades, functioned more as a constabulary than in its original intended role, needs to be merged with the Jamaica Constabulary Force (JCF) to increase the number of police personnel.

She also suggested the firing of incompetent cops and those who compromise the integrity of the force, tarnish its image and undermine its effectiveness.

"The new JCF personnel need to be properly trained in modern policing methods, including the respect of the rights of the citizens," she said.

Bennett also said that police should be deployed in communities, particularly those with high levels of crime, "to restore the rule of law" and proposed engagement in community-based policing "in order to rebuild the trust of the people by acting in a more proactive and professional manner".

She also suggested the introduction of a volunteer cadet scheme in which young people would be enlisted and trained in leadership, conflict resolution and crime prevention and detection

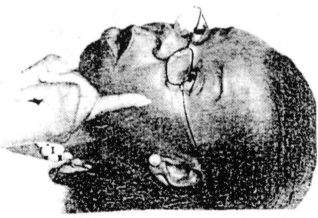

BENNETT...fire bad cops

"They would function as liaisons between the police and the community and be provided with a stipend," Bennett said.

NEWSDAY MARCH 29, 2002, page 47

CHIN LEE CREATES EXTRACT CRIME SQUAD

NEWSDAY Friday March 29, 2002 Page 47

By KEN CHEE HING

NATIONAL Security Minister Howard Chin Lee has announced the formation of a special Army/Police unit named the Extract Crime Squad (ECS) to carry out "intense, surgical strikes against criminals and crime organisations in the country."

Chin Lee made the disclosure during Wednesday's re-launch of the Crime Stoppers programme at Trinidad and Tobago Chamber of Commerce headquarters in Westmoorings.

The National Security Minister said the elite ECS will, acting on intelligence gathered from the Crime Stoppers programmes,

as well as existing intelligence bodies, in conjunction with Operation Anaconda, weed out the criminal elements in society.

"This unit will comprise 30 to 50 specially trained officers dedicated to the aim of conducting surgical removals of our various crime cancers plaguing the body of the society," Chin Lee said.

He added that Operation Anaconda will continue indefinitely with islandwide crime eradication raids every month and intense road-blocks throughout the country on a weekly basis.

The Crime Stoppers programme is a system where members of society can anonymously feed information to the police regarding criminal activities.

Based on this information, the police will act and make arrests and/or seizures of illegal items or stolen property.

Director of UWI's Centre of Criminology and Criminal Justice, Professor Ramesh Deosaran alluded to the fact that intelligence was vital to crime fighting and prevention.

The new Crime Stoppers programme is led by Martin George. Monetary rewards will be given to persons whose tip-offs lead to arrests and convictions of criminals.

The Trinidad and Tobago Chamber of Commerce yesterday pledged $250,000 to the Crime Stoppers programme.

NATIONAL Security Minister Howard Chin Lee delivers the feature address at yesterday's re-launch of Crime Stoppers.

VERSADEX III

Police Records Indexing and Information System

From

VERSATERM-Systems

A Division of FEDSCAN LTD.

971, Richmond Rd, Ottawa C. CANADA.

NEWSDAY Wednesday February 23, 2000 Page 49

TRINIDAD AND TOBAGO DEFENCE FORCE (REGIMENT)

TO GUARD & DEFEND

TO GUARD & DEFEND

CAREER OPPORTUNITY FOR COMMISSIONED OFFICERS

The Trinidad and Tobago Regiment is inviting applications from suitably qualified **MALE** nationals of Trinidad and Tobago to be considered for leadership positions in its Infantry Unit.

JOB SUMMARY

Organize, train and manage a group of 30 soldiers and mould them into an effective team.

THE CANDIDATE

The preferred candidates must be:-
- Committed to a career in the military.
- Results oriented.
- Flexible, thorough and able to work in a fast paced environment.
- Physically fit.
- Single and between the ages of 18-25 years.

MINIMUM QUALIFICATIONS

1. 5 GCE O'Level or CXC General Proficiency grades 1-3 (1998 onwards) which **MUST** include English Language and Mathematics.
   AND
2. 2 GCE A'Levels grades A to E excluding General Paper.
3. On selection candidates will undergo 12-16 months of training locally and/or abroad in either England or Canada.
4. On successful completion of the period of training the candidates will be commissioned to the rank of Second Lieutenant.
5. *NB Successful completion of any or all tests is in itself no guarantee of selection.*

COMPENSATION

The Regiment offers a competitive remuneration package, which includes:-
1. Basic Pay
   On entry $29,583.25 per annum
   On completion of training between $65,134.25 and $66,922.75 per annum.
2. Gratuity after 10 years service.
3. Gratuity and pension after 20 years service.
4. When married housing, traveling and meal allowances as well as, medical and dental services to the officer's family.

3. Application forms should be submitted by 13 March 2000 and should be addressed to:-

The Recruiting Officer
The Trinidad and Tobago Regiment
Camp Ogden
Long Circular Road
ST JAMES

CHAPTER 3.   DEMYSTIFYING THE MYSTIQUE OF FIREARMS

There are some countries which assume that if licensed firearms were to be allowed into fewer hands, fewer violent assaults and deaths will occur. That is a false premise hatched out of countrieswith certain historical tradition.

There maybe too, there is the belief of governments occupied with thephobia or fear notion that too many firearms in the hands of too many denizens can be unhealthy to control by state security forces in the event of civil insurrections. That perception of a government flops when there is no formula established by a government of who should own what?

The contrast and often criticised policy of the US Government successive administrations since its independence constitution was drawn up to indiscriminately allow all denizens the right to own firearms- note!" firearms" not "firearm." Nochecks and balances as to the character and background of potential firearm owners.

High powered automatic rifles were acquired with merely walking into a firearms dealers' stores with the money to pay. It is that madness of freeness that has created the scourge of criminality that has plagued the U.S.A until recent requirements for background checks and the banning of the purchase of assault rifles. There has been in recent times a tremendous decline in crime in the U.S.A in comparison to that of other countries with strict and restrictive firearms policies as will be shown later in this chapter.

The reason for this indiscriminate firearms US policy it is said stem from its early constitutional amendment as specified:

"BILL OF RIGHTS, THE FIRST 10 AMENDMENTS TO THE CONSTITUTION RATIFIED IN 1791.

AMENDMENT 2. THE RIGHT TO BEAR ARMS AND MAINTAIN STATE MILITIAS."

There is a present irony in England, the United Kingdom with its most restrictive firearms law and which pride itself in not arming its police service except for special purposes. This British policy has backfired now in that a major amount of firearm power now lie in the hands of criminals. The result of armed criminals, un-armed law-abiding citizens and un-armed police service has led to England having a higher crime rate than in the U.S.A.

The City of New York, U.S.A dramatic decrease in crime has been attributed to that city's former Mayor, Court Prosecutor Rudy Giuliani and its former Commissioner of Police Safir.

As I have been doing and shall do with each chapter, it is to provide supporting documentation for each chapter.Here are thus the following:

"Most crime worse in England than the US" NEWSDAY NEWSPAPER, OCTOBER 12, 1998.

"LONDON: You are more likely to be mugged in England than in the United States, according to a new crime study reported with some consternation in Britain yesterday.

The report by a Cambridge University Professor and a Statistician from the US Department of Justice…The Sunday Times reported the story at the top of its front page. It said Britain may have tougher gun laws but the US has longer prison sentences. COMMON SENSE SAYS THAT AMERICA IS THE MOST CRIME RIDDEN COUNTRY ON EARTH, WHILE BRITAIN IS AN OASIS OF TRANQUILLITY AND PEACE. COMMON SENSE IS WRONG, THE SUNDAY TIMES SAID IN AN EDITORIAL. 'WE URGENTLY NEED TO RE-EXAMINE OUR COSY ASSUMPTION ABOUT LAW AND ORDER.'

The Mail on Sunday reprinted some of the study's findings. They said that in 1995, the last time year for which complete statistics are available on both sides of the Atlantic. There were 20 assaults per 1000 people or households in England and Wales and only8.8 in the United States.

The rate of robbery is now 1.4 times higher England than in the United States, and the British burglary rate is nearly double America the report said.(REUTERS)."

The actual report of the London Newspaper is from the Sunday Times and states as follows:

"Official, more muggins in England than US" SUNDAY TIMES NEWSPAPER !! OCTOBER 1998,PAGE 1

ENGLISH PEOPLE ARE MORE LIKELY TO BE ROBBED OR ASSAULTED THAN AMERICANS, according to an official study that shatters the belief that England is a safe country. THE HOME OFFICE IS URGENTLY STUDYING A REPORT BY THE US DEPARTMENT OF JUSTICE WHICH SHOWS THAT SINCE 1981 CRIME RATES FOR ENGLAND AND WALES FOR MOST SERIOUS OFFENCES HAVE OVERTAKEN THOSE IN AMERICA.

It is a crime pattern that is being repeated across Europe. The 100-page report which took a year to compile is set to raise a furious`political debate about law enforcement in Britain.

Patrick Langan a senior statistician with the Department of Justice David Farrington a criminologist at Cambridge University and co-author of the report said the findings challenge the public view of crime levels in Britain."THE PICTURE HAS CHANGED DRAMATICALLY in the past 15 years. Then America had much crime rates, whereas now England is much higher."

The previous articles that I have quoted are for the year 1998, but this is the year 2003-what of the four years span has there been any change?. Well I shall now present two more recent reports from the London"Sunday Times Newspaper" interestingly the first article was written by the Editor of the Sunday Times Newspaper and titled:

"Crime's Ugly Rise" Sunday Times Newspaper January 6,2002 (Editorial by the Editor)

"The government's anti-crime strategy seems to be coming apart at the seams. Ministers deny it and claim that the overall figures for crime are falling. That was true when the last British Crime Survey was published a year ago, but London's dramatic figures show a worsening.

This is the topsy-turvy madness that prevents householders defending themselves from burglars in the middle of the night if they are considered to have used disproportionate force. The grieving family of Kevin Jackson, the Halifax man fatally stabbed in the head six times when he accosted car thieves outside his home, know the real horror of disproportionate force.The killers showed him no mercy.

Ordinary law-abiding citizens are entitled to feel THERE IS SOMETHING WRONG WITH A CRIMINAL JUSTICE SYSTEM THAT PUTS THE VICTIM AT A DISADVANTAGE. THE GROWING USE OF GUNS ESPECIALLY THOSE DRUG RELATED ones added a new and alarming dimension to the problem. BUT KNIVES AND OTHER WEAPONS CAN BE JUST AS DEADLY THE SCALE OF CRISIS IS BROUGHT HOME BY THE COMPARISON WE REPORT TODAY WITH NEW YORK, WHEN PEOPLE IN LONDON ARE SIX TIMES MORE LIKELY TO BE ASSAULTED OR ROBBED THAN PEOPLE IN NEW YORK, WE NEED SOLUTIONS FAST.

Dynamic leaders in the war against crime, MR BLAIR APPEARS TO THINK THAT BIGGER BUDGETS AND NEW PAY CONDITIONS WILL WORK,maybe, but he has had more than four years to turn things round and we are still waiting."

The other article I shall like to cite is from the London"Sunday Times Newspaper" excerpts are titled "Attacks raise fear level on streets,new victims feed alarm over crime" SUNDAY TIMES NEWSPAPER JANUARY 2002, PAGES 1,4, LONDON, ENGLAND.

"PEOPLE IN LONDON ARE SIX MORE TIMES LIKELY TO BEASSAULTED OR ROBBED THAN RESIDENTS OF NEW YORK,ONCE CONSIDERED THE MOST DANGEROUS CITY IN THE WORLD. IN LONDON THE NUMBER OF VIOLENT CRIME-DEFINED AS STREET ROBBERIES,ASSAULTS AND MURDERS PER PERSON ALSO OUTSTRIS THAT OF OTHER AMERICAN CITIES SUCH AS LOS ANGELES, CHICAGO AND DETROIT.

One factor is the number of police patrolling the streets, while London has 26,000, New York has 42,000. There is one police officer for every 190 people in New York and one for every 290 people in London."

But in 1985 one writer tried to put forward that England is and has always been a violent country in"Britain a violent country" by Daniel Nelson BARBADOS ADVOCATE NEWSAPER OCTOBER 15, 1985"The recent riots in Britain are not an isolated, an isolated phenomenon but must be seen as part of a longstanding tradition of violence in the country.

I have provided the reader with a comparison of a country which has boasted about its strict and restrictive firearms licensing policy-ENGLAND and another noted for its liberal and at first absurd non-selective, non-discrimination by quality of character firearm policy-USA. That policy has changed to allow rigid checks of quality character before firearm ownership is allowed. It nevertherless still liberal to the law-abiding.

Let me now delve into the realm of weaponry frequently used in woundings and often ending in murder. It is to me the very vicious cutlass or machete,

(a) THE CUTLASS/MACHETE   A MORE VICIOUS WEAPON THAN THE FIREARM:

A firearm is certainly not the only dangerous weapon, and it depends on the type of firearm such as the UZI SMG 9mm or.45 or its carbine model, the GALIL 7.62 mm semi -automatic sniper rifle loading a 25 rounds magazine just to make a few mentions.

There are other weapons that are just as deadly that do not require a license because they are so cheap to acquire and are really household equipment until they are used otherwise. But I wish to focus on the cutlass or machete(which is like a sword used in the olden days before the invention of firearms). You see,the cutlass/,\machete sharpened blade or dull blade, it is capable or has the capacity to severe the hand or head or limb with one strike or swipe or split a skull open into two. However it depens on the degree of force or velocity used. Keep in mind those two words used here synonymously with motion for you will soon understand this relationship between the power of a firearm and the movement of its projectile bullet, but this will be done later.

But why am I providing the reader with such morbid descriptions? Well, to show in time that THERE IS BASICLY ONE SINGLE FACTOR THAT STAND OUT ABOUT A FIREARM THAT DIFFER FROM OTHER WEAPONS AND THERE IS NO REAL MYSTIQUE ABOUT FIREARMS.

TO COMPARE THE VICIOUSNESS OF USE OF THE CUTLASS/MACHETE AS A FEARED WEAPON, let me give the reader some samples of its use in a variety of assaults or murders and the reports from newspapers and vivid pictures make gruesome telltales:

"Cutlass victim cries:I want new hands"NEWSDAY JULY 2,2000

"God put a hand,cries Sarabijtr Siewsankar whose HANDS WERE CUT OFF in a blooded attack in Siparia.(see NEWSDAY OCTOBER 11,97)
"Four chopped to death in one house NEWSDAY MAY 6,2001,PAGE 3" a 27 year-old woman, her four year-old daughter, her nine-year old handicapped step-son and her 62 year-old mother-in-law were brutally chopped to death at their home at Talparo.Alicia was found with more than 20 chop wounds...
"

"Cop's hand chopped off,man charged with attempted murder" NEWSDAY OCTOBER 18, 2001, PAGE 8
"An Arima man appeared in court charged with attempted murder

"BANDITS CHOP SAN JUAN COPS, CUTLASS ATTACK A REPRISAL ON POLICE" TRINIDAD GUARDIAN NOVEMBER 17, 1996, PAGES 1 AND 4
FIVE CUTLASS WEILDING BANDITS STORMED THE SAN JUAN POLICE SUB-STATION AND SEVERELY CHOPPED TWO POLICEMEN. The sub-station which houses the Crime Suppression Unit and the Service support Unit, police attached to these two units are normally armed with 9mm pistols and Uzis.
"MAN'S HAND SEVERED OUTSIDE RESTAURANT" WASHINGTON POST MAY 14,2002, PAGE B2,USA
A man was undergoing surgery TO HAVE A HAND RE-ATTACHED after he was slashed by an unknown assailant outside a Falls Church restaurant early in the morning, Fairfax Police said..."
8 CHILDREN DIE AS SCHOOL STABBING STUNS JAPAN" NEWSDAY JUNE 9,2001, PAGE 16 " IKEDA, JAPAN; Eight children were killed and 15 people injured in Japan's worst school tragedy when a middle-age man with a history of mental illness WENT ON A STABBING RAMPAGE AT AN ELEMENTARY SCHOOL.
The tragedy began when THE MAN WEILDING A 28CM KNIFE WALKED INTO A CLASS ROOM AND BEGAN STABBING CHILDREN THAT MEDIA SAID LASTED A LITTLE OVER TEN MINUTES..."
"MAN SLASHES NINE CHILDREN IN S KOREA CHURCH" NEWSDAY SEPTEMBER 5, 2002,PAGE 32
"SOEUL; A KNIFE WIELDING MAN WHO CLAIMED HE WAS DRIVEN BY VOICES TO KILL,SLASHED NINE YOUNG CHILDREN IN A CHURCH SCHOOL in the South Korean capital,police said."
So from the foregoing presentation one will see that other weapons other than a firearm can be used to hold,wound several persons at bay or"stand off" proximity makes the difference.
In Trinidad and Tobago the issuing of firearms is the domain and authority solely of the Commissioner of Police.
Most times to be a licensed firearm owner one must be a government minister,equivalent status or big businness owner
But there has been objections to this policy in the issuing of firearms.Anyone taking a dispassionate perusal of the policy can see that it is out-dated ,out-moded and rationally flawed. Even in the country of Jamaica this policy which is similar to their own,has drawn criticism.
I have ten "letters to newspaper editors" where the writers have vent their views on this issue-including an article by the Police Welfare Association in Trinidad and two articles from Jamaica, one an attorney at law and the other a councillor. Supporting documentation will accompany these statements in further pages.

In addition you willread from the accompanying articles, how off-duty police officers of junior rank below sergeant, have had firearm bandits break down the door of the officers' homes,robbed AND RAPED WIVES;and this goes for other homes where it is a prevalent occurrence. Maybe the Commissioner is of the assumption that a firearm to protect oneslf,family is too complicated, sophisticated and of costly value than the material possessions and lives of home owning law- abiding denizens.But when you read later down and see the visual documented cost of how cheap an ordinary firearm is and that its apparatus is no more complex than a car's carburettor then you will smile a cynical grin.I shall unravel all of this later in the chapter.

"Who should own a gun?"EXPRESS JULY 12, 1994, PAGE 9

"The Police Commisioner's recent statement to the Petroleum Dealers Association that he will only issue to them gun licenses ON HIS PERCEPTION OF THEIR NEED NOT THEIR WANT,,,The Commissioner stated that we should hire an armed guard, is he saying that a businessman,SETTLED FAMILY MAN WITH NOCRIMINAL RECORD IS LESS SUITED TO HOLD A FIREARM THAN A YOUNGMAN RECRUITED BY A SECURITY FIRM WITH LITTLE OR NO EDUCATION?..." DOORS CLOSED.

"Let more citizens own guns"NEWSDAY JULY 13,1997, P.9"...the Commissioner of Police admission of his in-ability to protect the good citizens of TT. Commissioner Mohommed said the help of the public was needed...

LAW ABIDING CITIZENS SHOULD NOT BE DEPRIVED OF OWNING an un-concealed weapon(long gun)...The fact is they the police are unable to protect the population in urban areas. THE TIME HAS COME FOR A NEW APPROACH TO CRIME FIGHTING IN TT WHICH DOES NOT INCLUSE THE ARBITRARY REJECTION OF ALL GUN PERMITS."Carlise Hall, New York

"Criminals not only after cash alone"NEWSDAY AUGUST 28,2001, PAGE 21.

"EVERY CIVILISED COUNTRY IN THE WORLD LIKE TRINIDAD AND TOBAGO with democratically elected government HAS CITIZENS OF IMPECCABLE CHARACTER... ALL DECENT LAW-ABIDING CITIZENS, competent in the use of firearms SHOULD QUALIFY AS HOLDERS OF LICENSED FIREARMS TO PROTECT THEIR FAMILY AND PROPERTY...the police cannot do it alone, it takes two hands to clap,Ellis Manigot,Trincity.

"Crime in TT likened to bubonic plague"NEWSDAY FEBRUARY 8,2002

"CITIZENS SHOULD BE ACCORDED THE PRIVILEGE OF ACQUIRING LICENCE FIREARMS WITH RESPECT TO THEIR SOCIAL,MORAL AND SPIRITUAL STANDING IN THEIR RESPECTIVE NEIGHBOURHOODS..."Lindsy Rampersad
Tacarigua

"COPS WANT TO TAKE THEIR GUNS HOME"EXPRESS FEBRUARY 5, 1998, PAGE 5

"POLICE OFFICERS WANT TO TAKE THEIR GUNS HOME WITH THEM SO THAT THEY CAN RESPOND TO THE CRIES IF THEIR NEIGHBOURS, INSTEAD OF REMAINING IMPOTENT WHEN FRIENDS AND FAMILY COME UNDER THE BARREL OF ARMED BANDITS,

This suggestion was made yesterday BY THE PRESIDENT OF THE POLICE WELFARE ASSOCIATION CPL WAYNE HAYDE,when he met with Public Administration Minister Wade Mark and Labour Minister Harry Partapt at the Central Police Station...
"

"Police commissioner Hilton Guy has issued a department order within the police service instructing that firearms issued to officers FROM THE RANK OF SGT DOWNWARD WHILE ON DUTY,SHOULD REMAIN AT THE VARIOUS STATIONS WHEN THEY FINISH THEIRT DUTY.ONLY OFFICERS FROM THE RANK OF INSPECTORS UPWARD ARE ALLOWED TO TAKE HOME FIREARMS.

The decision by the Commissioner came about following the shooting death of the wife of a police officer in South, Newsday learned that previously all Special Branch and OCNU were allowed to take home their service revolvers. COMMISSIONER GUY ALSO MADE IT CLEAR HE HAS TAKEN THE DECISION NOT TO ISSUE PRIVATE FIREARMS TO POLICE OFFICERS. He said that decision will remain in place while he is Commissioner,,,"

"Giving guns to people without training"NEWSDAY FEBRUARY 2,2002,PAGE 22

",,.for instance if you happen to be a jmagistrate,permanent secretary, member of the Senate or House of Representatives, you will be more or less granted a pistol or revolver almost automatically, and there is a long list of other persons so entitled. You must realise Ellis THAT THERE SOME CHOSEN INDIVIDUALS WHOSE LIVES ARE MORE VALUABLE YHAN THE LIVES OF MERE MORTALS..."Martin Kavanagh

Certified Firearms Instructor

La Romain

"Hunters plan legal action over refusal to gun licences" NEWSDAY SEPTEMBER 1, 2000, PAGE 15

"A group of hunters are contemplating legal action against the state for refusing them licences to obtain firearms.South Trinidad Hunters Association and attorney-at-law advised..."

"DISARMING JAMAICAN CITIZENS"GLEANER AUGUST 9,2000, JAMAICA.

"the Offensive Weapons Prohibition Act presently before Parliament Sub-Committee is worthy of debate and consideration before it is enacted into law. The intention of the bill is undoubtedly to disarm the whole citizenry of offensive weapons,protect the society and make it secure for people to go about their lawful business.IF I COULD BE CONVINCED THAT THE LAW WOULD ENSURE THAT NO ONE WOULD CARRY AN OFFENSIVE WEAPON AND EVERYBODY WILL BE SAFE THEN I COULD SUPPORT THE BILL...BUT IT WILL NOT AND THUS I CANNOT SUPPORT IT.CRIMINALS HAVE NO RESPECT FOR LAW.THE ACT WILL SIMPLY PUT LAW ABIDING CITIZENS AT EVEN GREATER RISK.

IT IS DANGEROUS TO WALK IN MANY COMMUNITIES TO RIDE BUSES AND TAXIS,WOMEN ARE HARASSED BY YOUNGMEN AND ARE SAVED FROM RAPE OR ROBBERY ONLY WHEN THEY PULL KNIVES,SCISSORS OR OTHER WEAPONS.

IN A ROTTENSOCIETY IN WHICH CRIMINALS HAVE THE UPPER HAND,IN WHICH THE SECURITY FORCES ARE UNABLE TO GIVE ADEQUATE PROTECTION, IT IS SIMPLY WRONG TO DISARM OUR CITIZENS AND LEAVE THEM WITHOUT THE MEANS TO DEFEND RHEMSELVES.

I THINK THE AUTHORITIES SHOULD EXAMINE ALTERNATIVES AND THE BETTER USE OF GUNS BY LAW-ABIDING CITIZENS AS AMEANS OF SELF-DEFENCE AND PROTECTION TO DEFEND THEIR FAMILIES AND PROPERTIES.THE ACT WILL SUCCEED ONLY IN MAKING IT SAFER TO THREATEN LAW-ABIDING CITIZENS.

THE HISTORY OF SIMILAR PROVISIONS IN ENGLAND, NORTHERN IRELAND AND TRINIDAD AND TOBAGO HAS NOT DEMONSTRATED THAT PEOPLE HAVE BEEN ANY MORE SECURE THAN BEFORE THE LEGISLATION.THE GUN COURT ACT WITH ITS THREAT OF LIFE IMPRISONMENT FOR POSSESSION OF GUNS, HAVE

NOT RELIEVED THE CRIMINALS OF THEIR DESIRE TO OWN ILLEGAL GUNS.THE GUN CONTROL LEGISLATIONS HAVE FAILED, WHY DO WE BELIEVE OFFENSIVE WEAPONS LEGISLATION WILL SUCCEED."

DELROY CHUCK IS AN ATTORNEY-AT-LAW OPPOSITION MEMBER OF PARLIAMENT.

'WE CAN'T DISARM GUNMEN, ARM THE PEOPLE" GLEANER SEPTEMBER 16,1996, PAGE B4, JAMAICA

"A CALL HAS COME FROM COUNCILLOR LENWORTH BLAKE, FOR THE GOVERNMENT TO REMOVE THE OBSTACLES FOR CITIZENS WANTING LEGAL FIRE POWER, SPEAKING IN THE CONTEXT OF RISING CRIMINAL ACTIVITY,HE DECLARED 'IF YOU CAN'T DISARM THE GUNMEN ARMTHE CITIZENRY,' TO SUPPORT FROM HIS COLLOGUES AT THE MONTHLY MEETING OF THE ST ELIZABETH PARISH COUNCIL.

ONE OF THE HARDEST THINGS IS TO GET A LEGAL FIREARM, ONE OF THE EASIEST IS TO GET AN ILLEGAL GUN."

I am impressed by the two Jamaicans' weighty statements and coming from the level of two public figures--lawyer/parliamentarian and a councillor.

The cynicism of old-fashion thinking in believing that more guns mean more violence, the fear of more accidents by stray bullets, ricochet and all sort of excusable hypotheses- even dis-allowing junior police officers--if a police officer or civilian want to wound or kill his wife or girlfriend in a domestic dispute he of she do not have to use a firearm,there are so many other implements in or around the house that can be used as lethal weapons,as so many incidents current and past have shown.

I shall now show the reader that both junior police officers and civilian citizens are at the mercy of gun toting and cutlass toting criminals aware fully that their victims do not have the firepower to keep them at a distance from harm.So they boldly breakdown doors or other entrances and proceed to attack. Here are a few examples:

"Police launch manhunt after cop's wife gang-raped"NEWSDAY MARCH 2,2002, PAGE 3

"NORTHERN DIVISION POLICE HAVE LAUNCHED A MANHUNT FOR FOUR MEN WHO DURING THE EARLY MORNING BROKE INTO A POLICEMAN'S HOME AND GANG-RAPED HIS WIFE.

Reports around 3am the constable attached to a North police station and his wife asleep,a crashing noise woke the couple up THEY WERE CONFRONTED BY FOUR MASKED MEN AND ARMED WITH CUTLASSES.WHILE TWO OF THE BQWNDITS HELD DOWN THE CONSTABLE,THEIR COHORTS DRAGGED THE SCREAMING WOMAN TO AN ADJOINING ROOM AND TOOK TURNS RAPING HER...

THE BANDITS STOLE A QUANTITY OF ITEMS INCLUDING THE POLICEMAN'S WALLET CONTAINING $1000. They ran out the house and minutes later sounds of a speeding car was heard..."

"Bandits terrorise cop"TRINIDAD GUARDIAN OCTOBER 5, 1995

"BANDITS TERRORSIED AN ARANGUEZ POLICE OFFICER AND HIS FAMILY FOR SOME TWO HOURS TUESDAY NIGHT,STEALING HIS VEHICLE THEN RETURNING TO SHOWER HIS HOUSE WITH MISSLES AFTER HE REPORTED THE MATTER.

'IT WAS VERY TRAUMATIC ,MY WIFE IS STILL IN SHOCK' SAID PC FAROUK KHAN OF HIS NIGHT OF TERROR WHICH BEGAN AROUND 1.15AM.KHAN ZAID HE WAS AWAKEN TO FIND FOUR MEN IN HIS GARAGE.ATTEMPTING TO STEAL HIS PICKUP VAN.HE SHOUTED AT THEM IDENTIFYING HIMSELF AS APOLICE OFFICER

BUT INSTEAD OF RUNNING AWAY,THE BANDITS BEGAN PELTING ROCKS WARNING HIM TO REMAIN INSIDE, THE MEN THENB DROVE OFF WITH THE VEHICLE.

BUT THE DRAMA DID NOT END THERE, ONE HOUR AFTER KHAN REPORTED THE MATTER TO THE SAN JUAN POLICE,THE BANDITS RETURNED, HIS HOUSE CAME UNDER A BARRAGE OF ROCKS AND BOTTLES THAT SMASHED WINDOWS,GLASS DOORS AND NUMBER OF HOUSEHOLD ITEMS. NEIGHBOURS AWAKENED ATTEMPTED TO INVESTIGATE WERE STONED AWAY BY THE BANDITS,BEFORE THEY DROVE OFF IN THE STOLEN VEHICLE.

KHAN SAID HE PLAN TO INSTALL BURGULAR PROOFING ON ALL DOORS AND WINDOWS OF HIS HOUSE.

"Police officer's home broken into, family terrorised by armed bandits" NEWSDAY FEBRUARY 14,1998, PAGE 5

"A POLICE OFFICER AND HIS FAMILY WERE TERRORISED BY A GANG OF ARMED BANDITS AT THEIR CUMUTO <u>HOME. .THE</u> HORRIFYING INCIDENT OCCURRED AFTER THE OFFICER RAISEED AN ALARM WHEN HE SAW THE BANDITS TRYING TO DRIVE AWAY WITH HIS CAR.

CPL ANDRE DEDERE WAS AT HIS HOME WITH FAMILY WHICH INCLUDED HIS WIFE,DAUGHTER AND SISTER,AT 3,50AM HE WAS AWAKEN BY A NOISE COMING FROM HIS GARAGE.ON LOOKING OUTSIDE HE SAW FIUR MEN BREAKING INTO HIS CAR,THE BANDITS SEEING CPL DEDIERE SHOUTED TO HIM TO GO BACK INTO THE HOUSE OR ELSE THEY WOULD SHOOT HIM.THE BANDITS ONE ARMED WITH A HANDGUN, THE OTHERS WITH CUTLASSES THEN TOOK TWO LARGE STONES AND BROKE DOWN THE FRONT DOOR OF THE HOUSE,ENTERED AND RUMMAGED THROUGH DRAWERS THEY ALSO ASSAULTED FEMALE MEMBERS OF THE FAMILY.

REPORTS THE INTRUDERS TOOK A TELEVISION,CD PLAYER AND JEWELRY WITH THEM.THE BANDITS THEN WENT BACK INTO THE CAR WHERE THEY STOLE THE TAPEDECK.WHILE THE BANDITS WERE LEAVING, A NEIGHBOUR WHO HEARD THE COMMOTION,PEEPED OUT HIS WINDOW,HE HAD HIS FRONT DOOR BROKEN DOWN BY THE BANDITS WHO THREW STONES AT IT..."

"Terror at Malabar"(editor's editorial) TRINIDAD GUARDIAN SEPTEMBER 20,1995,PAGE 8

"THE RESIDENTS OF MALABAR PHASE 111 WE ARE TOLD ARE TRUMATISED, MANY OF THEM ARE UNABLE TO GET A GOOD NIGHTS SLEEP, THE REASON; FEAR OF A MARAUDING GANG OF VIOLENT BANDITS, FAMILIES AWAKEN TO SHOCK OF BANDITS KICKING DOWN THEIR DOORS.WITHIN THE LAST FOUR WEEKS,BANDITS SMASHED THEIR WAY INTO FOUR HOUSES IN PHASE111,ATTACKING AND INJURING FAMILY MEMBERS AND ROBBING OF MONEY AND JEWELRY.

SATURDAY THE BANDITS SHOWED EXTRA CONTEMPT FOR THE LAW WHEN THEY INVADED THE HOMES OF TWO POLICE OFFICERS, CPL LESLIE CHARLES AWOKE AT 3.00 IN THE MORNING TO HIS FRONT DOOR BEING KICKED DOWN,HE WAS HELD UP BY A GANG OF FOUR ARMED MEN WHO PROCEDED TO LOOT HIS HOME OF A VIDEO RECORDER AND $5000 WORTH OF JEWELRY.

ON THE SAME NIGHT CPL CHRISTOPHER JONES ALSO FOUND HIMSELF CONFRONTED BY BANDITS WHO SMASHED DOWN HIS FRONT DOOR,JONES HOWEVER CHALLEBGED THE INTRUDERS WHO APPARENT NOT PREPARED FOR A FIGHT TURNED AND RAN..."

"San Juan robbery spree,woman jumps off her roof at gun point"TRINIDAD GUARDIAN AUGUST 31,1995

"ARMED BANDITS forced a woman to jump off 20 feet off her roof at gunpoint during a rampage at three homes yesterday in Barataria and San Juan.

THE GUNMEN TERRORISED THREE FAMILIES BEFORE RELIEVING THEM OF THOUSANDS OF DOLLARS IN JEWELRY,CASH AND OTHER ITEMS. THE WOMAN ALMA MAPP IS NOW WARDED AT HOSPITAL WITH A FRACTURED HIP,MRS MAPP TEEN SON SAID 'I HEARD THEM KICK DOWN THE DOOR,THE BANDITS ENTERED THE HOUSE,THEY RAMSACKED IT.' THE BANDITS TRAINED THE GUN ON MAPP,THEY ORDERED HER TO JUMP, THE WOMAN'S DAUGHTER JUMPED OFF THE ROOF ALSO.MAPP'S OTHER SON A POLICEMAN HAD ALREADY BEEN TIED UP IN A BEDROOM BY THE BANDITS...'

There are more reports that I could have included but I have to limit my input.So the reader is left to judge for themselves if it is a just policy to allow criminals to have the advantage in weaponry over law-abiding denizens, so much so that they dare even off-duty junior police officers to come out their homes and face the consequences. FIREARM POLICY RESPONSIBLE FOR CRIMES TO DECENT, DEFENCELESS LAW-ABIDING DENIZENS.

In order for me to dispel the mystique of firearms and de-mystify this demonized weapon, let me remind the reader that I have already exposed them to the viciousness of another demonized weapon or weapons ie the "Cutlass/machette" and the "knife" popular household items yet they can have a mean side to their use for with which many murders have been committed.

WHAT DOES THE BULLET IN A FIREARM, THE STONE OR STEEL BALL IN A SLINGSHOT, THE ARROW IN A CROSSBOW, THE ARROW IN A FISHNG GUN OR EVEN A STONE IN THE HAND HAVE IN COMMON? WHEN DISCHARGED THEY HAVE

(1) VELOCITY POTENTIAL (2) THEY CREATE DISTANCE BETWEEN THE USER WHO LAUNCHES THE PROJECTILE AND THE TRAGET/VICTIM (3) THEY HAVE LETHAL POTENTIAL TO DO DAMAGE TO THE OBJECT AIMED AT. WHAT STAND OUT ABOUT THE FIREARM AS TO THE OTHERS COMPARED IS THAT WHILE VELOCITY IS COMMON TO EACH,THE FIREARM HAS (1)A GREATER RATE OF VELOCITY

(1)THE RANGE DISTANCE IS ALSO GREATER(3) CAN BE SUCCESSIVE VOLLEY OF PROJECTILES DICHARGED. (4)THAT VELOCITY CAN BE UP-GRADED IN A FIREARM DEPENDING ON THE SHAPE AND INTERNAL COMPOSITION OF ITS AMMUNITION OR THE MECHANICS OF EACH FIREARM. (low velocity bullets as compared to high velocity bullets).

Please remember that in the games of lawn tennis, cricket, baseball javelin throw, shot put etc, the velocity speed of the ball pitched, bowled or thrown is already measured and it differs depending on the strength/style of the contestant. IN FIREARMS, VELOCITY IS MEASURED AS FPS(Feet or force per second).

Let me further demystify the firearm further. The bullet of the firearm differ in appearance and size and by different names, so too is the firearm. THE FIREARM INNER BARREL CIRCUMFERENCE OR BORE DIFFER AND BULLETS ARE MANUFACTURED TO FIT THAT BORE ALSO CALLED THE MUZZLE, THE SMALLEST IS the .22 that is in pistol or revolvers,rifles there larger bores such as: .38,.357magnum, .45,9mm etc.In shotguns there are measurements in guages of 12, 16,20.

There is another type of pistol or rifle but not of firepower but air/compressed air called air gun the smallest is the .177, but there are .20,.22size pellets and also can have high velovcity.

The mechanics of a bullet, is that it contains explosives of gunpower,primer of different measurement,grade, weight called grain,compressed into the inner casing of the bullet, while shot guns use cartridges with compressed gunpowder and steel bb balls or pellets.

In firearms there is a pin or firing pin part of the trigger/hammer, when the trigger is pulled and the firing pin moves forward it strikes the back `center of the bullet logged in the cylinder creating an explosion and moving the bullet out of the cylinder or barrel of the fire arm.it is this explosion which is seen as a flash coming from the barrel of the fire arm called muzzle energy flash and depending on the degree of bullet used and type of gun it can blind at night.Firearms carry safetly locks.

Firearm bullets are contoured differently and called by different names such as: jacketed, semi wadcutter, round nose, hollow point etc.The tip seen at the outside front of a bullet is really the slug made mostly of lead, it is this that enters the body when shot, Powder type made by different manufacturers is important as you have slow burning,fast burning powder,kickback or recoil can be experienced with certain high energy bullets and higher quality magnum firearms.

Barrel length differ also in pistols and shot guns,rifles such as in pistols 2",4",6" or even 8"(inches) and in shot guns/rifles barrels are as much as 35"(inches) long,

As I referred to velocity measured by ballistic experts vary from low velocity as 500FPS to high velocity of 1200FPS and more., the higher the number of velocity, the greater the distance of bullet travel and penetration. Three other aspects are (1) barrels are internally grooved in turns called rifling and has to do with accuracy of the bullet (2)Automatic and semi-automatic or repeater and single shot. In automatic bullets fly once you keep your finger on the trigger, in semi you have to pull the trigger (3)Number of bullets each pistol chamber holds.Some pistols chamber 5,6,15 or more,rifles can load 600rounds etc

SO I THINK THAT I HAVE DONE ENOUGH TO ALLOW THE READER TO UNDERSTAND THE FIREARM, AND THEREFORE I HAVE DE-MYSTIFY THE MYSTIQUE THAT YOU ARE LED TO BELIEVE THAT YOU HAVE TO HAVE SOME ESOTERIC KNOWLEDGE ABOUT A SIMPLE MECHANISM AND INEXPENSIVE EQUIPMENT. AS YOU WILL SEE THAT I SHALL DEAL WITH THE COST PRICE OF AN ORDINARY FIREARM LATER ON.(what training in firearm use do criminals have using illegal arms?)

NOW LET ME TURN TO THE LAW ON AIRGUNS IN THE REPUBLIC OF TRINIDAD AND TOBAGO. THE FIREARM(AIR WEAPONS LAW 16:01) ALLOWS ONLY SMOOTH BORE BARREL AND NOT RIFLED AND ONLY .177 OR 4.5 CALIBER. LET ME REMIND YOU AS I SAID BEFORE,RIFLING OF A FIREARM BARREL IS THAT THE INSIDE OF THE BARREL IS GROOVED IN TURNS ALLOWING THE EXIT OF THE BULLET/ PELLET/AMMUNITION TO SPIRAL OUT AND BE MORE ACCURATE RATHER THAN STRAY. JUDGE FOR YOUSELF READER- DO YOU FEEL THAT THE BRAIN OF A LAW-ABIDING ADULT IS SO THAT OF A CHILD? THAT EVEN WITH A PERMIT OF OWNERSHIP FROM THE COMMISSIONER OF POLICE THEY CAN ONLY BE TRUSTED WITH AN INACCURATE RATHER THAN MORE ACCURATE GUN THAT THEY HAVE SPENT THEIR MONEY ON.? I SUGGEST THAT THIS OLD-FASHION LAW BE CHANGED TO ALLOW RIFLED BULLET AIR WEAPONS.

I assume that government must be afraid that too many firearms in the hands of denizens of the country can spell fear of a civil insurrection that cannot be controlled by the security forces. Or are they afraid that law -abiding denizens will become snipers and be uncontrollable by the security forces?. THAT IS BECAUSE GOVERNMENT OF THIS THINKING WHOSE POLICY EXTEND TO THE HIGHEST ECHELON OF THE POLICE HAVE NOT STUDIED ANOTHER POLICY OF "alternative policing" I SUGGEST NOW(1)let the law-abiding denizens with years of stable family life of stable mind who own a lot of land and their own home and a suitable bank account own firearms(2)junior police officers with ten years service,stable family life be allowed to own firearms.(3)only .22 caliber be allowed to civilians and junior police officers(4)First division police officers upon retirement be allowed only .22 caliber(5) only the State Forces be allowed higher caliber automatics(5) a state agency be responsible to monitor firearms dealers inventories.

the Editor of the Sunday Times Newspaper(London)January 6, 2002 "Crime's ugly rise" and I quote here just two lines of the article "THE GROWING USE OF GUNS IN VIOLENT CRIMES—BUT KNIVES AND OTHER WEAPONS CAN BE JUST AS DEADLY."

I wish to insert below at this point the front cover of the WASHINGTON POST MAGAZINE JUNE 19, 1994 with the Words "Murder American Style" and see from that picture The number of weapons used for woundings:

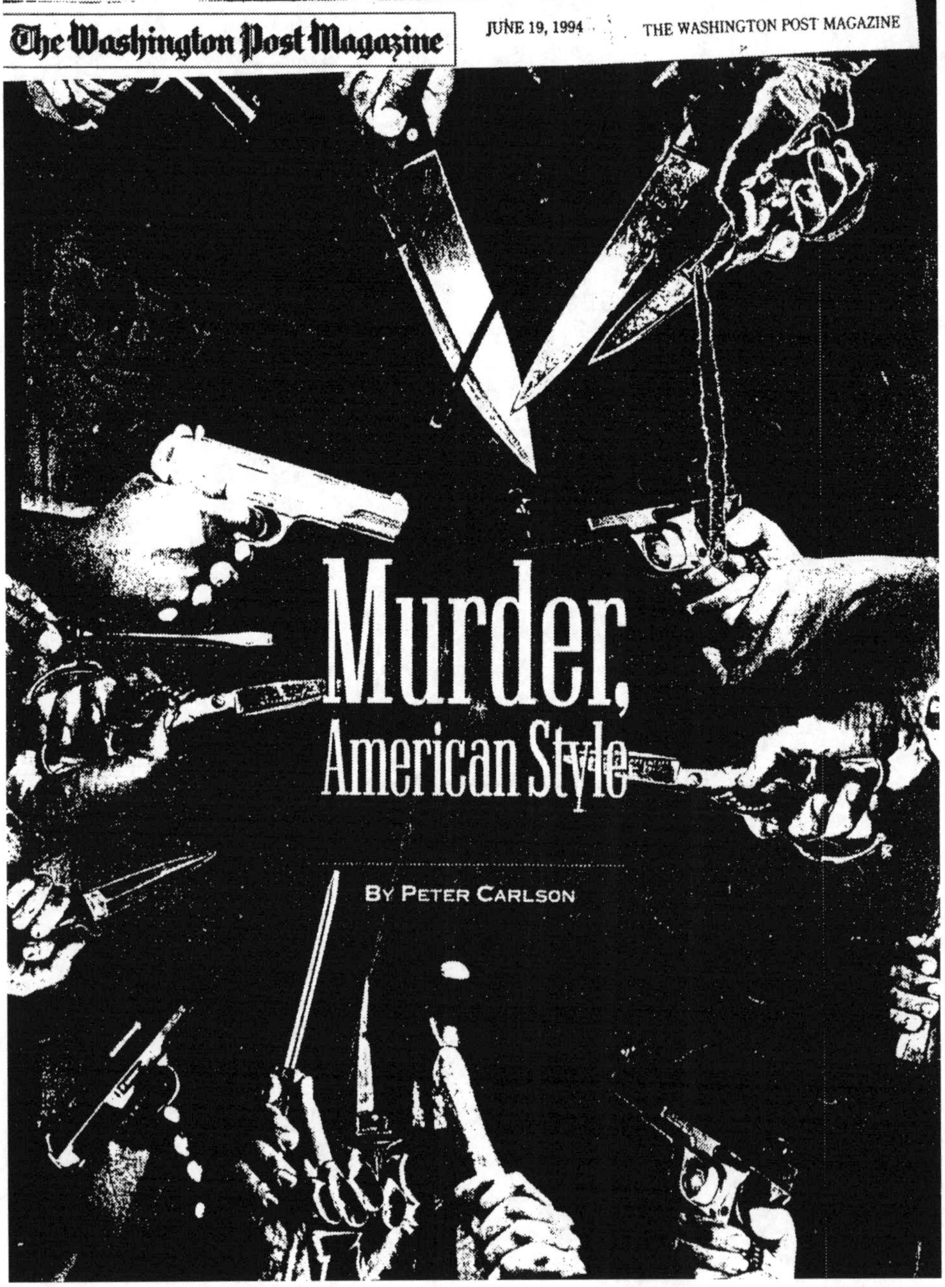

The Washington Post Magazine   JUNE 19, 1994   THE WASHINGTON POST MAGAZINE

Murder, American Style

BY PETER CARLSON

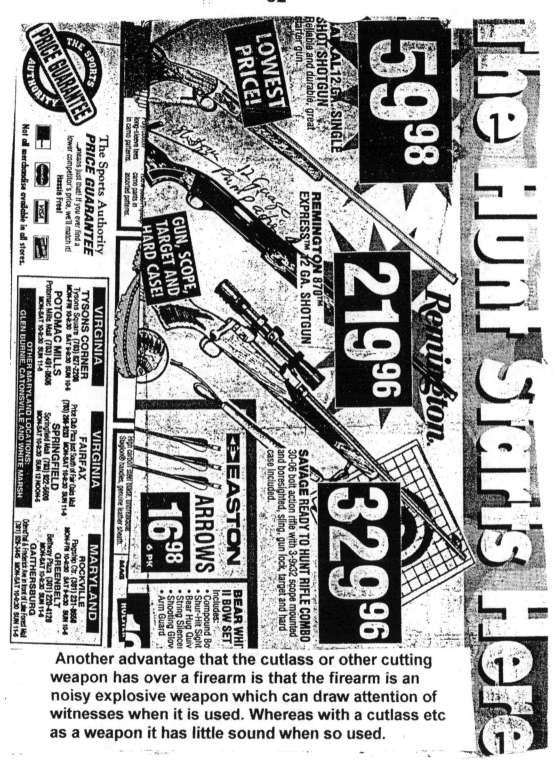

Another advantage that the cutlass or other cutting weapon has over a firearm is that the firearm is an noisy explosive weapon which can draw attention of witnesses when it is used. Whereas with a cutlass etc as a weapon it has little sound when so used.

46

I SHALL NOW SHOW YOU THAT LAW-ABIDING DENIZENS OWN HOUSE,LAND,CARS THAT ARE FAR MORE OF COST VALUE THAN AN ORDINARY FIREARM. IN ADDITION THEY DRIVE CARS ON SIX NARROW LANE HIGHWAYS WITH LESS THAN SIX FEET SEPARATING EACH VEHICLE GOING IN THE SAME DIRECTION WITH RARE FENDER ACCIDENTS, SO THEY CAN HOLD THEIR OWN WITH AIMING A GUN.

TRINIDAD
VALUATION OF FIREARMS COST
2003

INFORMATION QUOTATIONS SUPPLIED HERE ARE FROM
   (1)   SPORTS AND GAMES LTD, FIREARMS DEPARTMENT
   (2)   FIREARMS TRAINING INSTITUTE

NEITHER FIREARM DEALER STOCK THE SMALL BORE .22 CALIBER BECAUSE THEY FELT THAT CUSTOMERS WANTED AN ARMAMENT WITH GREATER STOPPING POWER. IN ADDITION I SOUGHT TO GET SOME OF THE CHEAPEST BRAND NAMES AND COST FOR YOU.
   (1)   SPORTS AND GAMES LTD STOCK MANUFACTURES OF:
         SMITH & WESSON, WALTHER, GLOCK ,SIG,SAUER,MOSSBERG,REMINGT ON CHEAPEST: .38 CALIBER—TT$4000.00(FOUR THOUSAND $) 9MM ""--- TT$6000.00(SIX THOUSAND)
         SHOT GUN 12GUAGE—TT$3000.00(three thousand $)
   (2)   FIREARMS TRAINING INSTITUTE STOCK:BERETTA, BROWNING,WINCHE STER,RUGER
         CHEAPEST:RUGER 9MM—TT$5000.00(FIVE THOUSAND $)
         BERETTA .380--TT$7000.00(SEVEN THOUSAND $)
         SHOT GUN—12 GUA-TT$1900.00(ONE THOUSAND 9 $)

SUNDAY TIMES MAY 13, 2001, ENGLAND

People in Britain face higher crime rates while having fewer officers per head than comparable countries

City	Population	No. of crimes	No. of officers	Officers per citizen
London	7,322,564	1,052,000	25,121	1 per 290
New York	7,285,000	288,000	45,535	1 per 161
Berlin	3,398,822	557,001	27,298	1 per 124
Chicago	2,821,032	180,932	13,366	1 per 211
Manchester	2,577,400	372,013	6,851	1 per 376
Sheffield	530,400	53,494	972	1 per 545

Gun crime in the UK

Offences involving firearms have risen by 40% since 1997. Armed robberies account for more than half the crimes

4,904 — 96/97
4,903 — 97/98
5,209 — 98/99
6,843 — 99/00

7,000
6,000
5,000
4,000

Gun law takes over in gangland drug wars

James Clark
Home Affairs Correspondent

GUN crime in Britain will escalate sharply as drug gangs battle for supremacy, police experts will warn ministers after the election. Police estimate that nearly 300,000 illegal guns or replicas capable of being reactivated are now in circulation.

The number of firearm offences increased from 4,903 in 1997 to 6,843 last year, but ministers will be told that a particularly high surge in murders using firearms in the past 18 months will continue, with more and more criminals prepared to use weapons to defend their businesses and territory.

Trafficking in the weapons is also on the increase, the National Criminal Intelligence Service (NCIS) will tell the prime minister in July, when it issues its confidential threat assessment.

The sharp warnings will be accompanied by new pleas from senior police officers for stricter gun laws. David

Mean streets: Nottingham has armed beat officers with handguns in a high-crime area

McCrone, deputy chief constable of Greater Manchester police and the UK's most senior police officer dealing with firearms, does not rule out the possibility of growing numbers of armed police on the beat if the situation does not change.

In recent weeks two men have been machinegunned to death in a residential street in north London, a pensioner was hit by a stray bullet during a shoot-out in Manchester and, in a residential cul-de-sac in Long-sight, Manchester. The divisional police headquarters is only 200 yards from her door. She is the first innocent

alarmed police in both cities.
Last Monday, Alice Carroll, 70, was shot in the back as a gunman opened fire on another man near her home in a quiet residential cul-de-sac in Longsight, Manchester. The divisional police headquarters is only 200 yards from her door.

'drive-by' shootings have signal police shootings in 1996.

head of the Association of Chief Police Officers (Acpo) committee on firearms, says: "I don't think armed British police are inevitable, but we need to do more to make sure that doesn't happen.

"Many criminals are now renting guns for killings. We see the same weapon being used in different parts of the country in different scenarios."

He will demand new laws to outlaw many replica guns and to ban the licence-free ownership of machines to reload bullets. Home-loaded rounds are most commonly used in gangland killings as legal or stolen rounds are less readily available since the ban on handguns was introduced in the wake of the Dunblane shootings in 1996.

NCIS will warn in July that there remains a "strong link" between firearm possession and drug trafficking. It will say that many young men carry weapons as a "fashion accessory" but use them in violent situations in the way that they might previously have used a knife. The largest number of guns is imported from western Europe, although more unusual weap-

British cities under the gun

SUNDAY TIMES APRIL 21,1996,ENGLAND 1996

The police are losing the fight against armed criminal gangs, writes John Burns

The two gunmen in Stephen Hardy's bedroom at 11pm last Tuesday paused before they shot him. There was a hurried conversation about the identity of Hardy, who was pinned to the floor alongside his girlfriend, with their one-year-old son asleep nearby. The masked gunmen were not sure if they had the right man.

"Shoot him anyway," one whispered fiercely. So they did — three times in the left leg, three in the right leg and once in the right arm. It was the type of routine punishment regularly doled out by Liverpool's increasingly violent gangsters. Since last weekend there have been four similar attacks, with a total of six men shot in the legs. What the gunmen did not appear to know was that their victim on this occasion was a police constable, and their mistake would focus a spotlight on their murky underworld.

One house looks much like another on the middle-class housing estate in West Derby, on the outskirts of Liverpool, to which Hardy and his family had recently moved. Until a few days ago, an individual under police investigation had been his near neighbour. The man, of similar age, had recently decided that he was no longer safe in his home. Police believe he may have been the real target of Tuesday night's attack.

"We don't know who was behind the attack yet and we don't have a motive," one Merseyside officer admitted. The problem for the police in Liverpool is that not every shooting is part of a drugs war between rival gangs. Criminals, who carry guns as fashion accessories, sometimes use them in the most trivial arguments. Insult a local thug's girlfriend or even give him a funny look in a nightclub and, chances are, he and his mates will be around later to spray your house with bullets.

The "straightener" was once a tradition among Liverpool's criminal fraternity. A grievance between two gangsters was sorted out by a fist fight, and that ended the matter. No longer; the losers of these fights now tend to escalate the disputes by resorting to guns.

That was why David Ungi, 36, met his death in Toxteth last May. Five weeks earlier he had won a "straightener" which had been intended to sort out a row over drinking rights at a former Conservative club. David Ungi was white and from Dingle; his rivals were black and from Toxteth. Colour was, however, incidental to the war that erupted between the gangs, police say.

Near Hardy's home is the set of Brookside, the Channel 4 soap opera. As the gang wars erupted Jimmy Corkhill, Brookside's resident drug dealer, bought a bulletproof vest. Corkhill's house was also attacked in a drive-past shooting of the kind that is seen in Bootle most weeks.

Detective Chief Superintendent Chris Smethurst said: "Our tactics are devoted exclusively to the recovery of illegally held firearms." The source of these guns is baffling the police. Even Tokarevs, standard military issue in China, have been seized. Many officers blame the end of the cold war for the glut of weaponry which is swamping Britain's inner cities. Some forces are investigating the possibility that gunsmiths are reactivating weapons that have

most violent inner-city area in Britain, the 10-year drugs war between the Doddingtons and the Gooch Close Gang is in a state of uneasy truce after the shooting of a leading Doddington member in January 1994. In the three years before that, more than 110 people were shot. In the two years since, there have been at least 40 shootings.

When the truce breaks down, the consequences are devastating. Only a bullet-proof vest prevented Darrell Laycock from becoming the second fatality in nine days last Christmas. Police, who found 27 spent cartridges at the scene of the attack, believe three people were shooting at Laycock — one with a shotgun and two using automatic weapons.

Superintendent Lilian King, head of community policing in Moss Side, believes one way to tackle the drug barons is to give police more powers to seize their assets. She has seen children as young as 13 being used to carry drugs and money on their mountain bikes.

LIVERPOOL SHOOTINGS LAST WEEK

1 Saturday April 13
Three men shot in legs at Glasshouse pub

2 Sunday April 14
Pregnant woman escaped unhurt after her house was shot at

3 4 Tuesday April 16
12.15 am: Man shot in legs
1.20 am: Another man shot in legs

Aintree

Peel Road

Stowbridge Close **5**

LIVERPOOL

Gidlow Road South **4**

Edge Lane **1**

Olive Lane **2**

Toxteth

5 Tuesday April 16
11pm: PC Stephen Hardy ordered out of bed and shot in arm and both legs

"We have had dealers driving expensive cars such as Porsches. If we take away their cars, jewellery and nice clothes, children will see these criminals in a different light," she said.

In Liverpool, police maintain a heavily armed presence in trouble spots to reassure the frightened local population. Most people are

By Kevin Helliker
THE WALL STREET JOURNAL

TORONTO STAR APRIL 23, 1994, CANADA

Their gun controls may be a model for the world, but British authorities concede they can't keep firearms out of criminals' hands. People are sharply divided about what to do

Armed in Britain

LONDON

WHILE walking his beat last October, Officer Patrick Dunne came across three drug dealers. They produced guns. The bobby had only a wooden truncheon. They laughed as they killed him.

In a nation so restrictive of guns that most police officers don't carry them, more and more criminals do. Incidents of armed robbery have more than doubled since 1983.

Guns are bought on the street these days as easily as drugs. Last month, a motorcyclist, stopped for a routine licence check here, shot and seriously wounded two police officers, neither of whom was armed.

The attempted holdup of a candy store last month was committed by a gun-toting assailant described as 8 years old.

A portrait of criminals holding guns on an unarmed populace haunts the halls of every U.S. gun-control debate.

And with the recent enactment of legislation requiring a five-day waiting period and background check for handgun purchases — the so-called Brady bill — that portrait will be used to argue against further regulation.

But in Britain, where criminals increasingly are better armed than anyone else, lawmakers are considering new ways of 'reducing the country's already minimal legal arsenal. Some members of Parliament, for instance, are arguing that home storage of firearms — currently illegal without a licence — ought to be banned.

This gamble is based on the premise that even criminals have a sense of fair play. Authorities concede that res-

and more frequently — just last month, police charged a 13-year-old with the fatal stabbing of an 85-year-old woman — Britain's sense of itself as more civilized than the U.S. is becoming harder to maintain.

Some neighborhoods here can be as rough as any street in America, as discovered this year by some Pennsylvania State University students enrolled at Britain's Manchester University.

After being held up at knifepoint, then at gunpoint, then beaten up and twice burglarized, they declared in the national press that they felt more vulnerable in Manchester than in New York.

Compared with London, New York is downright safe in one category: burglary.

In London, where many homes have been burglarized half a dozen times, and where psychologists specialize in treating children traumatized by such thefts, the rate is nearly twice as high as the Big Apple.

And burglars here are increasingly prefer striking when occupants are home, since alarms and locks tend to be disengaged

Hungerford in 1987.

Ryan's firearms certificate allowed him to own three pistols and two semi-automatic rifles, including the Russian-made Kalashnikov AK-47 that he used in the slaughter.

Margaret Thatcher's Conservative government responded to the killings by enacting the most draconian firearms act ever adopted in Britain, including outlawing semi-automatic weapons altogether.

In comparison, neither then-president George Bush — a member of the National Rifle

EACH sale of a firearm 'has to be recorded in a certain way,' he says, 'and every round of ammunition that is bought and sold has to be recorded.' Roberts estimates 'that such rules have raised his costs 30 per cent in recent years.

Despite such complaining, nobody in Britain's gun industry seems to favor deregulation. Lord Swansea, one of the strongest advocates of gun rights, says, 'You have to keep some sort of tab on ownership of all guns — not just handguns.'

In the same breath that Andrew Young, managing director of Browning/Winchester U.K. Ltd, complains about poor sales in Britain, he says he wouldn't favor arming all bobbies — even though his company has a contract to supply guns to them.

Currently, about one in 16 British police officers is trained to use arms, and operates in an elite force that responds to highly dangerous situations.

Following the murder of officer Dunne last October, a Police Review magazine survey found

that strong, either. The number of dealers has fallen 10 per cent in recent years, to 2,400.

And while no one will estimate the value of the British gun market, by all accounts it is small and 'on a 5 per cent to 10 per cent decline annually,' says Paul Roberts, chairman of John Rigby & Co., one of several world-renowned shotgun makers in Britain.

The company produces about 50 guns a year, about half of them for overseas customers. The $6,000 price-tag in part reflects the high cost of complying with regulations, Roberts says.

NEWSDAY OCTOBER 12,1998

Most crime worse in England than US

Newsday Oct 12-1998

LONDON: You are more likely to be mugged in England than in the United States, according to a new crime study reported with some consternation in Britain yesterday.

The study by a Cambridge University professor and a statistician from the US Department of Justice said crime rates for serious offences such as assault, burglary, robbery, and motor vehicle theft were all higher in England and Wales than in America.

Rape and murder rates were still higher in the United States, but Britain was gaining ground, said *The Sunday Times*, which reported the study at the top of its front page. It said Britain may have tougher gun laws, but the United States had longer prison sentences.

"Common sense says America is the most crime-ridden country on earth while Britain is an oasis of peace and tranquillity. Common sense is wrong," *The Sunday Times* said in an editorial.

"We urgently need to re-examine our cosy assumptions about law and order."

The Mail on Sunday reprinted some of the study's findings. They said that in 1995, the last year for which complete statistics were available on both sides of the Atlantic, there were 20 assaults per 1,000 people or households in England and Wales but just 8.8 in the United States.

The rate of robbery is now 1.4 times higher in England and Wales than in the United States, and the British burglary rate is nearly double America's, the report said.

(REUTERS)

Page 50 NEWSDAY Monday September 2, 2002

PEOPLE

NEWSDAY SEPTEMBER 2, 2002

Joan Collins fears 'crime-ridden' London

LONDON: Actress Joan Collins prefers life in New York over her birthplace of London which she denounces as dirty, crime-ridden and rife with violent thugs in an interview with the *Mail.*

The 69-year-old actress, who owns a flat in the fashionable west London neighbourhood of Belgravia, said she dreads walking even the few hundred yards to her hairdresser's for fear of being mugged. "Groups of muggers are frequently attacking people in the area

where I live. And the police don't appear to be able to do anything about it," she was quoted as saying.

"To be honest, I feel so much more comfortable there (in New York) than I do in London. I feel so much safer for a start." The veteran actress's comments came a day after one of Britain's top police officers said Prime Minister Tony Blair may fail in his pledge to bring the country's levels of street crime under control by the end of September.

London, in particular, has seen a sharp

rise in street crime, with offences up 40 percent earlier this year over the previous year. Recent figures indicate, however, it may have plateaued with police data showing street crime in the capital was down 8.6 percent between April and July.

Collins said she worries about the safety of her daughters, the eldest of whom, Tara Newley, was mugged for her watch in Notting Hill last year.

She is not the only celebrity victim of London street crime — thieves tried to grab a diamond necklace from US enter-

tainer Liza Minnelli while her car was stopped at a traffic light in March. Collins, who married fifth husband Percy Gibson in London in February, heaped particular scorn on the large numbers of "louts" on the capital's streets.

"Yobbism in London is rife. In New York, people are more polite, more respectful," she said.

THE SUNDAY TIMES

OCTOBER 11,1998,PAGE 1

No 9,085

11 OCTOBER 1998

(LONDON) Times News paper October 11, 1998, England

Official: more muggings in England than

by Nicholas Rufford Home Affairs Editor

The 100-page report, which took a year to compile, is set to launch a furious political debate about law enforcement in Britain. It shows that the most common types of serious offence — assault, robbery, burglary and motor vehicle theft — are higher in England and Wales than in America. Rape and murder rates are still higher in the United States — where gun ownership is prevalent — but the gap is narrowing.

"We are determined to learn the right lessons from the report and reverse this trend."

Many American cities, including New York, are safer than they were 10 years ago. In Britain, the reverse is true. The research, by two leading criminologists, one British and one American, also shows that the criminal justice system in Britain is worse at tackling crime. Someone committing a serious crime, other than mur-

der, is more likely to be caught, convicted and sent to jail in America than Britain.

Patrick Langan, a junior statistician with the Department of Justice, said the findings came as a huge surprise. "With most glary and automobile theft rates are getting on for double those people, the perception is that crime rates are much higher in the US."

the United States. In fact, rates are now higher in England for most types of major crime. The robbery rate in England and Wales, including muggings, is 40% higher. The assault, bur-

David Farrington, a criminologist at Cambridge University, co-author of the report, said the findings challenged the public view of crime levels in Britain. "The picture has changed dramatically in the past 15 years. Then, America had much higher rates, whereas now England is much higher."

The report is based on surveys of thousands of victims and data from police, courts and prison services over 15 years.

The report appears to be a vindication of tough American policies such as "zero tolerance" policing, "three strikes and you're out", which sends repeat offenders to jail for life, and frequent use of long custodial sentences.

A Home Office source confirmed the Tories for the 15-year increase in crime and de-cline in conviction rates: "The report is a graphic illustration of the Tories' failure on law and order. Not only has crime

Paxman's Progress — News Review, page 10

THE SUNDAY TIMES
JANUARY 6, 2002, LONDON, ENGLAND

Crime's ugly rise

The government's anti-crime strategy appears to be coming apart at the seams. Ministers deny it and claim that the figures for violent crime overall are falling. That was true when the last British Crime Survey was published a year ago, but London's latest figures show a dramatic worsening. Victims aged under 16, who are not included in the national crime survey, have become a prime target for mobile phone snatchers. Anybody who resists, as a 19-year-old woman did in east London on New Year's Day, may risk their lives in doing so. She was shot in the head and has still not been named because of fears for her safety. Official advice to mobile owners not to use their phones in public may be prudent, if depressing, but she was attacked at 5.30pm in a busy street. American research appears to show that resistance makes matters worse; in a study of 1m robberies in the United States, victims suffered more by resisting. People are faced with an awful dilemma: meekly hand over money and valuables or have a go and risk your life.

Last week's rash of crimes showed that this violence is not confined to London and other big cities. Nor is the fear of violence limited to direct physical attack. The 86-year-old Somerset woman who suffered a fatal heart attack after her purse was snatched in broad daylight as she walked home with her shopping was a victim of violence, even if the law says otherwise. So, in a different way, was the Essex landowner who was arrested for trying to unplug a music system being used by 60 ravers in his barn. The police excuse was that he, not them, risked causing a public order disturbance. "It wasn't so much a question of right and wrong," said a spokesman. Why not? Because the unruly trespass laws do not apply to fewer than 100 invaders.

This is the topsy-turvy madness that prevents householders defending themselves from burglars in the middle of the night if they are considered to have used disproportionate force. The grieving family of Kevin Jackson, the Halifax man fatally stabbed in the head six times when he accosted car thieves outside his home, knows the real horror of disproportionate force. The killers showed him no mercy. Ordinary law-abiding citizens are entitled to feel there is something wrong with a criminal justice system that puts the victim at a disadvantage. The growing use of guns in violent crimes — especially drug-related ones — adds a new and alarming dimension to the problem. But knives and other weapons can be just as deadly. The restraints on the police to stop and search for fear of inciting racial unrest do nothing to reassure a frightened public, whether black or white. In fact, ethnic minorities suffer disproportionately from these crimes and would welcome a tougher police line.

Tony Blair came to power promising to attack crime and the causes of crime. But violent crime is rising sharply and the promise of more police officers by next year sounds similar to his other as yet unfulfilled pledges to improve public services. Police resources in London have undoubtedly been stretched by terrorist threats, especially since September 11. That does not explain the shocking total of 212,000 cases of violence and robbery in the capital in the first 11 months of last year.

The scale of the crisis is brought home by the comparison we report today with New York, where a policy of zero tolerance has sent crime rates plummeting. When people in London are six times more likely to be assaulted or robbed than people in New York, we need solutions fast. The new Home Office quango chief, paid £200,000 a year to spur police forces to greater efficiency, will be worth every penny if he produces results. Nothing will change dramatically, however, without a new approach by chief constables and senior officers. They have become more anxious to avoid criticism and to say the right things politically than to be dynamic leaders in the war against crime. Mr Blair appears to think that bigger budgets and new pay and conditions will work. Maybe. But he has had more than four years to turn things round and we are still waiting.

Violent crime: assaults, murders and muggings

Attacks raise fear level

TIMES NEWSPAPER JANUARY 6, 2002
LONDON, ENGLAND

Crimes of violence in	2001	212,177		212,177	
London have increased by 28% in the past three years	2000	207,450			
	1999	204,322			
	1998	153,490			

London New York November 2001 · 20,061 · 3,673 · London New York Jan-Nov 2001 · 212,177 · 46,254

New victims feed alarm over crime

David Leppard and Jane Mulkerrins

PEOPLE in London are now six times more likely to be assaulted or robbed than residents of New York, once considered the most dangerous city in the world.

Amid growing concern over the rise in street crime, new police figures show that 2.5 people per 1,000 were victims of violent crime in London in November, compared to 0.4 per 1,000 in New York. The murder rate, however, is still higher in New York.

In London the number of assaults and muggings has risen by 28% in the past three years. But in New York, which has had a policy of "zero tolerance" to crime and more than 60% more police officers on the streets, violent crime is down by 32% over the same period.

In London the number of violent crimes — defined as street robberies, assaults and murders — are growing faster than in other American crime hotspots, such as Los Angeles, Chicago and Detroit.

The statistics will add to public concern after a series of violent crimes last week under-

lined the apparent inability of the police to act effectively. This weekend detectives were hunting an armed mugger who stole a 10-year-old's Christmas money and his friend's mobile telephone in southeast London.

A few days earlier police launched a murder hunt after Kevin Jackson died in a Halifax hospital. The father of two was stabbed in the head with a screwdriver by white youths after he tried to stop them stealing his mother-in-law's car.

The two incidents highlight an alarming increase in street robberies and violent crime.

In Birmingham in November there were 279 more street robberies than in November 2000. In Manchester muggings were up by 15%. Violent crime is worse in London, where in November there were 5,041 violent robberies, 168 per day, compared with 3,355 in November 2000, a 50% increase.

The scale of the epidemic has become more public. While London has 26,000 officers, New York has 42,000. There is one police

officer for every 190 people in New York, and one for every 290 people in London.

Policing methods are also different. Eight years ago Rudolph Giuliani, the recently retired mayor, introduced a policy of zero tolerance. Police officers were concentrated in neighbourhoods with high crime levels and even minor offenders, including fare dodgers, were prosecuted. Giuliani benefited as well from a fall in the teenage population and a decline in the use of crack cocaine. Crime during his tenure fell by 64%.

In London, policing has if anything become more liberal. Ever since the Macpherson re-

port branded the Metropolitan police as "institutionally racist" in the wake of the murder of the black teenager Stephen Lawrence, stop-and-search operations have declined sharply. Rank-and-file officers say the tool is essential in the war on street crime, but senior officers fear being branded racists.

Other factors are more subjective. Some psychologists blame a collapse in respect for authority and a general decline in moral standards. Ministers, however, say the number of muggings reflects the explosion in the use of mobile phones. They have called in manufacturers to demand they

introduce security features such as code numbers that render handsets useless if stolen. Home Office figures to be released this week will show that thefts of mobile phones have risen by almost 200% since 1995. In 1999 there were 5,000 muggings involving mobile phones. Last year there were 25,000.

Ian Blair, the Metropolitan police deputy commissioner, accepts there is a serious problem but argues that a big part of it can be explained by a shortage of officers. "What happened [was] equivalent to the short-age of officers," he said. "If you push that down too far it's a

very difficult road back." He points out that you are still four times more likely to be murdered in New York than in London and says his force arrested 27% more robbers in 2001 than in the previous year. But muggings in September, October and November still rose by 43% compared with the same period in the previous year.

Sir John Stevens, the Metropolitan police commissioner, recently told David Blunkett, the home secretary, that he will need a new law to tackle street robbers. He wants muggers to be treated like burglars, with an automatic prison sentence for anybody caught three times.

Police claim the surge in crime has been caused by a shortage of officers but ministers say muggings for/mobile phones are among a number of

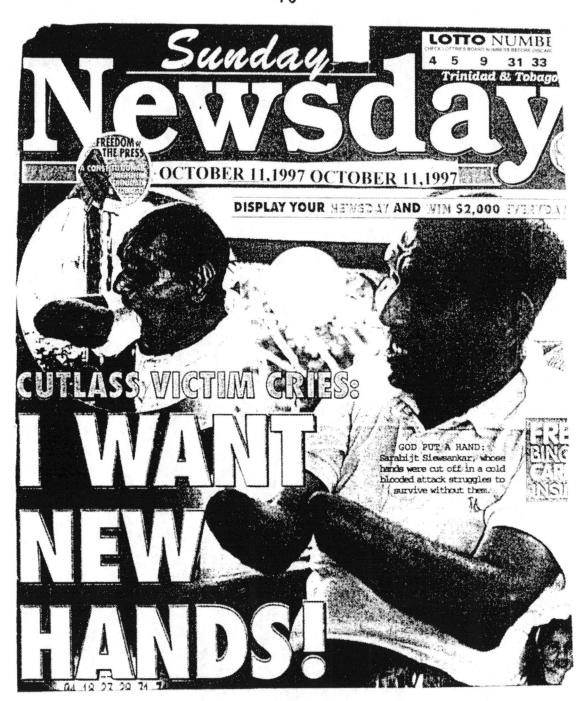

Man's arms chopped off in brutal attack

By RICHARD CHARAN

SARABJIT SIEUSANKAR, 65, of Mendez Village, Siparia, had both his arms completely severed yesterday when he was attacked by a man with a cutlass.

Sieusankar had just milked his cows and was returning from his garden with a bucket of fresh milk on his way to the village temple for prayers, when he was attacked by a man. He was also chopped on the face and back of the head.

Last night the elderly man, who is a retired Siparia Regional Corporation worker and described as a peaceful, devout Hindu, was fighting for his life at the San Fernando General Hospital, after doctors failed to re-attach the severed arms. The operation lasted eight hours.

A man living in a wooden shack near Sieusankar's garden, whose name was given as Basdeo Harripersad, witnessed the incident, and positively identified a suspect.

The attacker was last night still on the run, but, police, who have said that an arrest was expected last night.

Newsday was told that the suspect, about 45 years old, was a well known man from the village, who had made threats to "chop up" Sieusankar on many occasions over the years.

Police believe that Sieusankar was first chopped to the back of the neck and when he turned, recieved a vicious wound which cut him from his forehead across his nose to his chin. As he put up his hands to fend off the blows, police say, one arm was severed.

He was then chased along the road for about a quarter mile, bleeding profusely, and screaming out, when a second chop severed his other hand. The man was left writhing in the bushes at the side of the road, while his attacker ran off.

Although a crew from an oil company heard the screams, they did not react.

However, a neighbour responded and took Sieusankar in his taxi to the one hour journey from the deep south village, to the

POORANDAYE SIEUSANKAR, wife of Sarabjit Sieusankar, and their daughter hope for his recovery after both his hands were severed. Photo by AZLAN MOHAMMED.

hospital, but it was too late to re-attach it.

cattle", She explained that they both took weekly turns in going to their garden located half mile away, in Petrotrin owned lands, where they grew cassava, bananas, and corn, and minded their six head of cattle.

Recalling how she first heard of the gruesome chopping of her husband of 46 years, Pooransingh said that a young man from the village ran to her home and "tell me that he dead".

"When I gone to see him, they hold me back".

When she ran to the scene, she was prevented from seeing Sieusankar.

The woman said that her husband had over the past six months made daily pilgrimages to the Mendez Ganesh Temple, to participate in prayers.

Holding back tears, the woman said that when she went to the hospital, she was prevented from seeing her husband.

"On the way back home, I stop off at the temple, and I tell the pundit."

NEWS

Four chopped to death in one house

NEWSDAY MAY 6, 2001

BY NALINEE SEELAL

IN WHAT has been described as the "grisliest" murders for the year, a 27 year-old woman, her four-year-old daughter, her nine year-old handicapped step-son and her 62-year-old mother-in-law, were brutally chopped to death at their Alfred Dennis Trace, Talparo home early yesterday.

The mutilated bodies of Alicia James, her daughter Giselle Garcia, step-son Dillon Garcia and mother-in-law Catherine Garcia, were discovered by a neighbour around 9.30 am yesterday. Three bodies were found on the eastern side of the house in pools of blood while the body of Alicia was found at the front of her home with more than 20 chop wounds. Police have ruled out robbery as the motive for the murders as no valuables in the house were missing. The police are working on the theory that the killings were an act of revenge and investigators believe that they may be able to solve the brutal killings

UNDERTAKERS REMOVE the bodies of the two children chopped to death in a clear plastic bag while grandfather Raymond is restrained by relatives when he demanded to view their mutilated bodies.

the shocking, unbelievable news of the murders while working, and drove his car at dangerous speed to his home.

On his arrival, he looked on in horror as the body of his wife lay in gruesome death because he left early yesterday to sell his produce and escaped from the hands of the

physically restrained from the crime scene when he demanded to view the bodies of his wife, daughter-in-law and grandchildren.

He said that he was spared the gruesome death because he left early yesterday to sell his produce and escaped from the hands of the

THE BLOOD stains and the wheelchair which Dillon, 9, occupied and in which he was chopped to death.

"Why did they do this to me?" cried the elderly Garcia as he stared at the bodies of his loved ones being led away by undertakers.

Police investigators believe that the chopping deaths took place between 8 am and 9 am. They also believe that Alicia fought with the

have identify the killer or killers.

As tears filled her eyes yesterday, Pakeera said that she cannot believe that her son is gone. She cried as a clear plastic bag containing the bodies of her son and his sister were taken away to the hearse by undertakers.

NEWSDAY OCTOBER 18, 2001

Cop's hand chopped off —

MAN CHARGED WITH ATTEMPTED MURDER

By KEN CHEE HING

AN ARIMA MAN appeared in Court yesterday charged with the attempted murder of a Sangre Grande policeman, whose right hand was chopped off at the wrist on Monday.

Hector Devenish, 40, who told police he worked at the Ministry of Health, appeared in the Arima Court before Senior Magistrate Marcia Ayers-Caesar, charged with attempting to murder Police Constable Walter Bennet.

The charge was laid by Sgt Victor Greene of the Pinto Road police.

The charge against Devenish is that around 8 pm on Monday, he attacked and chopped Bennet at his (Bennet) father-in-law's home in Pinto Road, Arima.

After the case was called, Magistrate Ayers-Caesar adjourned the matter to Friday, when she will decide if to grant Devenish bail or not.

Yesterday, Magistrate Ayers-Caesar asked that police do a "race" to see if the accused had any criminal record.

Based on the officers' report, Magistrate Ayers-Caesar will rule on the issue of bail.

According to police reports, on Monday night Bennet went to the home of his father-in-law at Pinto Road, when he was attacked by a man who chopped him with a cutlass.

Bennet's right hand was chopped off from the wrist, and despite efforts by surgeons of the Port-of-Spain General hospital, the hand could not be reattached.

CHARGED: Hector Devenish, outside Arima Magistrate Court yesterday, where he appeared charged with attempting to murder PC Walter Bennet, whose right hand was chopped off on Monday. PHOTO BY KEN CHEE HING.

THE WASHINGTON POST TUESDAY, MAY 14, 2002
VIRGINIA

Man's Hand Severed Outside Restaurant

A man was undergoing surgery yesterday to have a hand reattached after he was slashed by an unknown assailant outside a Falls Church area restaurant early in the morning, Fairfax County police said.

The incident happened outside the Majestic Crab House, 2922 Annandale Rd., and occurred exactly one year after two men were shot to death outside the restaurant. The suspect in that shooting, Chong Le, has been charged with two counts of murder but remains at large. Investigators did not know yesterday whether any connection existed between the two crimes.

The victim in yesterday's attack, a 41-year-old man whose home town was not released, was walking to his car about 1:30 a.m. when another man approached him. Lt. Amy Lubas said it was unclear whether the victim knew his assailant, who fled in a white Honda Accord with Virginia license plate YZH-8840. Anyone with information about the incident may call Fairfax police at 703-691-2131.

FORENSIC MEDICINE

BY

KEITH SIMPSON,

M.A. (Oxon.), M.D. (Lond.), F.R.C.P.

F.C. Path., D.M.J.

PROFESSOR OF FORENSIC MEDICINE
TO THE UNIVERSITY OF LONDON

LONDON

EDWARD ARNOLD (PUBLISHERS) LTD

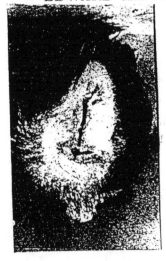 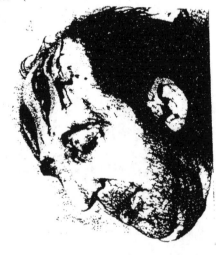

Fig. 38. Multiple axe wounds of the head

The single wound to the top of the head slanting sideways shows the length of the blade. The multiple wounds to the brow were inflicted after deceased had been disabled by the isolated first wound to the crown of the head

Bandits chop San Juan cops

TRINIDAD GUARDIAN NOVEMBER 17,1996

SUNDAY GUARDIAN, November 17, 1996, Page 15

By ROBERT ALONZO

FIVE CUTLASS wielding bandits yesterday stormed the San Juan Police Sub Station, near the busy Croisee area, and severely chopped two police men who were in the charge room.

Police believe the men invaded the station to take away arms and ammunition.

While the violent intruders were raining chops in, the lawmen they shouted "A day for Allah! A day for Allah!"

Two of them, aged... a 25-year-old Antiguan, the other aged... Village, San Juan, were held... armed member of the Crime Sup...

ered team of investigators to San Juan have appealed to the public to be on the lookout for suspected characters. Guy said persons with information leading to the arrest of the trio could contact any police station.

The suspect from San Juan was treated for gunshot injuries to the feet. Both men were under investigation.

...up last night.

Three blood stained cutlasses were recovered...

...drama unfolded sometime between 11:15 and 11:30 a.m. when the...

...into the charge room with cutlasses...

...police members of the Crime Sup...

...pression Unit (CSU) and Senior Sup...

Two of the men limped over the chopping Constables Marvin Hewitt and Irwin Roberts. Another man also...

...counter in the charge room and began...

TRINIDAD GUARDIAN NOVEMBER 17, 1996

POLICEMEN from the Scenes of Crime Unit (SCU) search for other clues outside the San Juan Sub Station yesterday after five men stormed the station and chopped two officers. *Photo by ALDWYN SIN PANG.*

Cutlass attack a reprisal on police officers

•ATTACK from Page 1.

Both Hewitt and Roberts received multiple wounds about the body. Inspector Michael Lambert, who heads CSU, and about nine of the officers were in an office at the back of the station and heard the "commotion."

Lambert and his team immediately responded. Shots were fired as the five cutlass wielding men were leaving the compound. Bullets shattered part of the front glass in front of the charge room and entered a police vehicle which was parked nearby.

Many shoppers and persons making their Saturday morning market had to scamper and duck for safety as gunshots rang out. No pedestrians were injured.

The police gave chase and two of the suspects were held a short distance away. Policemen from the entire North Eastern Division, including Senior Supt Welwyn Francis, who is in charge of that area, responded.

Chief of Defence Staff, Brigadier Carl Alfonso, also arrived and offered military assistance to Commissioner Mohammed.

The National Security helicopter was called in and a contingent of police officers went in search of the other three men.

The two injured policemen were conveyed to the Port-of-Spain General Hospital. Hewitt (CSU) was treated and discharged while Roberts (SSU) remained hospitalised last night.

The assailants came to the station on foot. But police suspect that the men had a getaway car parked a short distance away.

Assistant Commissioners David Jack, Everald Snaggs, Senior Supt Mervyn Ghatt, Supt Oswyn Allard, ASPs Maurice Piggot, Maurice Charles and Inspectors Fitzroy Phillips, Errol Denoon and Lance Lashley also joined and assisted.

Commissioner Mohammed said he was driving along the Lady Young Road when he heard about the incident on his wireless set.

The CSU officers had worked all night into the early hours of yesterday morning with their colleagues in Chaguanas who are investigating the reported kidnapping of San Juan businessman Wayne Winston Pirally.

Investigators believe that the five men had passed early yesterday morning by the station and saw all the CSU vehicles parked up.

They probably believed none of the officers were at the station and that it was a good time to relieve the two officers in the charge room of guns and ammunition. Senior officers are also working on the theory that the incident could have stemmed from a reprisal as CSU officers had been carrying out several raids and have been paying special attention to certain criminal elements over the past few weeks.

The police, with the assistance of the National Security helicopter, searched different parts of Morvant, San Juan, Barataria, Laventille and East Port-of-Spain for the three ————
Random ————

WIRE NEWSPAPER AUGUST 16,2002

Son suspected of hacking his dad to death

WIRE NEWSPAPERS   August 16, 2002

By AZAD ALI

POLICE are searching for a 15-year-old schoolboy who allegedly chopped his father to death at his home in Buenos Aires, Erin, yesterday.

area, who ordered its removal to the mortuary of San Fernando General Hospital.

corner of George and Streets, Port of Spain.

A gunman walked Emmanuel, an Emplo Training Programme (ETP)

A 15-YEAR-OLD schoolboy allegedly hacked his father Raymond Sieunarine (INSET) to death with this cutlass at their Erin home yesterday. The 40-year-old father of three died on the spot. (See Page 3)

Page 16 NEWSDAY Saturday, June 9, 2001

INTERNATIONAL NEWS

2001

NEWSDAY JUNE 9, 2001, page 16

8 CHILDREN DIE AS SCHOOL STABBING STUNS JAPAN

IKEDA, JAPAN: Eight children were killed and 15 people injured in Japan's worst school tragedy yesterday when a middle-aged man with a history of mental illness went on a stabbing rampage at an elementary school in western Japan.

The injured were mostly seven- and eight-year-old students at the school in Ikeda, a suburb of the western city of Osaka. Seven of those killed were girls and one was a six-year-old boy, Japanese media said.

Two teachers were also injured, police said, including one 25-year-old man who was in critical condition and underwent emergency surgery after the attack, considered unprecedented in tradition-ally safe Japan. Five children were also in critical condition, televi-sion reports said.

The tragedy began when the 37-year-old man, wielding a 28-cm knife,

JAPANESE children leaving their school compound.

walked into a classroom in mid-morning and began to stab children in a rampage that media said lasted a little over 10 minutes.

"He came in holding a knife and started stabbing," a first grade girl said.

One sixth-grade girl told *Reuters*: "We were listening to an announcement over the loudspeaker, and then it was broken into by a scream and a noise like a desk falling down."

"Then I heard someone scream from below, 'Run!'"

Several children ran into a nearby supermarket yelling and crying for help, witnesses said.

"One of the boys, whose back was stained with red blood, fell in front of the cashier. He was pale and did not speak a word," a shop clerk told a television reporter.

Police were holding in custody a 37-year-old man who they said had previously undergone treatment for schizophrenia. "We have arrested a suspect," said a local police spokesman.

It was the worst mass-killing in Japan since the 1995 fatal sarin gas attack on crowded Tokyo subways by the Aum Shinrikyo (Aum Supreme Truth) cult which left 12 dead and thousands ill.

The motive behind the incident was unclear, but NHK public broadcaster said that the suspect had told police he had taken 10 times the usual dosage of tranquilisers and was babbling. The suspect, with a history of mental illness, told police he wanted to suffer the death penalty for his crime. "I was fed up with everything," police quoted him as saying, adding that he had previously attempted to commit suicide. "I want to be put to death."

(REUTERS)

79

INTERNATIONAL NEWS

2002   NEWSDAY SEPTEMBER 5,2002,page32

Man slashes nine
children in S Korea church

SEOUL.: A knife-wielding man who claimed he was driven by voices urging him to kill, slashed nine young children yesterday in a church school cafeteria in the South Korean capital, police said.

"A deranged man rushed into the church cafeteria and slashed nine children who were having lunch," the detective in charge of the case told *Reuters* by telephone.

"Some of the kids are seriously injured," he added. The semi-official *Yonhap* news agency had earlier reported ten children wounded by the assailant, a 53-year-old jobless man who was arrested 30 minutes after the attack in the Gunja neighbourhood of eastern Seoul.

The agency said three of the children, including a six-year-old boy, had suffered severe head and neck injuries. All the victims were attending the church preschool.

Yonhap said the knife assault took place as 45 children and three adults were eating lunch in the church cafeteria.

The detective said 24 children and two teachers were present.

Yonhap quoted police as saying the man told them he had heard voices on Tuesday night telling him he would be killed unless he killed others.

"He said he was haunted by somebody else who tried to kill him. We are investigating him now," a second police officer told *Reuters*.

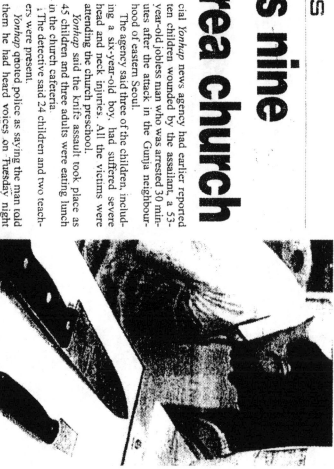

A JOBLESS man, 53, who attacked children at a church cafeteria, sits near bloodied knives at a Seoul police station as he waits to be questioned yesterday. REUTERS

EXPRESS 12,1994,page9

OPINION

Who should have a gun?

THE EDITOR: On the Police Commissioner's recent statement to the Petroleum Dealers' Association, that he will only issue gun licences to them on his perception of their need, not their want, may he explain to the public:

(1) the need for Dr Deosaran to have a licenced gun as opposed to a gas station owner—a number one prime target for armed robbery, never mind leaving it in a washroom at KFC?

(2) the need for the two young sons (under age 25 years) of a downtown fabric merchant to have licenced guns which they show off at weekend nightclubs?

(3) the need for the young, again 25-odd years old, and somewhat erratic son of an advertising executive to have just recently been granted a licenced gun by the Commissioner of Police.

The impact of not granting licences to legitimate businessmen is that in these tough economic times, with the almost emergency need for employment creation, and expansion of the economy, most of us business people are already quite wealthy, and will not put additional capital to work in investments that create employment if there is the slightest possibility of holdups and being left a sitting duck. Who needs the risk?

The Commissioner has stated that we should hire an armed guard. Is he saying that a businessman, usually a middle-aged, settled family man, with no criminal record, is less suited to hold a firearm licence than a young man recruited by a security firm with little or no education and paid five dollars per hour?

Maybe those people who get licences have a little more contact than most business owners who are under attack by armed criminals.

DOORS CLOSED.
GONE FISHING.

LETTERS

LETTERS

NEWSDAY JUNE 13, 1997, PAGE 9

Let more citizens own guns

THE EDITOR: I am frightened by the admission of the Commissioner of Police of his inability to protect the good citizens of TT. Commissioner Mohammed said the help of the public was needed... **"if we are able to arrest and bring before the courts criminals who feel that they can enter the homes of unsuspecting persons to commit murder, rape and wound and then escape without being apprehended."**

My understanding is that the murderers of Carlyle Bravo were not at all concerned about the likelihood that the occupants of the Bravo home might have been able to protect themselves. Bandits and lawbreakers in TT are confident that they can ply their trade as the law abiding citizen remains unarmed and cowering behind iron barricades that have become a part of the architecture of most Trinidad and Tobago homes. Small wonder ISPAT is doing so well. The bandits at the Bravo home casually stepped over the body of Mr Bravo and proceeded to terrorise Mrs Bravo and her family.

I am reminded of the experience of some of my clients two years ago when they visited for Carnival. On their way from the airport they discovered that they were being followed. They rushed to what they thought was the safety of the home where they were staying only to see the bandits follow them to the home, break down the door and proceed to rob them of their belongings, shooting one of them in the process. This home did not even have a cutlass for protection.

And so it goes. The killing of Stollmeyer, the two women in Westmoorings, the former Attorney General, etc.

A few weeks ago bandits entered the garage of a friend of mine and started to remove his car. Only because of his big mouth was he able to scare them off by shouting "thief". Of course, he dared not come out for fear of his life. Were he the owner of a shotgun or rifle the situation would have been quite different. I am not espousing that the people of Trinidad and Tobago be allowed to carry guns. However, I strongly believe that as part of one's human rights; one's inalienable rights;

Write to:

*Newsday
Chacon Street,
Port of Spain.*

one's right to quiet enjoyment, one should be entitled to be safe and secure in one's home — one's castle. Law abiding citizens should not be deprived of owning an unconcealed weapon (a long gun), particularly in remote areas where the police are unable to provide protection. The fact is that they (the police) are unable to protect the population of TT in urban areas.

I recall the recent incident where one entire family over powered a bandit and proceeded to beat him severely, only to be charged by the police with "excessive force". Of course the bandit's rights were fully protected by the police who were the ones unable to protect these citizens in the first place. The time has come for a new approach to crime fighting in TT which does not include the Police Commissioner's arbitrary rejection of all gun permits requests. Citizens the world over have a right to protect themselves when the Government is unable to do so.

CARLISLE HALL,
Brooklyn, NY

NEWSDAY Tuesday August 28, 2001 Page 21

Criminals not after cash alone

THE EDITOR: Every civilised country like Trinidad and Tobago which has a democratically elected government and which observes the rule of law, has citizens of impeccable character who served their country well in the armed forces and in the other protective services.

Such citizens of clean character who are competent in the use of firearms should automatically qualify as holders of licenced firearms for the protection of business.

their families and property from criminal elements. But the criteria for the granting of such licences have never been logically explained.

Preference seems to be given to certain people because of their social status, how much cash they hold in their possession and the area in which they reside or do

There are no "safe areas" in Trinidad and Tobago today.

The Westmoorings incident where two women were brutally raped and murdered in their homes in broad daylight is a good example of this.

Today's criminal is not only after your cash or property, but is also bent on raping your wife or daughter in the bargain. All decent, law-abiding citizens who are competent in the

use of firearms should qualify as holders of licenced firearms to protect their families and property.

After all, self-preservation is the first law of life.

When this is seen to be done, the police can then expect the greatest co-operation from such citizens in their fight against crime.

The Police cannot do it alone. It takes two hands to clap.

ELLIS MAINGOT
Trincity

WRITE TO:

Newsday,
Chacon Street,
Port-of-Spain

LETTERS

Crime in TT likened to Bubonic Plague

NEWSDAY FEBRUARY 8, 2002

THE EDITOR: As we advance on the precarious and unstable corridors of time, we are beginning to realise that crime is becoming like that of the Bubonic Plague. Men's hearts are becoming more and more fearful of the unholy stark realities of the modern criminal age.

That which is evil is soon learnt and the unexpected always happens. Apparently, nowhere in Trinidad and Tobago is safe anymore.

Men and women now find themselves ploughing the sands. At almost every nook and cranny, bandits are fully equipped to seize the just rewards of others.

These wicked, bold and vicious lawbreakers do not hesitate to show off their cloven hoofs to those they prey upon. Symposiums on crime should be organised at all

WRITE TO:

Newsday, Chacon Street, Port-of-Spain

levels and places of our communities. There is absolute strength in numbers so there has to be a coming together of our citizens to develop strategies to stem the life-threatening tide of this social problem. Certain crime targeted areas should be made private. Residents

should have access to their abodes by way of gates. Citizens should be accorded the privilege of acquiring licensed firearms with respect to their social, moral and spiritual standing in their respective neighbourhoods.

Security firms should be established within the communities. In this way, unemployed persons would be able go get lucrative employment.

At the same time, the protection of people's properties would be guaranteed. It is often said that bullies are generally cowards and that barking dogs seldom bite.

The fear of criminals must be rooted from our lives. By ongoing planning and extreme vigilance, criminals must be efficiently handled and made extinct.

LINDSEY RAMPERSAD
Tacarigua

Cops want to take their guns home

EXPRESS FEBRUARY 5, 1998, page 5

By ALVA VIARRUEL

Stingi

mu

By J
CAF
Sov

POLICE OFFICERS want guns to take home with them so that they can respond to the cries of their neighbours instead of remaining impotent when friends and family come under the barrel of armed bandits.

This suggestion was made yesterday by President of the Police Second Division Social and Welfare Association Cpl. Wayne Hayde, when he met with Public Administration Minister Wade Mark and Labour Minister Harry Partap at the association's Central Police station offices.

Hayde also pledged the loyalty of members of his organisation to ensure the "lawful and right policies of the government are carried out".

Mark and Partap met the association's executive as part of the dual agenda of both ministries to initiate "non-crisis meetings" with trade unions and associations representing public sector workers

During the discussion, Mark hinted that Government wants to change the 40-hour work week of members of the Police Service and intensify its recruitment drive to meet manpower shortages that have arisen with the expanding role of the service. He did not expand on the suggestion.

Hayde, in his opening remarks at the discussions, pledged the "loyal and faithful" support of police officers whom he said would continue to "work hard to

ensure...the government can carry out its mandate."

Hayde said while the Association's actions in the past may "appear to be antagonistic, it's our duty to perform for our members and we will not shirk that responsibility".

Among the grouses aired by Hayde and members of his executive were the regularisation of service for Special Reserve Police officers, an early retirement package and mandatory drug testing for all officers and the setting up of an employee assistance programme.

Hayde suggested that improving the recruitment process could stave off any manpower shortfall that may arise through attrition when the early retirement package is introduced. The association wants second division officers to have the right to retire after 20 years of service.

Mark described the retirement proposal which had been agreed upon with the past administration as "not unreasonable", but said Government needs first to assess "all the implications" of such a measure. Government is considering ways and means to create additional training facilities at the St James Barracks to expand on the number of recruits that can be admitted at any one time, he said.

Mark said the he was not surprised by the results of a UWI poll last year which showed an almost 50 per cent increase in public appreciation of the Police Service.

NEWSDAY JULY 30,2000, page 3

NEWSDAY Sunday July 30, 2000 Page 3

NEWS

NEW TOP COP DIRECTIVE —

NO GUNS FOR OFF-DUTY COPS

BY NALINEE SEELAL

POLICE COMMISSIONER Hilton Guy has issued a departmental order within the police service instructing that firearms issued to officers from the rank of Sgts downwards while on duty, should remain at the various stations when they finish their duties.

The Commissioner met with all heads of divisions recently and instructed that this order be adhered to.

Only officers from the rank of inspectors and upwards are allowed to take home firearms. Ag Inspectors are also allowed to take home firearms.

The decision by the Commissioner to issue the departmental order came about following the shooting death of the wife of a police officer in South.

OCNU officer Russel Mcalpin shot dead his wife with his service revolver and later turned the gun on himself.

Members of the public expressed outrage at the killing claiming that Mcalpin should not have been in possession of a firearm while off duty.

Sunday Newsday learned that previously all Special Branch and disciplinary charges.

OCNU officers were allowed to take home their service revolvers.

Commissioner Guy made it clear last week that he has also taken a decision not to issue private firearms to police officers.

He said that decision will remain in place while he is Commissioner of Police.

Some officers who previously took home their service revolvers have started adhering to the new regulation.

They are now required to sign off the weapons with the sentry on duty when they finish their duties, and those failing to do so could face disciplinary charges.

NEWS

NEWSDAY Friday September 1, 2000 Page 15

HUNTERS PLAN LEGAL ACTION OVER REFUSAL OF GUN LICENCES

BY AZARD ALI

A GROUP of hunters are contemplating legal action against the State for refusing them licences to obtain firearms.

At a meeting of the South Trinidad Hunters' Association (STHA) Friday night, an attorney-at-law advised them on what course of action they should take whenever the Commissioner of Police refuse to grant them gun licences.

Attorney Dr Charles Seepersad told the hunters that they have to compel the Police Commissioner to give reasons whenever a firearm users licence application is turned down.

Held at the home of STHA's President Abdool Aziz, the hunters contended that their applications for firearms licences are being turned down without reasons being given by the Commissioner.

Also at the meeting were several policemen, including Inspector Ashook Toll of South-West Division.

Charles told the hunters that though they can exercise the right to appeal to the Firearms Appeal Board, it was unfair to each hunter or applicant, not to be given reasons why he is being refused a firearm.

The new hunting season opens on October 1. An application for the firearm is made to the Commissioner of Police and it is either granted or refused.

"Let the applicant know why he is being refused. He is entitled to written reasons. Isn't that a right for someone to be told by a public authority, why he or she is being refused. And the reason should be given in writing the moment he or she is turned down," Seepersad said.

Stating that the person was of "bad" character is insufficient, he added. "What is he being accused of? Let the Commissioner say whether he has a previous conviction, or is known to be violent prone etc," Seepersad told the hunters.

Seepersad called on the hunters to bring pressure to bear on the Com-

Disarming Jamaican citizens

GLEANER AUGUST 9, 2000, JAMAICA

The Offensive Weapons (Prohibition) Act presently before a Parliamentary sub-committee is worthy of more debate and further considera-tion of the bill is undoubtedly to arm the whole citizenry of offensive weapons, protect the society and make it secure for people to go about lawful business. If I could be con-vinced that the law would ensure that no everyone would be safe, then I could support the bill. But, it will not and I cannot support its enactment.

Criminals have no respect for the law, and if we simply remember ister Peter Phillips' famous warning of "anyone who plays by the rules gets killed" then we know that the Act will law-abiding citizens at even greater risk. Nowadays, it is dangerous to walk many communities, to ride in taxis on the buses, and to go about one's lawful business. Women relate many frightening stories of being harassed, intimidated and manhandled by young-ry only when they pull their knives, or rob-

I contend that the Offensive Weapons Act is an assault on the individual's rights and freedoms, his right to antici-pate attacks and his freedom to carry the best means to defend against such attacks. Why shouldn't the ordinary citi-zen carry a knife, an ice pick, a screw-driver, scissors, etc., as a means of

In a rotten society, in which the crimi-nals have the upper hand, in which the security forces are unable to give ade-quate protection, it is simply wrong to disarm our citizens and leave them, without the means to defend themselves.

I think the authorities should, in fact, be examining alterna-tives and the better use of guns and weapons by law-abiding citizens as a means of self-defence and protection and, ultimately, to let criminals get their just desert, instead of the other way around.

To be sure, citizens need bet-ter weapons and more efficient means to secure and defend their families and properties, without having to resort to the area dons, securi-ty firms or the police.

I am aware that the government con-strated that people have been any more secure than before the legislations, Indeed, in these countries, violent crimes with the use of offensive weapons have not abated and in some years have actually increased. Indeed, our own history on gun control legisla-tion should have taught us that restric-tions on human freedom tend to hurt rather than help. The Gun Court Act, with its dreaded punishment of life imprisonment, and even certain execu-tion by the security forces for posses-sion of guns, has not relieved the crimi-nals of their desire to own, possess,

defence and protection? When one con-siders the violence, intimidation, fear, conflicts, robbery, rape, tension, tur-moil, volatility and insecurity in our communities, then the need to have protective measures become even more urgent.

That is why many young men and older folks carry weapons, not as a means of offence but as a means of defence

The Act, in my opinion, will succeed only in making it safer for criminals to threaten and hold up law-abiding citizens, especially old people, single women and disarmed young men.

Without a warrant

The tragedy of the proposed legisla-tion is that it will provide another path for the security forces to stop, search and humiliate innocent young men in our inner city communities. I pity the poor, young, black boys who will be further at the mercy of the security forces as virtually any article he carries can be deemed an offensive weapon and leaves him open to detention, a criminal charge and a date in court.

Moreover, motorists will suffer the same fate, as the proposed Act will empower the police to search vehicles, drivers and any passenger, without a warrant and if he has reasonable cause to suspect that an offensive weapon is being carried.

The Act itself makes the carrying or possession of a dagger, switchblade, flick knife, ratchet knife or Rambo knife, strictly prohibited. Perhaps, noth-ing would be wrong if the foregoing was the only prohibition and, in fact, many people believe that this is all the Act says and cannot understand why there is so much fuss about it.

Where the Act becomes offensive

carry and use illegal guns. If the gun control legislations have failed to achieve their objectives, why do we believe the offensive weapons legisla-tions will be any more effective?

however is in the further definition offensive weapons to mean "any article made or adapted for use for causing injury to the person or which is intended by the person having such article with him to cause such injury," which means that any pointed object, e.g. a broken bottle or a sharpened metal object, stick, can easily be interpreted by a police officer to be an offensive weapon and thereby lay a charge under the Act. The poor accused then has to go to court to give a reasonable excuse why he has the object on him.

I strongly believe that this Act will disarm citizens to their detriment. It will empower the security forces to search citizens for the most innocuous objects and further strain the relation-ship between the police and the citizen. It will force citizens to defy the law and to treat it with contempt, as inas-believe they have a natural right to defend themselves in whatever way they see reasonable and necessary.

This is another piece of legislation that is unlikely to stop the escalating crime wave and, like the gun control legislation, is more likely to make criminals mere lambs for criminal wolves to ravage. We, the people, should obey to its enactment.

Delroy Chuck is an attorney-at-law and Opposition Member of Parliament. He can be contacted at e-mail: Delchuck@Hotmail.com.

Bandits terrorise cop

BANDITS TER-RORISED an Aranguez police officer and his family for some two hours on Tuesday night, first stealing his vehicle, then returning to shower his house with missiles after he reported the matter.

"It was very traumatic. My wife is still in shock," said PC Farouk Khan of his night of terror, which began around 1.15 am on Wednesday.

Khan said he was awakened around to find four men in his garage attempting to steal his pick-up van.

He shouted at them, identifying himself as a police officer, but instead of running away the bandits began pelting rocks, warning him to remain inside. The men then drove off with the vehicle.

But the drama did not end there. One hour later, after Khan had reported the matter to his col-leagues at the San Juan Police Station, the bandits returned in his pick-up truck shouting they had "come back to kill."

Khan said his house then came under a heavy barrage of rocks, bottles and other objects that smashed windows and glass doors and a number of household items. Neighbours, awakened by the commotion and attempting to investigate, were also stoned away by the bandits, before they eventually drove off in the stolen vehicle.

Khan said yesterday he did not believe he had been specifically targetted by the bandits. He also could not say what may have prompted the men to return. But he said he planned to install burglar proofing on all the doors and windows of his house, as a result of the incident.

San Juan police are in-vestigations.

TRINIDAD GUARDIAN OCTOBER 5, 1995

NEWSDAY SEPTEMBER 23, 2002, p. 7

Gun stolen from police station

A .38 f   and six rounds of ammunition have been reported missing from the Besson Street Police Station, sources told *Newsday* yesterday.

Sources said the gun went missing Saturday night, but the discovery was only made around 8am yester-day by an officer in the charge room.

The weapon was issued to an offi-cer, and the person signed it off, but it could not be found. Senior officers remained tight-lipped, but said investigations are continuing.

THE GLEANER ● Monday, September 16, 1996, JAMAICA

GLEANER 16,1996

Inside the PARISH COUNCILS

'We can't disarm gunmen, arm the people'

WESTERN BUREAU - A call has come from Councillor, Lenworth Blake, for the Government to remove the obstacles for citizens wanting legal fire power.

Speaking in the context of the rising criminal activity, he declared, "If we can't disarm the gunmen, arm the citizenry", to support from his colleagues at the monthly meeting of the St. Elizabeth Parish Council, last Thursday.

The Council itself voiced concern and made its own suggestion on how to stem criminal activity in a resolution calling on the Government "to remove the obstacles for the restoration of capital punishment and for the restoration of flogging as among the appropriate measures to curb the rampant crime and violence in the country."

"One of the hardest things is to get a legal firearm, one of the easiest is to get an illegal gun," said Councillor Blake.

Meanwhile, the St. Elizabeth Parish Council, with immediate effect, has amalgamated its Roads and Works, and Water Supplies committees for reasons of efficiency. A similar exercise was carried out successfully in respect of the Health and Sanitation committees sometime ago, said Council Chairman, J.A.G Myers, who proposed the restructuring.

The amalgamated committee is now known as the Roads, Works and Water Supplies Committee, said Mayor Myers, and will operate with the same terms of reference. Councillor Donald Horne is the chairman and Uton Myers vice-chairman, and all members remain on the new committee.

The matter was ratified by the council Thursday's meeting.

NEWSDAY Saturday March 2, 2002 Page 3

POLICE LAUNCH MAN-HUNT AFTER —
Cop's wife gang-raped

NORTHERN Division police have launched a major manhunt for four men, who during the early morning hours yesterday, broke their way into a policeman's home and gang-raped his wife.

According to reports, around 3 am the Constable who is attached to a police station in Northern Division and his 26-year-old wife were asleep at their Arima home.

A loud crashing sound woke the couple up and they were confronted by the four bandits, all masked and armed with cutlasses.

While two of the bandits held down the Constable, their cohorts dragged the screaming woman to an adjoining room, ripped off her clothes and took turns raping her.

After the assault, the woman was forced to sit alongside her husband where they were guarded by one of the bandits, while the rest ransacked the house.

The bandits stole a quantity of items including the policeman's wallet which contained $1,100, his Police Identification Card and his bank cards.

They then warned the couple, that if any report was made to police, they would return to kill them. The bandits then ran out of the house and minutes later, sounds of a car speeding off was heard.

A report was made to the Pinto police station and a team of officers coordinated by Snr Supt Lloyd Coutain and ASP Gregory Correia went to the victim's home and began investigations.

The rape victim was taken to a medical institution where she was examined by the District Medical Officer (DMO) who confirmed that she was sexually assaulted.

Up to late yesterday no arrests had been made and Cpl Charles of the Pinto Police Post is continuing investigations.

NEWSDAY   **SATURDAY FEBRUARY 14, 1998   PAGE 5**

Police officer's home broken into

Family terrorised by armed bandits

By KEN CHEE HING

A POLICE officer and his family were terrorised by a gang of armed bandits at their Cumuto home on Thursday morning. The horrifying incident occurred after the officer raised an alarm when he saw the bandits trying to drive away with his car.

Cpl Andre Dediere attached to the Community Policing Unit in Port-of-Spain was at his Little Cora Road, Cumuto home with his family which included his wife, daughter and sister on Thursday at 3.50 am when he was awakened by a noise coming from his garage.

On looking outside he saw four men breaking into his motorcar. The bandits, on seeing Cpl Dediere, shouted to him ordering him to go back into the house or else they would shoot him.

The bandits, one armed with a handgun and the rest with cutlasses then picked up two large stones and broke down the front door of the house.

The bandits entered the house and immediately started rummaging through drawers. They also assaulted the female members of the family.

According to the report the intruders took a television set, a CD player and jewellery with the overall estimated value of the stolen items amounting to over $10,000. They then left the house threatening the family to keep their mouths shut or else they would come back.

The bandits then went back to the car where they stole a tapedeck. While the bandits were leaving a neighbour who heard the commotion and peeped out his window to see what was going on, had his front door broken down by the bandits who threw stones at it.

They also beat up two men who were walking to work at the time and saw what was going on. Following the incident, a party of Cumuto officers headed by Sgt Karim and including Sgt George and Cpl Stewart visited the scene. Some of the family members were taken to a medical denture for treatment.

Sgt Karim of the Cumuto Police Station is continuing enquires.

Page 8. TRINIDAD GUARDIAN, Wednesday, September 20, 1995

Trinidad Guardian

NATIONAL NEWSPAPER OF TRINIDAD AND TOBAGO

Established September 2, 1917

22-24 St. Vincent Street, Port of Spain.

Terror at Malabar

THE residents of Phase III, Malabar, we are told, are traumatised; many of them are unable to get a good night's sleep and some are suffering from a prolonged case of diarrhoea. The reason: Fear of a marauding gang of violent bandits.

The Police must move immediately to stop this kind of terrorism.

Malabar has been the hunting ground for armed intruders for more than two years now, but in more recent times the invasion and pillaging of homes in the area has become a more frequent nightmare, with families waking up to the shock of bandits kicking down their doors.

Extra Contempt

Within the last few weeks, for example, bandits smashed their way into four houses in Phase III, attacking and injuring family members and robbing them of money and jewelry. On the night of August 18, Amoco employee Martin Sanovich, his wife and their children became the victims of terror in their own home, as they were robbed of $1,200 in jewelry and $1,000 in cash by a gang of armed men. Sanovich was beaten and tied up before the intruders began searching his home.

About half an hour later, the bandits broke into the home of Osborne George and his companion Sharon Greaves. When they found George uncooperative, the gunmen pumped bullets into his abdomen and right thigh. Then they ransacked his house, taking $200 in cash and $1,500 in jewelry. The men also drove away in George's Laurel motor car which they later abandoned under the Laventille flyover.

Last Saturday, the Malabar bandits showed an extra contempt for the law when they invaded the homes of two police officers. Corporal Leslie Charles awoke at three in the morning to the sound of his front door being kicked in. He was held up by a gang of four armed men who proceeded to loot his home of a video recorder and jewelry valued at $5,000.

On the same night, Corporal Christopher Jones also found himself confronted by bandits who had smashed down his front door. Jones, however, challenged the intruders who, apparently not prepared for a fight, turned and ran.

Increasing attacks such as these, coming after a long history of crime in Malabar, are sufficient cause for the fear and trauma which now infect residents of the area. According to police statistics, a total of 146 serious offences — robberies, rapes, woundings — was reported at Malabar in 1994, making that housing settlement in the East one of the most crime ridden in the country. So far this year, the Police have received 129 reports of serious crime in the district.

These incidents also expose the impotence of the Police post which was established at Malabar several months ago to deal with rising crime in the area. Not only is the post undermanned but it is handicapped by a seemingly pervasive deficiency of the Service — no vehicles to respond to crime reports.

Armed Bandits

It would be an exercise in futility if the present effort to set up similar posts in "high crime areas" across the country results in the same kind of scenario as the one at Malabar. These mini-stations must be adequately manned and equipped to respond rapidly to reports of crime within their jurisdictions. Their mere presence alone is not enough.

Clearly, a gang of armed bandits has chosen Malabar as their special turf. Councillor Yvonne Lezama has identified a set of abandoned factory buildings on the outskirts of Malabar as a possible base of operations for these criminals. If Senior Supt Carrington is to respond adequately to Lezama's delegation, the Police must become proactive in the area and launch a counterattack on the bandits.

Indeed, this must be the approach in every residential district where this kind of crime is on the rise. Banditry, looting and terrorism in the homes of our citizens demands that kind of response.

Balgobin: My gun saved me

EXPRESS JULY 29 2002, page 3

By DARRYL HEERALAL

A GUNMAN attacked ice-cream manufacturer Wilbur Balgobin at his Chaguanas home on Saturday night and the businessman is convinced that he was saved from being abducted because he had his firearm with him.

The founder of the Willie's Ice Cream chain was able to scare off his attacker by firing two shots at him with his licensed Smith and Wesson 9 mm pistol.

"If I did not have a firearm I would have most certainly been kid-napped," Balgobin told the *Express* while recounting the incident yesterday.

The attacker mistook the businessman's friend, Stephen Ramaya for him.

The attack on the 46-year-old businessman took place around 9 p.m. at his home on Eastern Avenue, Lange Park just two hours after Balgobin had returned from busi-ness in Barbados.

Balgobin and Ramaya, who were going to the Shipwreck Pub on Chin Chin Road, Cunupia, were just about to leave Balgobin's home when the gunman attacked.

Ramaya's car was parked outside Balgobin's

BUSINESSMAN Wilbur Balgobin, left, speaks to the *Express* at his Lange Park home yester-day, in the company of a friend.
Photo: STEPHEN DOOBAY

his car and was waiting on Balgobin to drive out of his garage, as they had planned to use their own cars for the trip.

Balgobin recalled he

gate at the end of Eastern Avenue, which is a cul-de-sac.

Balgobin's Audi was parked in the garage. Ramaya had gone to

had just sat down in his car when he heard some-one shouting "we come for you tonight, open the door, open the door".

Balgobin said he came

out of his car, turned around and saw that the gunman had his weapon pointed at Ramaya.

"I point my weapon at him too and shout out 'Papa I have a gun and all'," Balgobin said.

Recounting the series of events that followed, Balgobin said he and the gunman squared off "eye to eye" for about four to five seconds pointing their guns at each other.

"I fire off a warning shot and the gunman scamper off," Balgobin said.

Balgobin said he ran inside the house but, before doing so, fired another shot into the air.

"The second shot was to make sure the kidnap-per get the message," he explained.

Ramaya told the *Express* yesterday that when he saw the gunman coming he locked his door and had his hand on the lever to lower the seat in case the gunman fired a shot.

When the gunman turned to Balgobin, Ramaya said, he drove off, but returned about 15 minutes later.

Once inside, Balgobin telephoned the police but described their response as "unacceptable".

"The police take about 30 minutes to come, I call

them and tell them who I am and about the shoot-ing and they take that long... that is madness," Balgobin said.

Balgobin has won sev-eral local and internation-al awards, including Entrepreneur of the Year in 1997 and the Prime Minister's Exporter of the Year award in 1998.

Since the incident Balgobin has hired pri-vate security for protec-tion.

Balgobin echoed the call from many business-men for firearms since the recent spate of kidnap-pings.

"It is necessary for the government and Minister of National Security to send a cogent signal to bandits," Balgobin said. "This is totally unaccept-able.

He added: "This may sound barbaric but I think we have to deal with them in accordance with the words of Winston Churchill that if men's passion cannot be ruled by love they must be cured by fear.

"It must be an eye for an eye a tooth for a tooth."

The attack on Balgobin comes three days after kidnap victim, Bhudath "Bob" Ramlogan, escaped from his abductors at a house at the nearby Ring Road in Lange Park.

EXPRESS Monday, July 29, 2002 Page 5

Two injured in Molotov attack

TWO people were injured after gunmen shot up their house and threw a Molotov cocktail inside on Saturday night.

According to reports, two men shot up the home of Radesh Ramjattan at Freeman Road, St Augustine, around 9 p.m., then went to the home of his mother-in-law Jean Dalip and did the same.

Ramjattan and Dalip live next door to one another. Ramjattan, whose house was the first to come under attack, was not at home at the time.

The gunmen moved next door and fired at Dalip's house, and threw a molotov cocktail into the home before driving off.

Dalip and Darrel Bridgelal were inside the house and suffered minor burns. Both are hospitalised.

Neighbours formed a bucket brigade and extinguished the fire.

It is believed the attack was the result of an ongoing dispute.

Sgt Don Lezama, of St Joseph CID, is investigating.

—DH

Bandits rob South cops

EXPRESS JULY 29,2002, page 5

SOUTHERN police remained tight-lipped yesterday about an incident involving a police sergeant and a woman police officer who were held up by four men at Garth Road, Princes Town.

The *Express* learnt that around 11 p.m. on Saturday the sergeant and the female police were seated in the sergeant's private car at Garth Road when they were attacked by four men.

dragged out of his car and beaten about his body, while his female companion was relieved of $250 in cash.

After the incident the men made their escape in the sergeant's car.

Both officers were treated at the San Fernando General Hospital and discharged.

Insp Williams, of the Princes Town Police Station, is investigating.

Businessmen protest for guns

BY DARRYL HEERALAL

PROTEST greeted National Security Minister Howard Chin Lee in Chaguanas on Thursday night as he was about to address Central businessmen on the escalating crime situation in the borough.

Chin Lee delivered the feature address at a meeting of businessmen organised by the Greater Chaguanas Chamber of Industry and Commerce at the Kam Po Chinese restaurant.

A handful of demonstrators carrying placards gathered outside the restaurant.

"It is important we realise Chaguanas under siege from these criminals and nobody safe anymore," one of the protesters said.

One of the placards read: "We want guns for protection not to shoot foot."

Three years ago Chin Lee accidentally shot himself in the foot.

On Wednesday the businessmen called on Commissioner of Police Hilton Guy to hasten the processing of gun licences.

On Thursday night, Guy declined comment on the call by the businessmen for gun licences, saying he was the one who has to "adjudicate" in the processing of the licences.

The protesters felt Chin Lee was not doing enough about the "crime siege" in Chaguanas and wanted more action from him.

Inside, Chin Lee sought to assure the businessmen that his Ministry was doing all it could to arrest the escalating crime wave.

HOWARD CHIN LEE...
spoke of plans to fight crime

form a crime committee and meet at least twice monthly with the police to come up with solutions to the increasing crime problem.

Selwyn "Robocop" Alexis, who claimed to have information on who kidnapped businessman Kenneth Medford, showed up outside the restaurant to speak with Chin Lee.

When Chin Lee was told that Alexis was outside, the Minister's driver took the car around to the back entrance to the restaurant.

Alexis, the media and some of the protesters followed the car to the back.

There was a heavy presence of uniformed police officers at that entrance and, after about fifteen minutes, the driver went back around to the front of the restaurant.

The small crowd again followed the car.

As he was leaving, Chin Lee shook hands with Alexis but did not speak to him.

Alexis did not get his chance to give Chin Lee any information but was told by Guy that he could come to the Commissioner's office to speak about the kidnapping.

Yesterday Alexis said he would visit Guy next week.

Anaconda has had "no effect in Chaguanas" and that Central police were ill equipped and under-staffed.

Chin Lee responded by saying that government has sourced new police vehicles some of which will be assigned to the Central Police Division.

Guy suggested that the Greater Chaguanas Chamber

NAIDU POWDER protests in front of Kam Po restaurant, Chaguanas on Thursday night. He and others were protesing the inability of the Government to deal with crime.
Photo: KRISHNA MAHARAJ

EXPRESS MAY 18,2002,page 4

Trinidad Guardian May 17. 2002, page 3

TRINIDAD GUARDIAN • FRIDAY, MAY 17, 2002 • 3

News

PM rejects gun talk

By GAIL ALEXANDER

PRIME MINISTER Patrick Manning has rejected a call by Central businessmen for guns to fight crime.

Giving guns, he said, will breed more violence.

At yesterday's post-Cabinet briefing, Manning said: "We don't believe as a government that the solution to any problem of violence would be the issue of more guns. All that does is make more guns available in the wider community and instead it breeds more violence."

Adding that he deeply regrets what has taken place in Central Trinidad, Manning referred to a recent kidnapping in the area involving businessman Kenneth Medford who Manning said was a friend of his. He said he regrets the state of anxiety that exists in Central Trinidad.

Manning added: "As has been suggested by their colleagues elsewhere — don't panic. And, in making the same suggestion to the Central businessmen, I wish to assure that Government is doing what it can to the best our ability."

He said the authorities have special facilities with regard to the kidnapping problem and Government is trying to ensure this does not become the normal pattern in T&T.

"The authorities are quite capable of treating with these issues."

On the issue of sidewalk vending, Manning said Cabinet agreed yesterday that a six-member ministerial team will meet with vendors to arrive at a solution to the problem as soon as possible.

Firstly, they will deal with vending in Port-of-Spain, and then the issue of vending in the country, overall.

Members are Ministers Lenny Saith, John Rahael, Howard Chin Lee, Conrad Enill, Penny Beckles and Jarrette Narine.

He said the team recognises that while there is legal framework on vending, there are also sociological considerations and that the situation cannot have a totally legal or law enforcement approach "..but there must be some element of trying to satisfy the need that clearly exists..." he added.

In the interim, he said, Government will talk with the Local Government authorities to see if, while discussions are going on, there could be "some kind of truce" between authorities and venders. (*See Page 4*)

TRINIDAD GUARDIAN AUGUST 3, 2002

Chin Lee's hypocrisy

ANAND RAMLOGAN
anand@tstt.net.tt

> 'What criteria qualifies Chin Lee to own a personal firearm but would disqualify Chaguanas businessmen from getting theirs?'

"Firearms stand next in importance to the Constitution itself. They are American people's liberty, teeth and keystone under independence"

— 1st US President George Washington

"Among the many misdeeds of British rule in India's history will look upon the act of depriving a whole nation of arms as the blackest"

— Mahatma Gandhi's autobiography.

HOWARD CHIN LEE literally shot into the limelight when he recently shot himself in the foot with his personal firearm. As a flourishing businessman, Chin Lee felt it necessary to arm himself against potential criminal attacks. He equipped himself with a firearm to protect and defend his property, life, wealth and family.

This, of course, did not happen here. Why not? Is it one law for Chin Lee and another for Balgobin?

What secret criteria, pray tell, qualifies businessman Chin Lee to own a personal firearm but would, at the same time, disqualify Chaguanas businessmen from getting theirs?

Precisely what entitles Chin Lee and others to the privilege of having a gun to defend their lives, businesses and property, but disentitles the Chaguanas businessmen?

The Chaguanas businessmen are under attack. The recent spate of kidnappings and robberies in Chaguanas has terrorised them. Like Chin Lee, they have worked hard and sacrificed their entire lives to build their business. How can Chin Lee pompously pronounce that they do not deserve firearms?

If Chin Lee truly believes "guns are not the answer", then he should lead by example and hand in his own firearm.

If, as Minister of National Security, Chin Lee cannot feel sufficiently safe and secure to do without a personal gun, what message is he sending to the rest of us?

HOWARD CHIN LEE,
Minister of National Security

Our Constitution does not give us such a right, but it does guarantee "the right of the individual to life, liberty, security of the person and enjoyment of property".

Are we enjoying these rights? We have become prisoners in our own homes. Windows with burglar-proofing, steel doors, pit bulls, expensive private security (for the rich) and self-imposed curfews have become the norm for law-abiding citizens.

While Chin Lee is fighting tooth and nail against issuing guns to the Chaguanas businessmen, he moves with his finger on the trigger of his own personal gun.

He piously contends guns are not the solution to the crime problem, but hasn't even spared a thought for the hundreds of illegal guns the criminals have when they confront these businessmen.

Perhaps he just assumed the criminals have licences for these guns and that after the 40-day fete, the bandits will simply bow to him and throw their guns down at his feet. What a great crime plan!

CHAPTER 4. YOUTH CURFEW, SAVING THE CHILDREN FOR THE FUTURE

(A) What business does a 16-year-old have out-doors at night after 9.30pm? it's dangerous out there!

When I was growing-up as a boy, by the time dusk,the gloaming or twilight time set in at about 6.30pm-7.00pm when night was at hand, I had to be in doors at my parents home. This was the norm for all my friends and presumably it was taken to be the norm of our society then.

Today it seems as if times have changed and youths of many countries which consider their society liberal and liberated enjoy"sweet liberty" out-doors beyond midnight and into the wee hours of the morning. The parents of these children either condone this past bed-time latitude, cannot control their children or are parents who are bad examples to their children.

This juvenile liberty is condoned even by civil liberties organistions in the name of civil rights and as champions and guardians of such liberties enshrined constitutionally. They go as far as the courts to protest the introduction of such laws and to justify the rights of juveniles to be out-of-doors at anytime as long as they do not get into trouble--even when chiefs of police,mayors and government officials endorse such laws as a method of curbing juvenile crime. It is good to know that those objectionable challenges have been dismissed by for example the US Supreme Court which has allowed laws on juvenile curfew to be implemented.

Today youth curfews exist by law in many cities in the USA, partial in England and some other countries as you will read for yourself the documentation to follow. I believe that one of my recommendations is the national introduction of juvenile curfew laws that will keep youths from bad company and influences prone under the cover of darkness.

The pages to follow will give you (a) number of reports of disastrous dangerous consequences that befell some youths when they ventured out to parties or have fun late at night into the morning's dawn. (b)curfew laws in some countries.

(1) "We are failing as parents" TRINIDAD GUARDIAN JANUARY 14, 1996(letter to the editor)

"A recent report of a most abominable crime, rape against a 14-year-old girl of Petit Valley by 14 youths in the last days of the year 1995...

Why was a GIRL 14 YEARS OUT ON THE BRIAN LARA PROMENADE AT THAT HOUR OUTSIDE THE SANCITY OF HER HOME AND WITHOUT SECURITY OF HER PARENTS?

I suggest that we as parents and adults have failed to keep good family values..."

Ramesh Patrick Mathura.

(2) "ill judgement" NEWSDAY JANUARY 4,1998

"We condemn outright the alleged RAPE OF A 14-YEAR-OLD GIRL which took place IN THE EARLY HOURS OF NEW YEARS DAY. Why did her parents or guardian ALLOW HER TO BE OUT AT THE UNGODLY HOUR OF 3.15AM and relatively un-protected? WHY WAS A MINOR PERMITTED TO BE AT A PARTY UNTIL THE WEE HOURS OF THE MORNING AND ALLOWED TO WALK HOME THROUGH LONELY HOURS UNPROTECTED.

While we cannot condemn too strongly her alleged rape,WE MUST CENSURE HER PARENTS/GUARDIANS.

TO PERMIT A 14-YEAR-OLD GIRL TO WALK HOME AT 3.15AM IN THE MORNING with two teenage Youths,PERMITTING A 14-YEAR-OLD TO BE AT A PARTY UNTIL AFTER MIDNIGHT AND THEN WEND HER WAY HOME WITHOUT FAMILY PROTECTION…"

(3) "Mormon gets 12 years for rape"INDEPENDENT
MARCH 12, 1997
"A Mormon counsellor was jailed for 12 years by Justice Volney after he WAS FOUND GUILTY OF RAPING A 14-YEAR-OLD GIRL in Sangre Grande seven years ago.

According to the state's case presented by prosecutor Maria Wilson, on December 22,1990, THE GIRL WAS WAITING FOR TRANSPORT TO GO HOME AROUND 4.00AM AFTER ATTENDING A PARTY. When she stopped a white

When she stopped a white corolla car driven by Morang. There were two men in the car whom she knew who lived further up from her. Morang passed her stop and dropped off the two men,he turned around the car and when they reached a deserted area,Morang and the girl came out the car.He then pushed her against the trunk of the car,ripped off her clothes before raping her. The girl made a report to the police and Morang was arrested and charged…"

(4) "15-year-old raped" TRINIDAD GUARDIAN APRIL 26,1999
"A 15-YEAR-OLD GIRL WAS RAPED AFTER RETURNING FROM A PARTY. Police reported that the girl from Maracas,St Joseph WENT TO A PARTY WITH SOME FRIENDS,

After the party she accepted a ride home with a male friend.Police said the victim's friend drove to an area close to Johnson and Johnson factory where he alleged raped her and later drove her home.

The girl told her parents about the incident, a report was made to the Arouca Police Station, A man has been held…"

(5) "11-year-old missing" NEWSDAY DECEMBER 19,1998
"A Morvant woman IS CALLING ON HER 11-YEAR-OLD DAUGHTER WHO RAN AWAY FROM HOME on Friday to return to the safety of her home. MONICA TOLD NEWSDAY THAT ON FRIDAY HER DAUGHTER ASKED TO GO TO THE BRIAN LARA PROMENADE,SHE TOLD HER TO RETURN BY 8.00PM. When Kimika failed to return, a frantic Monica and two friends WENT IN SEARCH OF THE GIRL.

THEY SAW HER WALKING ALONG INDEPENDENCE SQUARE BUT WHEN THEYCALLED OUT TO HER SHE RAN AND DISAPPEARED IN THE CROWD. Monica has lodged a report with Besson St Police…"

(6) "Police probe rape report"EXPRESS AUGUST 10,1998 "Police are investigating a gang-rape report OF A 17-YEAR-OLD WOMAN BY THREE MEN. THE WOMAN WAS UP TO LATE YESTERDAY AT HOSPITAL , THE GIRL WHO LIVES in Petit Valley SAID SHE AND HER 14 -YEAR-OLD SISTER BOARDED

A TAXI AROUND 4.00AM YESTERDAY NEAR MORVANT JUNCTION,THERE WERE THREE MEN IN THE TAXI, ANOTHER DRIVING. THEY WERE TAKEN TO AN ISOLATED AREA WHERE THE 14-YEAR-OLD MANAGED TO ESCAPE. THE 17-YEAR-OLD WAS THEN ALLEGED RAPED BY THE THREE MEN.

(7) "Rapist on the prowl, two women raped in Arouca" NEWSDAY DECEMBER 15,1998

"TWO VICTIMS AGES 16 AND 26 WERE RAPED within half an hour of each other in the Arouca District. Police reports revealed that AROUND 4.00AM THE 16-YEAR-OLD LEFT HER HOME TO VISIT A FRIEND. While walking along Railway Road, SHE WAS AMBUSHED BY FOUR MEN who PULLED HER INTO SOME BUSHES and robbed her of $40. THE MEN THEN TOOK TURNS IN RAPING THE TEEN AGER.She was left by her four attackers who then fled the Scene…"

(8) "Five charged with rape of 15-year-old" TRINIDAD GUARDIAN OCTOBER 8,1996

"A 15-YEAR-OLD POINT FORTIN SENIOR COMPREHENSIVE SCHOOL STUDENT WAS RAPED AND BUGGERED BY FIVE MEN ON HER WAY HOME AFTER A PARTY AT CLIFTON HILL EARLY SUNDAY MORNING.

THE GIRL WAS RETURNING HOME FROM A FETE WHEN SHE WAS ACCOSTED BY FIVE MEN WHO PULLED HER INTO A TRACK. THE MEN RAPED AND BUGGERED THE SCHOOL GIRL BEFORE LEAVING HER BLEEDING ON THE TRACK…"

(9) "Cops hunt rape suspect" NEWSDAY FEBRUARY 15, 2000

"AFTER BEING SUPPLIED WITH ALCOHOL,A 16-YEAR-OLD GIRL WAS TAKEN HOME BY AN ELDERLY MAN SHE MET AT A BAR. BY THE TIME THE GIRL BEGAN TO SOBER-UP, THE MAN HAD RAPED HER AND WAS ATTEMPTING TO SEXUALLY ASSAULT HER A SECOND TIME. THE ASSAULT IS ALLEGED TO HAVE OCCURRED EARLY SUNDAY MORNING.

According to reports THE SECONDARY SCHOOL STUDENT WENT TO A WELL KNOWN CHAGUANAS NIGHT SPOT WITH FRIENDS. SHE MET A MAN WHO OFFERED HER DRINKS THROUGH-OUT THE NIGHT,EARLY SUNDAY MORNING after escaping the man's clutches, she went to the police and reported the matter. She was medically examined and rape was confirmed.,police are searching for a suspect…"

(10) "Khan: Girls getting drugged in discos and clubs" NEWSDAY SEPTEMBER 22,2001

"Junior Minister of Health Dr Fuad Khan expressed concern about ready access to Estacy drugs at discos and clubs. Speaking during debate on the 2001/02 budget, he welcomed enforcement of the law relating to the selling of alcohol to minors.

Khan claimed…THE DRUGGING OF HIS 17-YEAR-OLD DAUGHTER A MONTH AGO. HIS DAUGHTER HAD TO BE TAKEN HOME BY FRIENDS WHEN SHE FAINTED FOLLOWING A PARTY AT A POPULAR NIGHT CLUB…"

(11) "Brother of victim testifies"EXPRESS JULY 3,1998

"After Jason Johnson told accused Brad Boyce 'rock so nah white boy' Boyce with a semi-folded fist hit Johnson on the head.

JOHNSON'S 16-YEAR-OLD BROTHER STEPHEN TOLD A COURT YESTERDAY. STEPHEN JOHNSON WAS 14-YEARS-OLD AT THE TIME OF THE INCIDENT.HE SAID AROUND 11.30PM ON AUGUST 31,1996, HIS

BROTHER Jason, a friend Christopher AND HIMSELF WENT TO THE EDGE NIGHT CLUB TO PARTY.

THE WITNESS TESTIFIED HE(STEPHEN) CARRIED A MEAT CHOPPER FOR PROTECTION AS THERE HAD BEEN AN INCIDENT BETWEEN HIMSELF AND SIX BOYS SIX WEEKS BEFORE. JASON HE SAID DID NOT KNOW ABOUT THE MEAT CHOPPER AND HE(STEPHEN) REVEALED HE HAD A WEAPON ON HIM. JASON HE SAID BECAME ANNOYED AND TOOK THE MEAT CHOPPER FROM HIM AND HID IT UNDER THE STEPS

THE STEPS LEADING UP TO THE NIGHT CLUB, AND THE THREE PARTIED UNTIL 3.45AM. STEPHEN ADMITTED THAT JASON WAS A LITTLE TIPSY WHEN THE THREE CAME OUT INTO THE CAR PARK.

BRAD BOYCE HAS BEEN CHARGED WITH MURDER…"

(12) "A sister cries for the murder of her 14-year-old brother, Benji was a nice boy" EXPRESS FEBRUARY 15,1997

"BENJIMAN WILLIAM BENJAMIN WAS THE 14-YEAR-OLD BOY WHO WAS STASBBED TO DEASTH ON JOUVERT MORNING. Benji's sister Shurlar said ..'it was the first time that he went on his own,' she recalled she begged him to stay and jump with them, 'we always carried Benji to jouvert, but this time he said he was going to lime with friends and that I would see him later.'

THE NEXT TIME SHE SAW HER BROTHER, HE WAS LYING ON A SLAB IN THE MORGUE. HE GOT ONE STAB TO HIS BELLY,ONE BY HIS CHEST,ONE IN HIS BACK AND TWO TO HIS HEAD. according to police report,Benji got into AN ARGUMENT WITH ANOTHER MAN OVER A WOMAN,HE WAS APPARENTLY CAUGHT WINING WITH A WOMAN. HE WAS DUE TO START HIS FIRST TERM AT THE SAN JUAN GOVERNMENT SCHOOL

(13) "School boy 15 stabbed to death" NEWSDAY APRIL 8,2002

"SCHOOL BOY MIGUEL MARTINEZ BECAME THE FIRST MURDER VICTIM FOR THE YEAR WHEN HE WAS STABBED TO DEATH DURING A PARTY IN BUCCON ON TUESDAY. THE FORM ONE STUDENT WAS STABBED TO DEATH LATE TUESDAY NIGHT AT A BUCCON BEACH BAR,TOBAGO DURING A FIGHT WITH ANOTHER TEENAGER AT A MASSIVE FETE.

Eyewitnesses said that martinez BEGAN ARGUING WITH ANOTHER TEENAGER APPARENTLY OVER A SAID THAT MARTINEZ BEGAN ARGUING WITH ANOTHER TEENAGER APPARENTLY OVER A GIRL WITH WHOM THE TEENAGERS WERE BOTH FAMILIAR.

According to police report, THE TEEN PULLED OUT AN ICEPICK AND STABBED MARTINEZ TWICE IN THE CHEST BEFORE MAKING HIS ESCAPE IN THE CROWD

(14) "Teen stabbed to death over girl" NEWSDAY NOVEMBER 24,1998

"AN ARGUMENT OVER A TEENAGE GIRL RESULTED IN THE STABBING DEATH OF A 17-YEAR-OLD SANTA CRUZ TEENAGER Nicholas Bumper Joseph.JOSEPH LEFT HIS HOME ON SATURDAY NIGHT TELLING HIS STEP-FATHER THAT HE HE WAS GOING TO A SCHOOL BAZAAR

While there an argument broke out between Nicholas and a group of men, the group threatened to kill Nicholas over the girl. THE GROUP OF TEENAGERS REPORTED CHASED NICHOLAS THROUGH THE STREETS OF BARATARIA AS HE WAS MAKING HIS WAY HOME EARLY SUNDAY MORNING, POLICE

REPORTS REVEALED THAT AROUND 1.30AM NICHOLAS ATTEMPTED TO HIDE,HE WAS CORNERED BY THE MEN,ONE OF THE MEN STAB NICHOLAS IN THE BACK KILLING HIM INSTANTLY…"

I have concluded the listing of examples of youths under 18 years who were out late at night and into the early morning hours. Cases of girls who were raped, one 11-year-old girl ran away from home and boys killed,except for the 14-year-old brother who was out late after mid night with his brother and friend and who testified in court that he saw his brother killed when he was struck in the head.

The above cases represent a few reports that came into highlight in the media, but I am sure that there are many too ashamed of rape or other sexual assaults and have left things quite out of the news media.Habits of sad episodes are there,look around your neighbourhoods and listen when it is carnival and fete time and see the youths defying the late nights.

I shall now introduce the other section of allowing the reader to digest curfew laws reported in various countries.

SAID THAT MARTINEZ BEGAN ARGUING WITH ANOTHER TEENAGER APPARENTLY OVER A GIRL WITH WHOM THE TEENAGERS WERE BOTH FAMILIAR.

According to police report, THE TEEN PULLED OUT AN ICEPICK AND STABBED MARTINEZ TWICE IN THE CHEST BEFORE MAKING HIS ESCAPE IN THE CROWD

(15)" "Teen stabbed to death over girl" NEWSDAY NOVEMBER 24,1998
"AN ARGUMENT OVER A TEENAGE GIRL RESULTED IN THE STABBING DEATH OF A 17-YEAR-OLD SANTA CRUZ TEENAGER Nicholas Bumper Joseph.JOSEPH LEFT HIS HOME ON SATURDAY NIGHT TELLING HIS STEP-FATHER THAT HE HE WAS GOING TO A SCHOOL BAZAAR
While there an argument broke out between Nicholas and a group of men, the group threatened to kill Nicholas over the girl. THE GROUP OF TEENAGERS REPORTED CHASED NICHOLAS THROUGH THE STREETS OF BARATARIA AS HE WAS MAKING HIS WAY HOME EARLY SUNDAY MORNING, POLICE REPORTS REVEALED THAT AROUND 1.30AM NICHOLAS ATTEMPTED TO HIDE,HE WAS CORNERED BY THE MEN,ONE OF THE MEN STAB NICHOLAS IN THE BACK KILLING HIM INSTANTLY…"

I have concluded the listing of examples of youths under 18 years who were out late at night and into the early morning hours. Cases of girls who were raped, one 11-year-old girl ran away from home and boys killed,except for the 14-year-old brother who was out late after mid night with his brother and friend and who testified in court that he saw his brother killed when he was struck in the head.

The above cases represent a few reports that came into highlight in the media, but I am sure that there are many too ashamed of rape or other sexual assaults and have left things quite out of the news media.Habits of sad episodes are there,look around your neighbourhoods and listen when it is carnival and fete time and see the youths defying the late nights.

I shall now introduce the other section of allowing the reader to digest curfew laws reported in various countries.

(b) "Curfew for young Belizeans" NEWSDAY AUGUST 14, 2000
"BELIZE CITY, BELIZE: The Belize town of San Pedro has earned a reputation as a happy go lucky tourist destination. BUT SOME OF ITS KIDS ARE A PROBLEM

SOME ARE ON THE STREETS VERY LATE AT NIGHT. NOW A CURFEW IS PLANNED FROM SEPTEMBER TO KEEP THE YOUNGSTERS OFF THE STREETS. TV STATION CHANNEL 5 SAYS, it quoted Patty Arcco, Area Representative of Belize Rural South as saying 'THIS EXERCISE WE FIND NECESSARY, BECAUSE WE ARE FINDING TEENAGE PREGNANCY HAS INCREASED IN ADDITION TO THE ABUSE OF DRUGS,ESPECIALLY ALCOHOL IN MINORS. IT IS INCREASING.'

WE ARE SEEING MORE CHILDREN AT THE AGE OF TEN, FIFTEEN AND EVEN EIGHT YEARS OLD ON THE STREETS, TWO,THREE O'CLOCK IN THE MORNING.BUT WE AS AUTHORITIES COULD ONLY DO SO MUCH, SO WE ARE ASKING PARENTS TO TAKE CONTROL OF WHERE THEIR CHILDREN ARE."

"Curfew for St Kitts children" EXPRESS FEBRUARY 7 2001

"THE DEFENCE FORCE OF ST KITTS RECENTLY LAUNCHED A CAMPAIGN TO KEEP CHILDREN OFF THE STREETS AFTER 10.00PM. THE ACTION LED TO THE DETENTION OF SIX CHILDREN UNDER THE AGE OF 15 YEARS FOUND LOITERING ON THE STREETS OF BASSETERRE AFTER 10.00PM.

THE CHILDREN WERE HANDED OVER TO THE POLICE THE EXERCISE IS TO BE AN EFFORT TO PREVENT YOUNG PERSONS IN THE SOCIETY FROM PICKING UP

BAD HABITS,RUBBING SHOULDERS WITH CRIMINALS\AND YIELDING TO TEMPTATION. This project is supported

By the CRIMINAL AMENDMENT ACT PASSED December 20 1976. THE ACT PROVIDES FOR A BOY OR GIRL UNDER THE AGE OF 15 YEARS WHO ARE FOUND WONDERING OR LOITERING ON THE STREETS AFTER 10.00PM TO BE STOPPED AND TAKEN TO THE POLICE STATION.

IF HE OR SHE FAILS TO SHOW SATISFACTORY REASON FOR BEING OUT AT THAT HOUR, THE CHILD IS NOT RELEASED UNTIL A PARENT OR GUARDIAN OF THE CHILD SHOWS UP.

THE PARENT OR GUARDIAN OF THE CHILD IS FINED EC$200 IF THE CHILD IS FOUND REPEATEDLY OUT AFTER 10.00PM AT NIGHT."

CARIBBEAN WEEK
ST KITTS/NEVIS

"Cali under curfew" TRINIDAD GUARDIAN APRIL 9, 1997

"BOGATA: Cana-Reuter. AUTHORITIES HAVE CLAMPED AN OVERNIGHT CURFEW ON CALI,COLOMBIA'S SECOND LARGEST CITY, IN AN ATTEMPT TO CURB VIOLENT CRIME INVOLVING MINORS, LOCAL MEDIA REPORTED.

BOGATA'S EL TIEMPO NEWSPAPER SAID THE CURFEW BANNING ANONE UNDER THE AGE OF 18 YEARS FROM OFF THE STREETS OF CALI BETWEEN 11.30PM AND 5.00AM WOULD TAKE EFFECT ON TUESDAY NIGHT AND LAST INDEFINITELY. THE NEWSPAPER SAID THAT POLICE STATISTICS INDICATED THAT 70 PERCENT OF CRIMES COMMITTED IN CALI, INVOLVED ADOLOCENTS BETWEEN THE AGES OF 12 AND 17 TEARS OLD..."

"Boy thief among the first to face tearaway curfew" TIMES 6 SEPTEMBER 1998,ENGLAND.

"A SEVEN YEAR-OLD BOY THIEF THAT HAS BEEN ARRESTED MORE THAN TEN TIMES COULD BE AMONG THE FIRST TARGETS OF A NEW CURFEW RULES WHICH BECOME LAW ON SEPTEMBER 30. THE CURFEW LAW IS ANOTHER ATTEMPT TO GIVE AUTHORITIES ANOTHER OPTION AND TO MAKE PARENTS RESPONSIBLE FOR THEIR CHILDREN.UNDER THE LAW,CURFEWS WILL BE IMPOSED ON NEIGHBOURHOODS IN WHICH YOUNGSTERS ARE CAUSING TROUBLE RATHER

THAN INDIVIDUALS THEMSELVES. THE LAW WILL OPERATE BETWEEN 9.00PM AND 6.00AM IN WHICH YOUNGSTERS FOUND AT THESE TIMES ARE AT RISK OF BEING PICKED UP BY SPECIAL POLICE...It is important to see this provision as only one part of the legislation. Part of the CRIME AND DISORDER ACT. The legislation forms part of a key element of Jack Straw's CLAMPDOWN ON JUVENILE CRIME, A GROWING PROBLEM IN BRITAIN..."

"Invasion of the super-predators,they are young,brutal and remorseless...what can be done to combat the new generation of child gangsters..."TIMES FEBRUARY 16, 1997, LONDON,ENGLAND

"Michael Howard,the Home Secretary now plans to give magistrates wide-ranging new powers AIMED AT FORCING PARENTS TO TAKE MORE RESPONSIBILITY FOR THEIR CHILDREN. THOSE WHO FAIL TO CONTROL THEIR UNRULY CHILDREN COULD EVEN FIND THEMSELVES CONFINED TO THEIR OWN HOMES UNDER CURFEW ENFORCED BY ELECTRONIC TAGGING.

Howard's new measures to be announced will include new powers for courts to issue 'parental control orders' which WILL FORCE MOTHERS AND FATHERS TO ENSURE THAT THEIR JUVENILE DELINQUENTS ARE KEPT UNDER STRICT CURFEWS. PARENTS WHO BREACH SUCH ORDERS COULD BE FINED 1000(British pounds) AND BE SUBJECT TO CURFEWS THEMSELVES.THEIR MOVEMENTS COULD BE MONITORED BY ELECTRONIC TAGS STRAPPED TO THEIR ANKLES..."

"Young and ruthless"SUNDAY SUN JUNE 2,1996 CANADA

"Will we too one day have to think about enforcing CURFEW LAWS ON OUR KIDS? ONTARIO ALREADY HAS A CURFEW UNDER THE "CHILD AND FAMILY SERVICES ACT" IT CAN PREVENT A CHILD INDER 16 YEARS FROM BEING ON THE STREETS BETWEEN MIDNIGHT AND 7.00AM..."

ENGLAND
CRIME AND DISORDER ACT 1998,
CHAPTER 37,LOCAL CHILD CURFEW SCHEMES 14-

(2) This subsection applies to a ban on children of specified ages(under 10) being in a public place within a specified area-
- (a) during specified hours(between 9pm and 6am) and
- (b) otherwise than under the effective control of a parent or responsible person aged 18 years or over (6) A notice given under a local child curfew scheme may specify different hours in relation to children of different ages...

1998 No.2327(c.53)
CRIMINAL LAW,ENGLAND AND WALES
CRIMINAL LAW, SCOTLAND

CRIMINAL LAW,NORTHERN IRELAND
The Crime and Disorder Act 1998 Commencement No.2 and Transitional Provisions
Order 1998
Made 19th September 1998.

Trinidad and Tobago, 1986-1995
Central Statistical Office

PUBLIC ORDER

TABLE 50. PERSONS COMMITTED TO PRISON BY SEX AND TYPE OF COMMITTAL, 1986-1995

Period	Number of persons committed to prison during the year			Type of committal						To penal imprisonment[1] Expenditure $000		
				For safe custody[2] remanded		For debt[3]		In default of fines				
	Both sexes	Male	Female	Male	Female	Male	Female	Male	Female	Total	Staff	Main-tenance
	(1)	(2)	(3)	(4)	(5)	(6)	(7)	(8)	(9)	(9)	(10)	(11)
1986 ...	6 264	5 903	361	3 782	313	13	2	807	35	51 095	47 457	3 638
1987 ...	6 945	6 666	279	4 194	207	31	5	815	45	47 812	43 710	4 102
1988 ...	5 715	5 397	318	2 579	264	17	5	1 002	15	47 647	43 270	4 377
1989 ...	15 506	15 205	301	12 525	181	18	-	1 006	22	44 257	39 385	4 872
1990 ...	36 679	36 381	298	33 279	207	15	6	952	24	45 656	39 935	5 721
1991 ...	16 027	14 987	1 040	11 932	926	6	4	1 185	35	57 829	49 673	8 156
1992 ...	20 359	19 216	1 143	15 214	1 053	8	2	1 712	32	66 333	59 161	7 172
1993 ...	26 179	24 956	1 223	21 717	1 135	17	1	1 451	37	61 855	55 383	6 472
1994 ...	21 083	19 106	1 977	15 798	1 875	2	-	1 169	25	74 693	66 436	8 257
1995 ...	21 293	20 877	416	17 260	336	20	4	1 247	26	91 263	77 218	14 045

[1] For further analysis of persons committed to penal imprisonment. (See Table 52).
[2] Persons awaiting trial, deportation and execution.
[3] Persons convicted may also be awaiting trial. Hence the figures could be duplicated in other columns and would not necessarily add to the total.

Source: 4.3

110

TRINIDAD GUARDIAN JANUARY 14, 1996

again according to the report.

(4) Why was a girl of 14 years on the Brian Lara Promenade at that hour outside of the sanctity of her home and without the security of her parents?

I suggest we as parents and adults, have failed our youths by doing nothing to prevent a crime like this. We have failed to keep good family values, respect for women and children and passed on this total lack of discipline to a new generation of young people who believe that "win the lotto and reach the sky" is all that life consists of. Young people have no respect for police, teachers, laws (natural, constitutional and statutory). We have allowed a whole generation in our island, to believe that crime pays.

(5) Have we institutional corruption and crime? I believe we have.

We must make changes constitutionally, and in our homes. Discipline must be practiced and respect for authority enforced. We must make sure that justice, tempered with mercy, must prevail. This must be swiftly carried out to destroy the already accepted concept of a "9 day country". This can be proved by the number of abominable similar crimes committed last year that are already forgotten.

The present new government needs, in my opinion, to proceed to fulfill their manifesto promises by:

(1) Destroying institutionalised crime and corruption.

(2) By bringing back the necessary "out dated, old-fashioned methods to reinforce home and school discipline. Children must go to school. Police must have the right to "pickup" children (under 16 years) who are not in school and on the streets.

(3) The Attorney General and the Chief Justice must proceed with quick, effective,

We're failing as parents, adults

out late

THE EDITOR: A recent report of the most abominable crime — rape — against a 14-year-old girl of Petit Valley by 14 youths (boys, youngmen) was in my opinion not well highlighted in another newspaper in the last three days of the year 1995. The report has prompted, in my mind, several questions that we must answer to avoid such occurrences in this New Year, 1996.

(1) Is it so difficult to identify and arrest these alleged perpetrators in view of the facts presented in the report? These youths were armed — more reason to arrest them.

(2) Are the police so poorly informed and slow to move? I do not think so. They are hindered and obstructed in such cases by people who protect these youths.

(3) How many more "budding Lincoln Guerras" are we going to let go? This girl was so beaten, raped, escaped and caught, raped and beaten

RAMESH MATHURA.   **PATRICK**

92

Page 8 NEWSDAY Sunday January 4, 1998

Ill judgement

WE CONDEMN OUTRIGHT the alleged rape of a 14-year-old girl, which, reportedly, took place in the early hours of New Year's Day, but, nonetheless, question why her parents or guardians allowed her to be out at the ungodly hour of 3.15 am, and relatively unprotected?

Why was a minor permitted to be at a party until the wee hours of the morning? And to worsen matters, allowed to walk home through lonely areas relatively unprotected.

And while we cannot condemn too strongly her alleged rape we must censure the parents or guardians. For even though we hold to the view that all females should be able to walk the roads of Trinidad and Tobago without molestation, today's reality of increasing sexual assaults on women and girls, even in their own homes, demands caution.

At the risk of seeming old fashioned we insist that parents and guardians must assume full responsibility for the upbringing and putting into effect of safety measures for their children, particularly their daughters.

Increasingly, all women and girls are, potentially, at risk today and to allow a 14-year-old girl to walk home at 3.15 in the morning, accompanied only by two teenaged youths, is to intensify the odds against her.

And in the case of parents and guardians clearly there must be a family compact the basic terms of which would allow for the protection of their children through upholding and guidance, the instituting of safety measures and the instilling of ideas for their own safety.

Clearly, permitting a 14-year-old girl to be at a party until way after midnight and then wend her way home without adult family protection violated the terms of that compact.

The Independent

Mormon gets 12 years for rape

WEDNESDAY, MARCH 12, 1997   PAGE 5

BY DARREN BAHAW

A MORMON counsellor was spared punishment of the whip but jailed for 12 years by Justice Herbert Volney after he was found guilty yesterday in the Port-of-Spain Second Assize Court, of raping a 14-year-old girl seven years ago in Sangre Grande.

John Morang, 40, a father of four young children, of Coalmine Village, Sangre Grande, nervously took off his watch and handed it to his attorney, glanced at his wife, relatives and members of his church organisation in the courtroom before being led away by police.

Justice Volney told Morang, the sole bread-winner of his family, that he was a man he had to protect society from but the evidence in the trial was not tantamount to the maximum penalty of life imprisonment.

The Judge said Morang, an electronic technician, had not shown any remorse during the trial and

even up to the time he was found guilty.

Instead "he chose to rub salt in the wounds of the victim suggesting that she had made up this whole thing."

Justice Volney took into consideration "a stirring plea for mercy" from Morang's attorney Christlyn Moore that her client had never had any previous brushes with the law nor he had any criminal matters pending.

Moore said that Morang's church had supported him throughout the episode and members including foreign missionaries and local parishioners were willing to come forward to testify to his character. Several members of the Church of Jesus Christ of Latter Day Saints were outside the court all day awaiting the verdict.

However, he dismissed the plea for a non-custodial sentence saying that "in this country whoever commits the offence of rape goes straight to jail...the question is how long."

The judge told the defence attorney that her plea for mercy centered around the prisoner, his family and his church but "not of the victim who was subjected to the indignity of the debasing act by the

prisoner."

He said that the victim wept throughout the trial, adding that, "she is still hurting."

According to the State's case presented by prosecutor Maria Wilson, on December 23, 1990, the victim was waiting for transportation to go home around 4 am after attending a party, when she stopped a White Corolla car driven by Morang.

Sitting in the back seat were two men she knew from her district.

The car proceeded towards Coalmine Village.

However, when she neared her stop, Morang continued driving and told her he would drop off the two men who lived higher up the same road before dropping her off.

After Morang dropped off the two men he turned around and drove in the direction of the girl's home but passed her stop and headed to Rampartap Trace.

When they arrived at the deserted area, Moran and the girl

came out of the car and he shoved her in the back seat. She attempted to escape but fell down and bruised her leg and elbow.

Morang then pushed her against the trunk of his car and ripped off her clothing before raping her. The victim testified that she was raped for 30 minutes.

He then gave her back her clothes and dropped her home.

The girl made a report to the Sangre Grande Police Station shortly after.

She told the court that while returning from the doctor's office, on Paul Street, in company with PC Verlin Belle, she saw Morang driving the same car near her taxi stand.

He was arrested by PC Belle and later charged. Police seized the bloodstained underwear Morang was wearing earlier that day and also the victims panties which were sent to the Forensic analyst for examination. Both blood stains were of the same blood type as the victim.

HERBERT VOLNEY...
straight jail for rapists

113

TRINIDAD GUARDIAN OCTOBER 8, 1996

Five charged with rape of 15-year-old

Trinidad Guardian October 8 1996

A 15-YEAR-old Point Fortin Senior Comprehensive student was raped and buggered by five men as she made her way home after a party at Clifton Hill on Sunday morning.

The girl was returning home around 2.30 am following the fete when she was accosted by five men who pulled her into a track near the Triple K Bar.

Police said the men raped and buggered the school girl before leaving her bleeding on the track.

She was rescued by passers by and reported the matter to the Point Fortin Police. Following investigations by Cpl. Cooper, five young men, all of Point Fortin, and between the ages of 19-21 were arrested and charged with rape, buggery and serious indecency.

When they appeared before Magistrate Lee Kim in the Point Fortin Magistrate Court yesterday Court Prosecutor Acting Inspector Gregory Christopher objected to bail on the grounds that the offences were "too serious."

Magistrate Lee Kim upheld his objection and advised the young men of their rights to apply to a Judge in Chambers for bail. They were then remanded in custody to reappear on Thursday in the La Brea Magistrate Court.

TRINIDAD GURDIAN APRIL 26, 1999

15-year-old raped

By SAVITRI SOOKRAJ

A 15-YEAR-OLD girl was raped early yesterday morning after returning home from a party.

Police reported that the girl, from Maracas, St Joseph, went to a party with some friends. After the party she accepted a ride home with a male friend, said to be in his 20s.

Police said the victim's friend drove to an area close to the Johnson and Johnson factory, off the Churchill Roosevelt Highway, where he allegedly raped her. He then took her home. The girl subsequently told her parents about the incident.

A report was made to PCs Hazarie, Ralph and WPC Mungroo of the Arouca Police Station. Police have held a man for the alleged attack. He was expected to be charged yesterday.

114

Two women raped in Arouca

NEWSDAY DECEMBER 15, 1998, p 4

By NALINEE SEELAL

TWO VICTIMS ages 16 and 26 were raped within half an hour of each other in the Arouca district early yesterday.

Police reports revealed that around 4 am, the 16-year-old girl left her Arouca home to visit a friend.

While walking along Railway Road, Arouca, she was ambushed by four men who pulled her into some bushes and robbed her of $40.

The men then took turns in raping the teenager.

She was left in the bushes by her four attackers who fled the scene by running away.

The girl managed to clothe herself and made her way to her home where she reported the rape.

She was taken to the Arouca Police Station where she lodged a formal report.

Later she was examined by a district medical officer.

Almost half an hour after the rape of the 16-year-old girl, a 26-year-old woman was walking along Farm Road, Arouca, when she was attacked by a man armed with a knife.

The woman was raped by the man who fled the scene after carrying out the assault.

Sgt Peter Grant and PC Mungroo of the Arouca Police Station carried out a seach for the rapists yesterday.

Police believe that a gang of men operating in the Arouca district are responsible for the rape of the 16-year-old.

They have not linked the two rapes, but they are calling on young women to travel in groups when venturing out of their home at nights or during the early hours of the morning.

Police have increased patrols in the Arouca district as a result of the two rapes.

Guy: We need co-operation and help to survive

By SASCHA WILSON

POLICE COMMISSIONER Hilton Guy indicated that police were bombarded with things that cause them to think and reevaluate their strategy, outlook and approaches to make an impression in order to do their work.

He was speaking at Acting Commissioner of Police Cecil Carrington's need co-operation and help from all of us to survive." Guy said, "No man is an island," adding that the times we live in clearly typifies this statement.

"Our resources are scarce, we do not have all to discharge our responsibilities but we are blessed with citizens who make the shortfall bearable," he indicated.

Guy thanked all the citizens for their

Cops hunt rape suspect

NEWSDAY FEBRUARY 15, 2000, p 6

AFTER being supplied with alcohol, a 16-year-old girl was taken home by an elderly man she met at a bar. By the time the girl began to sober up, the man had raped her and was attempting to sexually assault her a second time.

The assault is alleged to have occurred early Sunday morning.

According to reports, the secondary school student went to a well known Chaguanas night spot with friends. She met the man who offered her drinks throughout the night.

Early Sunday morning, the girl was taken to the man's house.

After escaping the man's clutches, the girl went to the Chaguanas CID, where she reported the matter. She was medically examined and rape confirmed.

Police are now searching for a suspect.

Schoolboy stabbed to death

Guardian May 30, 2003

GEISHA KOWLESSAR

A 15-YEAR-OLD schoolboy was stabbed to death after he assaulted a prostitute, police said yesterday.

The family of Junior Langford, however, maintains he was attacked while on his way home from cricket practice.

Investigators up to late yesterday evening were searching west Trinidad for a female suspect.

Langford's death brings to 90 the number of people murdered to date.

Senior investigators believe Langford, of Nizam Avenue, El Socorro, may have tried to solicit the prostitute.

"We received information he approached the person and said he had only $80. But when the woman told him that was not enough, he slapped and pushed her," a senior officer said yesterday.

"They began fighting and the woman allegedly pulled out an ice pick from her handbag. Langford was stabbed once in the chest, the officer said.

Police said the women may have also witnessed the incident.

A party of officers led by ACP Crime Oswyn Allard cordoned off the area for several hours.

Officers discovered Langford lying on his back in a pool of blood.

Langford's family insist he had gone to cricket practice.

Langford's 16-year-old sister Keisha could not control her grief on hearing of the death of her younger brother.

"The teenager was a Form Two student of the Tranquillity Government Secondary School.

Brother of victim testifies

EXPRESS JULY 3, 1998, p 3

BY OLIVIA MEJAS

AFTER Jason Johnson told accused Brad Boyce, "Rock so, nah white boy," Boyce, with a semi-folded fist, retaliated by hitting Johnson in the head.

Johnson's 16-year-old brother Stephen Van Luc Johnson told a court yesterday that before Boyce hit his brother, he (Boyce) told Jason: "Like one ah allyuh want to get it tonight."

Boyce, Stephen Johnson said, then walked up to Jason, "hopped back, came down and lash Jason in his head".

The witness was made to demonstrate to the court how Boyce delivered the blow.

Johnson said that after the blow, Jason held onto the left side of his head, took about two steps backward and fell down on his back.

"I walk up about 15-20 seconds after and saw Jason beating up. His hands was moving all over the place and his legs beating up.

"He was bleeding through his nose and mouth, air was sounding like it was coming through his ears and his lips started to swell.

"Brad watched down on the floor and walked off, I was trying to speak to Jason but he wasn't responding at all," Johnson said.

In her opening address to the jury, Assistant DPP Carla Brown-Antoine said the State intended to prove that Boyce committed an unjustifiable act when he struck Johnson that night.

Johnson, she said, died from cerebro cranial trauma, a blunt force injury to the head, which, in pathologist Dr Hughvon Des Vignes's opinion, caused his

brain to dislodge, "twist and move", hitting the right inside part of his head.

The damage, the assistant DPP said, caused Johnson to fall into a coma for two weeks and then die.

Stephen Johnson, who was 14 at the time of the incident, said around 11:30 p.m. on August 31, 1996, his brother Jason, a friend—Christopher "Conkie" D'Abreau—and himself went to The Edge to party.

Stephen Johnson broke down in tears when he told the court that Jason had told him that it would be his "last party".

The witness said he carried a Chinese chopper with him for protection as there had been an incident between himself and six boys two weeks before.

Jason, he said, didn't know about the chopper, until their eldest brother, Sean, had dropped them off at the mall's carpark and he (Stephen)

revealed he had a weapon with him.

Jason, he said, became annoyed, took the chopper and hid it behind an ice-box under the steps leading to the night club and the three partied until 3:45 a.m.

Stephen Johnson admitted that Jason was "a little tipsy" when the three had come out into the carpark to wait for their friend Pablo Henry to give them a drop home.

D'Abreau, he said, became involved in an altercation with about six or seven youths and was eventually taken back inside the club by a bouncer of the club.

Stephen Johnson said D'Abreau was eventually released and was returning to them in the car park when he (Johnson) heard cursing and saw Boyce, a committee member of the club, coming towards them saying, "What the f--- wrong with allyuh. All yuh mother c--- banned, not to f--- ing come back here."

Jason, Stephen Johnson said, was cursing too and had turned around and started walking towards Boyce, saying "we don't f---ing, bound to come back to yuh club."

"There was a further exchange and the incident occurred, he said, adding that neither Boyce nor Jason had anything in their hands.

His brother, he said, was eventually put in a taxi and taken to the Port of Spain General Hospital and he returned to his home and told his parents about the incident.

Johnson will be further cross-examined when the trial resumes today at 9 a.m.

STEPHEN VAN LUC JOHNSON, brother of murder victim Jason Johnson, leaves the Hall of Justice yesterday. *Photo: STEVE McPHIE*

At a glance

ACCUSED: Brad Boyce, 20, of Bel Air Gardens, La Remaine

THE CHARGE: Manslaughter of 19-year-old Jason Johnson of Woodbrook on September 15, 1996. Johnson died from injuries inflicted to his head outside The Edge nightclub, Long Circular Mall, on September 1, 1996.

STATE ATTORNEYS: Assistant DPP Carla Brown-Antoine and Aveson Quinlan.

DEFENCE ATTORNEYS: Karl Hudson-Phillips QC, Gerald Stewart, Elaine Greene.

JUDGE: Herbert Volney

JURY: Five men, four women

COURT: Port of Spain Second Criminal Court, Hall of Justice.

A sister's cry for her murdered 14-year-old brother

Benji was a nice boy

EXPRESS FEBRUARY 15, 1997, p 5

BY UCILL CAMBRIDGE

SHARLAR BENJAMIN came up the gap to her family's house, climbed the wooden stairs, went inside, and started to bawl.

"Everybody bawling, nobody could believe what happen to Benji," she exclaimed.

"Benji" William Jouvert, as it was the first time he ever went off on his own. She recalled she begged him to stay and jump up with them.

"We always use to carry Benji to Jouvert with us. When we reach in town this time I was with my aunt and us. He said he was going to go with some friends," practically begged him to stay with me, but he told me he was going with his friends and that

to capture the person responsible for the death of 15-year-old Anthony Williams of Eastern Quarry, Laventille, who was gunned down last November while on his way home from school.

Benji's sister, Sharlar, 24 said it was practically Benji's first time the ever went off on his own. She recalled she begged her woman in the area who was returning from the early morning celebrations.

As she passed the yard of the house, she called out to Benji's 11-year-old brother who was outside in the yard. He then went

would see him later."

The next time she saw her brother he was dead, he get stab up in town."

Residents in the Gonzales area—closer to St Babb's Laventille than Belmont—all seem to hold one opinion about the deceased. "He was a nice boy."

Climbing the hill to get to the house, one young lady called out: "All you from the papers?

"You all have to do something about what the papers saying about Benji. Knowing

inside and relayed the news he got from the woman that, "Benji in no fight with nobody dead, he get stab up in town."

the type of person he was I sure he didn't get in no fight with nobody over no woman!"

According to a police report, Benji got into an argument with another man over a woman. The report said he was apparently caught winning with the woman during Dimanche Gras. They said the altercation escalated into a fight which led to the youth being stabbed.

But one police source said yesterday that the stabbing did not occur during that

the type of person he was incident. He admitted there was a dispute over some young lady, but that matter had passed, when something else happened which led to the young man being killed.

"I cannot imagine any reason why somebody would want to kill my brother," Sharlar Benjamin told the *Express*. She said her brother was the type of person who took nothing seriously.

"He was always laughing, always on 'kicks'. He was14, but you would think he was

NEWSDAY APRIL 1, 2002, p4

SCHOOLBOY, 15, STABBED TO DEATH

By SAMPSON NANTON
Tobago Bureau

SCHOOLBOY Miguel Martinez, 15, became the first murder victim in Tobago for the year, when he was stabbed to death during a party in Buccoo on Tuesday night.

The Form One student was stabbed to death late Tuesday night at a Buccoo Beach Bar, Tobago, during an altercation with another teenager at a massive fete to culminate the Easter season in Tobago.

Miguel Martinez of John Gully Street, Delaford, died on the spot after being stabbed twice in his chest at 11.45 pm.

Eyewitnesses said that Martinez had begun arguing with another teenager, apparently over a girl with whom the teenagers were both familiar.

According to police reports, the teenager pulled out an ice-pick and stabbed Martinez twice in his chest, before making his escape by running through the crowd.

On one occasion, a relative of Martinez fainted on seeing his body and had to be treated by medical personnel present.

As promoters began shutting down the many music systems on hand one by one just after 1 am, more and more people made their way ground near the goat race track. Officers and ambulance personnel had a tough time controlling the large crowd of people who shoved their way towards the body, most of whom had been alerted only by the presence of the police.

Two police jeeps and an ambulance arrived on the scene within 15 minutes and had to ease through the crowd, which police estimated to be between 10,000 and 15,000, before reaching the body, which was lying face up on the towards the scene.

One DJ even announced to the crowd that "there is a murder across the road".

The prompt ending of the festival created huge traffic problems in the existing areas as the thousands left for home.

A close schoolmate of Martinez, who attended the Pentecostal Light and Life Secondary School, a new school opened to accommodate the universal secondary education system, told *Newsday* that he was planning to return to school next week, after being absent for some time. The friend described Martinez as a friendly person who "used to get along with everybody in school".

Efforts to contact Martinez's parents proved futile yesterday, as they were engaged in a series of duties at the hospital and with the police.

Cpl Vincel Edwards of the Old Grange Police Station is investigating the matter. PC's Arthur, Roberts, Wallace and Clarke visited the scene. Up to yesterday, police were searching for the suspect.

TEEN STABBED TO DEATH OVER GIRL

Page 4 NEWSDAY Tuesday November 24, 1998

By NALINEE SEELAL

AN ARGUMENT over a teenage girl resulted in the stabbing death of 17-year-old Santa Cruz teenager Nicholas "Bumper" Joseph.

His murder brings to 84 the number of people killed for the year so far.

Joseph left his La Canoe Road, Santa Cruz home on Saturday night, telling his stepfather Roland Munroe that he was going to a school bazaar in Barataria.

While at the bazaar, an argument broke out between Nicholas and a group of men. The group threatened to kill Nicholas during a heated argument over a teenage girl.

A pastor of a church who was at the bazaar spoke to the group of five men and begged them to desist from any form of violence.

The group of teenagers reportedly chased Nicholas through the streets of Barataria as he was making his way home early Sunday morning.

Police reports revealed that around 1.30 am Nicholas attempted to hide by running into a fenced yard at Luis Avenue, Barataria.

He was cornered by the group of men who began planassing him with a cutlass. One of the men then stabbed Nicholas in the back which killed him instantly.

Residents of Luis Avenue who heard the screams of Nicholas alerted the E 999 police, and when officers went to the scene they found the lifeless body of Nicholas.

The body was viewed by a district medical officer and removed to the Forensic Science Centre.

Yesterday Annmarie Munroe, the mother of Nicholas, held on to her nine-year-old daughter Yolande and cried constantly as she spoke about her son.

Munroe told *Newsday* that she learnt of her son's murder while viewing the 7 pm news on television on Sunday.

She claimed that from the description of the clothes of the dead man she suspected that it was her son, Nicholas.

According to Munroe, on Sunday she cooked a meal of roti, curried channa and curried chicken which is Nicholas' favourite food.

She added that she put aside some food for her son, but during the day she felt a bit unhappy and was unsure why.

The mother of five related that it was when a neighbour broke the news to her that Nicholas was dead she started crying hysterically and went to the Barataria Police Station accompanied by the same neighbour, where she confirmed the stabbing death.

At the Santa Cruz home where Nicholas lived, his stepfather Roland and his younger brothers and sisters were in a state of shock over the murder.

They claimed that Nicholas kept the family together with his sense of humour and his ability to make everyone smile.

He was also helpful around the house. Nicholas was supposed to start his first job as a welder yesterday, and the money earned would have assisted this family.

Police investigators told *Newsday* that they are searching for a teenage girl who could assist them in pointing out the group of men responsible for the stabbing death of Nicholas.

Yesterday, a party of officers led by Inspector Anchoor Ali combed the Barataria and Santa Cruz areas in search of the girl.

EXPRESS FEBRUARY 7,2001,page 3

Caribbean Week
St Kitts/Nevis,

Curfew for St Kitts children

THE Defence Force of St Kitts recently launched a campaign to keep children off the streets after 10 p.m.

The action led to the detention of six children under the age of 15 years, found loitering on the streets of Basseterre after 10 p.m. They were handed over to the police. The exercise is said to be an effort to "prevent young persons in the society from picking up bad habits, rubbing shoulders with criminals and yielding to temptation."

"This project is supported by the Criminal Law Amendment Act, passed in December 20, 1976. The act provides for a boy or girl under the age of 15 who are found wandering or loitering on the streets after 10 p.m. to be stopped and taken to a police station.

The parent or guardian of the child is fined EC $200 if that child is repeatedly found out after 10 p.m. at nights.

NEWSDAY AUGUST 14,2000

CURFEW FOR YOUNG BELIZEANS

BELIZE CITY, BELIZE: The Belize town of San Pedro has earned a reputation as a happy go lucky tourist destination where fun is the order of the day, TV station *Channel 5* says.

But some of its kids are a problem — some are on the streets very late at night.

Now a curfew is planned from September 1 to keep the youngsters off the street, *Channel 5* reported.

It quoted Patty Arceo, Area Representative of Belize Rural South, as saying: "This exercise, we find it necessary because we are finding that teenage pregnancy has increased on the island, in addition to the abuse of drugs, especially alcohol in minors, it is increasing.

"We are seeing children at the age of ten, fifteen, sometimes eight years old on our streets, two, three o'clock in the morning.

"We had launched a campaign before, where we were asking parents to take care of their children, be more responsible, because, let's face it, if anything happens to these children, the first thing that they want to blame is the authorities.

"But we as authorities can only do so much, so we are in reality asking the parents to take control of where their children are.

(CANA)

121

TRINIDAD GUARDIAN APRIL 9.1997

Cali under curfew

BOGOTA, Cana-Reuter—AUTHORITIES have clamped an overnight curfew on Cali, Colombia's second largest city, in an attempt to curb violent crime involving minors, local media reported yesterday.

Bogota's *El Tiempo* newspaper said the curfew, banning anyone under 18 from the streets of Cali between 11.30 pm and 5 am, would take effect on Tuesday night and last indefinitely.

The newspaper said police statistics indicated that 70 percent of crimes in Cali involved adolescents aged between 12 and 17 and 1,243 minors were arrested in the city last year

TIMES SEPTEMBER 6,1998, ENGLAND

Boy thief among first to face tearaway curfew

by Maeve Sheehan

A SEVEN-year-old thief, who has been arrested more than 10 times, could be among the first targets of new curfew rules which become law on September 30.

The boy was apprehended after complaints that he stole purses from elderly ladies at bus stops and smashed car windows to steal radios. The child, who cannot be identified, lives in Newcastle where police have been warned to maintain a special watch for him.

"His family have been through police hands and they do not think that what this kid is doing is wrong," said one police officer.

The seven-year-old is just one of hundreds of problem under-10s across Britain who police and local authorities are considering placing under curfew using the new law. Such children cannot currently be prosecuted for their crimes as they are below the legal age of criminal responsibility. Until now the only option has been to make them the subject of care proceedings — a move often regarded as too drastic.

The curfew law is an attempt to give authorities another option and to make parents take responsibility for their children. Under the law, curfews will be imposed in neighbourhoods in which youngsters are causing trouble rather than on individuals themselves. The laws would operate between 9pm and 6am, with youngsters found outside these times at risk of being picked up by special police patrols.

After making an arrest the officers would first have to take a child to his or her home but if their parents were absent or seemed incapable of looking after them, they could be taken to police cells. Their parents would subsequently be expected to meet police and

identified 20 children under 10 who could have curfews imposed around their homes and haunts.

Among the worst offenders on the list is an eight-year-old boy who has been apprehended by police four times in the past year. He has twice been caught trying to steal cars and once tried to set a building alight. On another occasion he caused £9,500 damage by smashing most of the windows of an empty office block.

Ian Vickery, a police inspector in Middlesbrough, said the curfew rules would be useful if applied with "extreme caution". He added: "Curfews will be used very sparingly here. We want to get youngsters on our side. About 35% of those arrested have addresses which also appear on the domestic violence register."

In London the Metropolitan police arrested under-10s on 36 occasions between April and June this year. In 1997 police in Northumbria made 463 child arrests, with the youngest being just five years old.

The Association of Chief Police Officers gave a cautious welcome to the legislation. A spokesman said: "We will be seeking the views of police officers. It is important to see this provision as only one part of the legislation."

Part of the Crime and Disorder Act, the legislation forms a key element of Jack Straw's clampdown on juvenile crime, a growing problem in Britain. Home Office figures released in May revealed that one in five attacks on people or property was committed by children aged 15 or under.

Despite such figures, there is strong criticism of the proposed laws. Mike Thomas, chairman of the National Association for Youth Justice, said the measures were excessive. "It is

TIMES FEBRUARY 16,1997,ENGLAND

Invasion of the Superpredators

They're young, brutal and remorseless. They commit crimes by the dozen and get away with most of them. What can be done to combat the new generation of child gangsters dubbed "superpredators"? Report by **Stephen Grey**

Times 16 February 1997, Pg10. England
Curfew

Michael Howard, the Home Secretary, new plans to give magistrates wide-ranging new powers aimed at forcing new powers to take more severe jagging.

A STUDY by police in Northumberland last year

Prosecuting authorities and courts have also shown them-selves increasingly reluctant to take the firm measures that might be regarded as a deterrent.

laws enforced by electronic

America. A firm believer in "humiliation punishments", he allows the victims of bur-glaries to visit the burglars' homes and help themselves to

A 15-YEAR-OLD girl named Rachel experienced the American idea of bringing offenders and victims together last week. Nervous and embarrassed with her mother at her side, she was met at a police station in Milton Keynes by Tim O'Rourke, the security manager of an HMV store from which she had sto-len a £15 compact disc.

O'Rourke told her that shoplifters cost the retail trade £2 billion a year, putting prices up and jobs at risk. "I never realised so many people could be affected." Rachel re-plied. "I just thought I could get away with it"

She has never been in trou-ble with the police before and is unlikely to offend again. Only one shoplifter in eight is subjected to such confronta-tions in Milton Keynes has been caught doing so, com-pared with two in three dealt with in other ways.

The superpredators, who would laugh in the face of their victims, are a different proposition. In the run-up to the general election, both To-ries and Labour are drawing up tougher policies to counter serial offenders.

Howard, measures, to be announced in a green paper within a fortnight will include new powers for courts to issue "parental control orders" which could force mothers and fathers to ensure that juvenile delinquents were kept to strict curfews. Parents who breached such orders could be fined £1,000 and

Crime and Disorder Act 1998 (c. 37) ENGLAND.

1998 Chapter 37 - *continued*

PART I, PREVENTION OF CRIME AND DISORDER - *continued*

Youth crime and disorder - continued

back to previous text

Appeals against child safety orders

13. - (1) An appeal shall lie to the High Court against the making by a magistrates' court of a child safety order; and on such an appeal the High Court-

(a) may make such orders as may be necessary to give effect to its determination of the appeal; and

(b) may also make such incidental or consequential orders as appear to it to be just.

(2) Any order of the High Court made on an appeal under this section (other than one directing that an application be re-heard by a magistrates' court) shall, for the purposes of subsections (4) to (6) of section 12 above, be treated as if it were an order of the magistrates' court from which the appeal was brought and not an order of the High Court.

(3) Subsections (6) and (7) of section 10 above shall apply for the purposes of subsection (1) above as they apply for the purposes of subsection (1)(a) of that section.

Local child curfew schemes.

14. - (1) A local authority may make a scheme (a "local child curfew scheme") for enabling the authority-

(a) subject to and in accordance with the provisions of the scheme; and

(b) if, after such consultation as is required by the scheme, the authority considers it necessary to do so for the purpose of maintaining order,

to give a notice imposing, for a specified period (not exceeding 90 days), a ban to which subsection (2) below applies.

NB ✓ (2) This subsection applies to a ban on children of specified ages (under 10) being in a public place within a specified area-

✓ (a) during specified hours (between 9 pm and 6 am); and

(b) otherwise than under the effective control of a parent or

Offenders facing justice by committee

TORONTO STAR FEBRUARY 4,1999,CANADA

Tories embrace New Democrat idea for youths

By Joel Ruimy
QUEEN'S PARK BUREAU CHIEF

Ontario will soon be putting some non-violent first-time young offenders through "youth justice committees" instead of criminal courts, Premier Mike Harris has announced.

The tribunals would have the power to order young offenders to apologize and make cash restitution to victims, do community work, observe curfews or get counselling.

Youths going through these tribunals instead of the courts would avoid imprisonment, which some experts say often leads to a life of more serious crime.

A pilot program, launched by the NDP government of then-premier Bob Rae, has been running successfully in Cornwall since 1995. Yesterday's announcement extends the tribunals to Toronto, Barrie, Port Colborne, Kitchener and Ottawa this fall.

got to restructure and close old hospitals and build new ones and we're certainly doing that, too."

The announcement even won plaudits yesterday from Liberal Leader Dalton McGuinty, a criminal lawyer who often defended young offenders in Ottawa before becoming party leader.

"I think that holds some promise," he said, adding that "it's worked in other jurisdictions.

"The traditional means of incarceration provide an outstanding education in criminality. We should be looking at alternatives wherever possible to divert young offenders from the existing system.

"I think that's a good start."

The program wouldn't be automatic for all young offenders, defined as being aged 12 to 17. Youths would go through the new system only on the recommendation of police before charges are laid, or crown attorneys after charges are laid.

Youths accused of shoplifting, possession of stolen goods, mischief, fraud, or causing a disturbance would be eligible.

Ineligible charges include break and enter, joy riding, weapons offences, assault, stalking and drunk driving. Those have to go to court.

'There's absolutely no question that violent youth crime ... increased dramatically over the last 10 years.'

Young and ruthless

SUNDAY SUN JUNE 2, 1996, p 18, CANADA

NOT ON THE FENCE. Youth crime expert Metro Police Sgt. John Muise, in front of East York Collegiate, says problem is growing.

Curfew

It's becoming all too familiar in this global village: Kids killing other kids, or other brutal crimes of violence committed by youngsters.

But the recent claims that an 11-year-old Metro boy participated in the gang rape of a 13-year-old girl has been a focus for new concerns about whether youth violence in our own city is spiraling out of control.

Will we too one day have to think about enforcing curfews for our kids? Ontario already has a curfew under the Child and Family Services Act, but the law is rarely enforced. It can prevent a child under 16 from being on the streets between

olence, but generally it was one young man squaring off with another," Muise said. "At the worst it was probably fists and boots, but the likelihood of weapons was slim to nil."

Crimes of violence for those 12 to 17 have increased 133.5% from 1986 to 1994, he said. However, from 1994 to the present, Statistics Canada figures show the rate has re-

mained fairly constant, at around 14,000 "violent" offences yearly by youths in Canada.

Yet Metro Police have released figures showing that violent crimes, particularly robberies, rose dramatically between 1985 and 1995.

"You can write some of it off to increased community awareness, and as a result of

more reporting.

"But you know what: You can't write it all off," said the 20-year veteran police officer.

"We have had officers that have been attacked by groups of young people, and that's something that wouldn't have been any-where near as likely to happen 15 years ago.

"Those that would downplay the seriousness of youth violence, and the very obvious change from years gone by, do a tremendous disservice to young people, in particular youthful victims and potential youthful victims," Muise said.

Stuart Auty, Ontario chairman of the Safe School Task Force, said questioning whether there is a problem is "outrageous."

"That is like being in a pit of denial ... we have never seen the kinds of weaponry and the kinds of outcomes of that weaponry in the schools before. We haven't."

127

Curfews keep U.S. kids off city streets

TORONTO STAR AUGUST 17, 1997, pages A1, A12

By KATHLEEN KENNA
WASHINGTON BUREAU

Sunday Special

NEW ORLEANS — It's The Big Easy for adults only — this city is tough on kids.

Anyone aged 16 and under risks jail time if they're caught outdoors after 9 on week nights this summer.

"Lockdown," as some teens call it, is 11 p.m. every Friday and Saturday, but it's cut back to 8 p.m. during school term.

That means no late movies, no Superdome rock concerts, no neighborhood basketball games at dusk and not even walking the family pooch.

In a city famous for non-stop partying where adults can drink booze on the street and sex-club dancers bare almost everything on the sidewalk, Mayor Marc Morial has declared: This play-

ground is NOT for kids.

Since Morial introduced the scheme in mid-1994 after his first election campaign, New Orleans has boasted about having the toughest curfew in the United States.

Legislators and police from across the nation have used this city of almost 500,000 as a model for similar laws. A 1995 study by the U.S. Conference of Mayors found almost 300 cities have curfews and most were imposed in the past few years.

Britain also is studying New Orleans' curfew, but there's no evidence Canadian communities intend to follow.

President Bill Clinton, has

praised curfews as a way of curbing crime in a violence-plagued country, where 16 children are murdered by guns every day.

"The evidence shows that wherever these curfews are in place, they're working," Clinton said in a speech in New Orleans last summer to 10,000 members of the Women's International Convention of the Church of God in Christ. "Children's lives have been saved and their futures have been rescued."

Despite wild rhetoric about kids running rampant on America's streets, juvenile arrests account for only about 6 per cent of the U.S. total for violent crime.

"One half of 1 per cent of kids in the United States are arrested

☛ **Please see Curfew, A12**

ON PATROL: Uniformed officers walk through New Orleans' crowded streets at night.

KATHLEEN KENNA / TORONTO STAR

NEWSDAY MARCH 23, 1999

US Supreme Court lets stand juvenile curfew law

WASHINGTON: The US Supreme Court yesterday let stand a juvenile curfew law, rejecting arguments that the ordinance violates the constitutional rights of minors and their parents.

Confronted with an issue of growing importance as more cities nationwide impose curfews, the high court rejected a constitutional challenge by the American Civil Liberties Union (ACLU) to the law in Charlottesville, Virginia.

The justices without comment or dissent declined to review a US appeals court ruling that the law, which seeks to reduce juvenile crime and violence, passes constitutional muster.

The two-year-old law requires juveniles who are 16 or younger to be off the streets between midnight and 5 am on week nights and 1 am and 5 am on weekends.

The law contains eight exceptions, including when a minor is accompanied by a parent, is involved in an emergency or is running an errand for a parent, as long as the minor has a signed note.

The law allows juveniles to undertake employment or to attend supervised activities sponsored by schools and civic, religious or other public organisations.

The ACLU argued in the appeal that the curfew "deprives parents of their historically fundamental right to direct the rearing of their children". It also said the law "discriminates against minors in matters of fundamental freedoms".

But the Supreme Court sided with Charlottesville, which said it wanted to reduce crime. The city said its authority may extend into areas where parents have a corresponding responsibility to supervise and protect their children.

(REUTERS)

TORONTO STAR JULY 7,1996, CANADA

REUBEN GREENBERG: Charleston, S.C. police chief says rehabilitation is a waste of time and poverty and deprivation do not justify criminal behavior.

Tough-talking ~~CURFEW~~ police chief has crime on the run in Charleston

Toronto Star July 7. 1996

BY MARTIN WALKER
SPECIAL TO THE STAR

CHARLESTON, S.C. — Want to spank your child? Call the cops and they will make a house call to watch approvingly. It's part of their job "to reinforce parental authority."

Want to visit someone in a public housing block? There is a guardhouse where they'll check with the resident before letting you in, just like the gated and secured communities for the wealthy.

Want to be paroled from prison? If your crime was committed in the city of Charleston, the local police have a unit whose sole job is to attend parole hearings and oppose on principle all parole applications for serious offences.

Want to skip school? The police of this South Carolina city where the American Civil War started have standing orders to pick up people of school age. During school hours, they are taken back to school. After midnight, they are taken home.

"Black parents really like it, because they used to believe that cops take white kids home and black kids to jail," says police Chief Reuben Greenberg.

Once a self-confessed liberal sociology professor, Greenberg is one of America's best-known and toughest cops.

The American fashion for teenage curfews began in Charleston, part of a strategy of aggressive and effective policing that has made this coastal Southern city of more than 70,000 people a giant experiment in law and order.

marry, but they had children and the family kept the faith.

Despite his success at battling crime, Greenberg is perhaps best known for his apprehension of a bicycle thief while wearing his in-line skates.

Using the skates is, he maintains, an efficient way to patrol. He also insists his police officers wear running shoes on the beat, and the way to win promotion is through Greenberg's own Flying Squad of officers who can run down their prey.

'It is our job to . . . take away the anonymity of the criminal'

Greenberg's fame flows partly from his innovative tactics, partly from his insistence on reinforcing parental discipline, and partly from his skill at self-promotion and public relations. But the bottom line is Charleston's crime rates have dropped further and faster than any other small- or medium-sized city in the U.S.

Rates of murder and armed robbery, and of lesser crimes like burglary, have tumbled back to levels last seen in the 1950s. When the crack cocaine epidemic sent the crime rates shooting back up, Greenberg's force drove them down with two new tactics.

The first was to put a uniformed cop on every street known as a place where drugs were dealt. The officers just stood there asking people for their names and addresses.

"Your purpose there is not to ask him any questions, really. It's to let him know that you recognize he's there and if something happens he's one of the people you're going to be looking at as the perpetrator."

The goal was also to exert a constant presence that would drive drug dealers off the streets. Next, every drug raid became an exercise in punitive fiscal damage.

"Old-style policing is to kick in the door and make arrests. But that's not enough. You have to make drug dealing or prostitution or gambling a way to lose money, not make money," Greenberg says.

Enforcing a law which says police may confiscate anything that brings "aid and comfort to criminal operations," the police in Charleston took everything: cars, carpets, furniture, clothing, telephones, computers, even the air-conditioners.

"We started with a list of crimes that we thought destroyed the quality of life in the public-housing projects — drug dealing, burglary, armed robbery and rape," he says.

Anyone convicted of a crime is automatically evicted from public housing.

"That's my constituency. Those ladies who have worked hard all their lives, probably cleaning somebody's floors. They deserve not to be prisoners in their own homes."

In his book, *Take Back Our Streets*, Greenberg argues that crime is a simple contest between good and evil, and that poverty and deprivation do not justify criminal behavior.

"Crime occurs because somebody is a low-down, good-for-nothing son of a bitch. There doesn't have to be any other motive," he insists. Hence his determination to cut down on parole and keep criminals in prison. "Rehabilitation," he says, "is bullshit."

"I used to be a great liberal, like most Berkeley graduates," he says, and recalls taunting cops as a student on civil rights marches. "But then, when I went out in the world, things didn't work out that way."

But the Charleston police do not have a licence to be aggressive. Every use of force, from drawing a gun to using a choke hold, has to be justified in a written report. In one five-year period, Greenberg's police did not fire a shot.

In the past five years, when many U.S. cities have seen the death toll rise for black teenagers, Charleston has seen only one person under the age of 7 murdered, and he was killed by an adult.

In the last term not one handgun was found in schools, after Greenberg announced a plan offering a $100 reward for any child who reported another with a weapon.

"Kids are the greatest snitches in the world," he says. 'Before, the more people who knew you had a gun, the greater your prestige. Now, the more people who know, the more likely you are to be turned in."

Charleston's main concern now is that a larger city will hire their police chief away.

OBSERVER NEWS SERVICE

WASHINGTON POST JULY 28,1995,USA

Retooled Curfew Law in Baltimore

■ Baltimore Mayor Kurt L. Schmoke yesterday signed a rewritten juvenile curfew law designed to pass constitutional muster after a Frederick ordinance similar to Baltimore's old law was thrown out by Maryland's highest court.

The new measure, effective immediately, bans children 16 or younger from city streets from 11 p.m. to 6 a.m. weeknights and midnight to 6 a.m. on weekends. D.C. police began enforcing a similar curfew July 16.

Baltimore police suspended the city's old curfew July 7, when the Maryland Court of Appeals struck down a nearly identical Frederick ordinance that it called unconstitutionally vague.

The Baltimore and District laws contain more specific language. Both are based on a Dallas curfew upheld by the 5th U.S. Circuit Court of Appeals in 1993.

131

D.C. Curfew For Youths Starts Sept. 7

WASHINGTON POST AUGUST 12, 1999, USA

By BILL MILLER
Washington Post Staff Writer

D.C. police will begin enforcing the city's juvenile curfew law on Sept. 7—the day after Labor Day—after launching an effort to educate the public and to train officers about its strict provisions, officials said yesterday.

Mayor Anthony A. Williams (D) and Police Chief Charles H. Ramsey have decided to delay enforcement of the law until after the school year begins, even though recent court orders give them discretion to act immediately. The curfew prohibits youths 16 and younger from being in public places from 11 p.m. to 6 a.m. on Sundays through Thursdays and from midnight to 6 a.m. on Fridays and Saturdays.

The law, enacted with much fanfare in the summer of 1995, was in effect only 15 months before it was struck down as unconstitutional by a federal judge. That ruling was reversed in June by the D.C. Circuit Court of Appeals, and an injunction barring enforcement of the curfew was lifted last week.

Executive Assistant Police Chief Terrance W. Gainer said yesterday the D.C. government is printing brochures about the law and plans to distribute them as part of a public awareness effort that coincides with school registration. Police officers also will be trained within the next few weeks, he said.

When the law first was introduced, officers from the department's youth division took youths who were picked up after hours to their homes or special detention centers. This time, Gainer said, the neighborhood patrol officers who pick up the youths will be expected to contact parents or other family members. If that fails, the youths will remain overnight in police district facilities. The goal is to address any underlying problems, he said.

"Locking people up is not the answer," Gainer said. "We want to figure out why they're doing what they're doing. We want to get more involved and learn what we as a government can do to make things right for the family."

Juveniles who violate the curfew can be ordered to do 25 hours of community service. But the law is more directed toward reining them in through parents and guardians, who can be punished with fines up to $500 and ordered to perform community service or undergo counseling. The law has several exceptions, including emergencies, errands requested by a parent or guardian, travel to and from work, and attendance at chaperoned school events.

The law, passed unanimously by the D.C. Council and highly touted by then-Mayor Marion Barry, was

Pr. George's Police Begin to Enforce Juvenile Curfew

WASHINGTON POST JULY 2,1996,USA

By Philip P. Pan
Washington Post Staff Writer

Prince George's County police last night began enforcing the county's new youth curfew, a law that threatens parents of teenagers out past 10 p.m. with stiff fines in an effort to fight rising juvenile violence in Washington's most crime-plagued suburb.

Although a handful of local municipalities have curfew laws, Prince George's County is the first of Washington's major suburban jurisdictions to experiment with restricting the nighttime activities of juveniles as an anti-crime measure.

The District adopted a juvenile curfew last summer, but police officials say the city's officers are too busy with emergency calls to vigorously enforce it. In the first three months of 1996, D.C. police picked up about one juvenile nightly, and none was formally charged with violating the curfew.

It's unclear whether a curfew law will prove more effective in Prince George's County, a diverse, sprawling community where crime is con-

See CURFEW, B5, Col. 3

"The officers of Prince George's County are as busy and probably busier than any jurisdiction around here," Farrell said. "What we're asking them to do is make a good-faith effort to use this ordinance as a tool in their normal duties. In places where you have groups of youngsters hanging out in the middle of the night, this is a perfect tool to move them on.

Loitering

"We're serious," he said. "We're not going to just let this law sit on the books."

The curfew ordinance, passed unanimously by the County Council in November, requires those younger than 17 to be off the streets and out of other public areas from 10 p.m. to 5 a.m. on weeknights and by midnight on weekend nights.

Once enforcement is in full swing,

ordinance will
ing and will be
it the parents
fines of $50,
sequent viola-
low a youth to
ld be fined as

have argued
titutional and
ers have said
rbing rise in
county, espe-

les were slain
rge's County,
year before,
those arrests
s were juve-
counted for a
ggravated as-
police said.

years, we've
ffenders drop
crimes rise,"
ge Robert H.
s the juvenile
: Is this cur-
rents to now
rol their chil-
to do so in the

wer depends
police enforce

took effect at
police officials
tion campaign
should precede enforcement. A brochure explaining the curfew was sent with report cards last month to all county students in the eighth through 10th grades.

The curfew ordinance has several exemptions for juveniles who are working after hours or are engaged in other adult-supervised activities with the permission of a parent. Parents are supposed to notify police in advance and obtain official employment or "exception" cards for their children, but most police stations did not have them ready yet.

FOR MORE INFORMATION

To read a 1995 Post article about Laurel's enaction of a curfew, visit The Post's site on the World Wide Web at http://washingtonpost.com

The Washington Post

SUNDAY, OCTOBER 20, 1996   M T

Pr. William Suggests Sweeping Curfew Enforcement

Under Plan, Police Would Do Late-Night Roundups of Teenagers in Public Places

Washington Post October 20-1996, pages B1,B2

By Leef Smith and Michael D. Shear
Washington Post Staff Writers

Prince William County police would conduct unannounced, late-night sweeps to round up teenagers loitering after hours in public places

several smaller communities in the Washington area. But unlike the proposal in Prince William, none of the curfews in other communities assigns officers specifically to go out and catch violators.

In addition to conducting periodic roundups,

Parents and business owners also could be charged under the proposed law. Those who knowingly permit a young person to violate the curfew could be charged with a misdemeanor, which carries a maximum of six months in jail or fines of as much as $1,000.

Another Crack at a Curfew Law

WASHINGTON POST SEPTEMBER 8, 1999, USA *page A22*

TEN YEARS AGO, the District twice launched an effort to put a curfew law for juveniles on the books. Officials would have made it illegal for those 18 and younger to be on the city streets between 11 p.m. and 6 a.m. on weeknights and between midnight and 6 a.m. on weekends, except in connection with "legitimate" employment or unless they had documents showing good reason to be on the streets. Both efforts failed to pass judicial muster. Undeterred, the city began enforcing a new curfew law last night.

Old concerns remain. The new statute, which was upheld by the D.C. Circuit Court of Appeals in June, is a lot like the old laws rejected by U.S. District Judge Charles Richey in 1989. Under today's rules, juveniles can't be outdoors from 11 p.m. to 6 a.m. Sunday through Thursday, and from midnight on weekends, without adult supervision. This time the cutoff is age 16 rather than 18. And the law holds parents and guardians more accountable, subjecting them to fines and other sanctions for youth curfew violations. As with the old law, this ordinance also contains exceptions for emergencies, travel to and from work, parent-approved errands and attendance at chaperoned school events.

The passage of a decade hasn't changed the fact that the curfew law, as Judge Richey explained in 1989, "subjects the District's juveniles to virtual house arrest each night." True, minors don't have the same constitutional rights adults do. But the freedom of movement of law-abiding youths has been curbed as a result of this new law. There are added concerns. Will the curfew compound problems for a Metropolitan Police Department already feared missing in action in certain communities? Children caught violating the new law will be taken to station houses or, if under 12, to the D.C. Department of Child and Family Services. Will that divert already scarce police officers from street patrols? Will enforcement of the curfew depend upon the neighborhood?

Advocates expect the law to have a positive effect on juvenile crime rates. Let's hope that occurs. The way in which the law is enforced bears close watching.

CHAPTER 5. POPULATION GROWTH,FAMILY LIFE AS A BREEDING GROUND FOR CRIME.

The subjects to be covered in this chapter are very serious ones, for they are the bedrock or foundation upon which a country its government, its inhabitants, its economics and its social fabric of society are interwoven.

I do not care who may advance a theory that the world still has virgin lands for cultivation and potential mineral wealth, as well as the sea is still rich for harvesting of its resources to sustain its inhabitants, this is not what the United Nations, Food and Agriculture Organisation(F.A.O)or the United Nations, Population Division is stating. On the contrary these agencies speak about depletion. Few countries have climbed the ladder of economic prosperity without the possessing of national natural resources. and they are dependent for success.

It is a fact that people who breed multiple children will have to provide for multiple mouths, the more you impregnate, the more you will have to find food, clothing, shealter, schooling, employment health and that is more finance either rich or poor. But if you are poor, all the ills of society will fall upon yourself and your children and that is what many poor girls and women are doing around the world, especially getting caught in love relations with young men who are un-employed, dealing in drugs and other crimes and then bringing problems home for their parents, often to a single parent mother now grandmother who herself fell into the same type of love trap so the vicious cycle continues,

In all of this it is the state, the church, social organisation which have to act as substitute parent and ultimately taxpayers money which has to be spent to provide the sustenance of living.

I see it before my eyes,girls-school girls falling for young men loitering by street corners or whom they may think own a car but it is not,young men spewing obscenities from their mouth and just using their smooth, soothing words to get "another female Meat" and with television and education in this modern age they fall for it. Mothers at 16 years, grand mothers at 32 years,luck and smart is it if one of these girls wisely choose a young man who has good character and a stable job.

These girls seem to be mesmerised by the "child father" syndrome, often influencing their weak minded friends to do so like so. Luck is the one who may have made one error and end up with one child, but there are those who as fast as they fall out with the child's father,the girl ends up with a child for another un-employed or temporary employed, un-savory character man.

To make a living she may end up prostituting, or a stripper in a night club. What kind of home will children of these mothers and fathers grow up in? what kind of guidance of character will they receive? rare is a child who in such adverse environment surmount their surroundings and come out un-tainted. Of course there are poor parents who train their children to be good denizens of the country, for it is the law-abiding denizens especially those who maintain stable family life and with two children as an ideal family unit that the social success of a cohesive progressing nation is dependent upon.

Two articles I shall like to mention but not quote, for the reader will have the chance to do so further in the chapter from the source itself. These articles are timely and serve as a warning to young women and men alike. One of the articles I lost the source of its origin but nevertheless it is useful:

"Girls beware of sweet talking limers" HEARTLINE/LOVE PROBLEMS write Dear Christine DAILY NATION NEWSPAPER SEPTEMBER 19,1990, BARBADOS

"Young girls beware of those sweet talking men"

With all these children being born in a country, governments are called upon to monitor the natality rate in the country,The United Nations, Population Division, Economic and Social Information Policy Analysis, monitoring is done on each country's annual average increase or annual growth rate, birth rate and death rate.This aspect also has the concern of the Family Planning Association.

In many cases where women are "head of household" or single parent, taxpayers money from the state's treasury play a subsidising role such as welfare schemes or public assistance.

What many of these girls should have done is upon completion of high school, instead of running crotch long into sexual liaisons to make child,they should have used their head to take a course that will provide them for their future of self-dependence, rather than dependence upon a man who often fail.

Do you know what is the annual admission of school age children from primary schools? Well for example in 1999,the statistics was 30,339 students who sat the common qualifying exam; 21,393 gained places in high school. The "Annual Statistical Digest" showed that over 14,000 were placed in primary schools, and these figures approximate are constant each year.Government has a task at hand in finding more school places, building more schools and assisting if necessary to find jobs when the high school graduates and non-graduates leave school. Of course this is not government's role, for governments do not make children,parents do. The onus therefore is on the parent/parents.

Check the number of birth certificate of children, in many instances, the father's name does not appear, only the mother's name, it takes two to make a child,with the exception of a test tube baby, every father's name must be on the office register of the doctor and the birth certificate. The only excuse is in rape cases or paternity cases where DNA must be used. The establishment of a National DNA Database must be set-up. It is time men stop escaping their responsibility and child maintenance noose. Readings on this compulsory birth certificate of both parents and DNA database are to follow and in recommendations at end of chapters.

The limiting of the number of houses in home settlements and the numbering of every house is important to cut down on urban sprawl,rural, hill side squatting and to allow police to be more able to manage,patrol and control. This is the responsibility of the Local Government/Municipal Councils according to the Act No.21 which governs house numbering, demolition of abandoned buildings and clearance of abandoned lots unkept by absentee landlords and now effectively doing a good job of maintaining is the Community Environmental Protection and Enhancement Programme(CEPEP).

Many poor families leave nothing by way of a will and die intestate without leaving stocks,bonds, life insurance, real estate for the children as inheritors. So that the choices made in who will be your children's father or mother is vital to the stability of the family unit,the propsperity of that unit and ultimately that of the country. Crime in many instances can be traced back to the type of parents and home environment that children are reared in though not necessarily so in all cases.

The ideal family is the mother, father and two children in the home with good character and steady employment.It is better to be poor and have good character, than to be wealthy and have bad character.

Loitering nuisance, noise nuisances will be dealt with in the recommendations at the end of al chapters.

There are many case reports for the reader to digest in this chapter in their original form to support what I am saying, but I shall like to include only two here:

"Painful choices, Denise Jordan is off welfare, but what about her daughter? WASHINGTON POST OCTOBER 19, 1997, AGES A 1 AND A 16,USA

"Tonight 34-year-old Denise Jordan understands too well the urge to make a baby disappear.Denise 15-YEAR-OLD DAUGHTER HAS TWO CHILDREN. Kyisha holds in her arms her 9-month-old son and in her belly a five months of another life…"

"From love affair at age 13, to years of domestic abuse, if I have to live my life all over again, I would listen to my parents"NEWSDAY JANUARY 6,2000,PAGE 8

"When Angel Maharaj fell in love with her neighbour Stanley Harewood at 13 years of age, and went across to his home to begin in common-law relationship, little did she know it would end as a sordid domestic violence story. It began in 1982 at Brechin Castle,California and came to a disastrous end on Monday night.

According to Angela 'life with him at first was good, but as time went and children came, living with him was hell.'Her parents, brothers and sisters never approved of the relationship.

POPULATION GROWTH, FAMILY LIFE AS A BREEDING GROUND FOR CRIME.

138

24. WEDNESDAY, SEPTEMBER 19, 1990. DAILY NATION. BARBADOS ;

HEARTLINE / Love problems? Write to Dear Christine / c/o the NATION

sweet talking timers girls beware

Dear Christine:

PLEASE PUBLISH my letter as soon as possible so that I can warn all those young ladies about these terrible creatures called men. Why did God put men on this earth? He could have made a way that women could have babies without the help of the man.

Oh yes, they'll tell you how much they love you, but the truth is they are only out to have sex with you. One of their tricks is to call you night and day which causes you to say to yourself "this guy really loves me because although I reject him, he still comes back begging me to go out with him."

But young girls, men are only doing this because they feel there isn't a woman on this earth that they cannot get and they won't give up until they get you in bed or wherever.

They appear very sweet and loving but when they get what they want, they're off and running. So from one teenager to another, I appeal to you not to let these men take you for a ride. They aren't worth it. I am still at school and I am not prepared to let a man turn my head or cause me any pain. — C.T.

those young girls from first to fifth form that "lime" in the River Road van stand on mornings with those undesirables on bicycles.

They feel that those guys like them, but they are only interested in their bodies. The first and second formers are the most gullible.

I am not telling you teenage girls to be lesbians, I am just telling you to be very careful with these good-for-nothing men out there.

I am especially appealing to

Dear CT:

You write and say, "from my experience" so I gather you have been personally hurt by one or some of these sweet talking guys. It isn't the talk that causes the pain and embarrassment, it is what follows when those girls are gullible.

Not one of those guys who invariably are not working has anything to offer any girl and the girls are being very stupid if

- I am 16 years old and from my experience I can tell all you teenagers reading this column that the men of today are only out to use you, because when you really need them, they'll be out of sight.

Young girls beware of sweet-talking men

Dear Auntie Brenda,

I am writing about what happened to me because I want other young girls to beware of sweet-talking men, and above all, to honour their mothers.

I am 21 now but I was 14 when I met the father of my first child. I was in school and he was unemployed since he had not long left school and did not have a job as yet. He used to hang out with some fellows near to my school and he would interfere with me when I pass.

Eventually, I started talking to him and we became friends. I was a virgin and he was the first man to have sex with me. My mother found out because I started staying away from school to spend time with him and the teachers told her that I was absent too many days.

She beat me unmercifully and told me to try and get a good education and stop minding a man who could not give me anything. But young and foolish, I ignored her and then I got pregnant.

I was 15 then and my mother supported me until my son was born, but when I refused to stop seeing my boyfriend, she asked me to leave her house. I went to live with my boyfriend but after a year, he took up with somebody else and put me out of his mother's house.

I went back to my mother and she took me in. I got a job and things were going alright until I butt up on Boyfriend No. 2 — another sweet-talker with no job. He was always looking for a job, he told me, and I spent a lot of my money on him instead of helping my mother in the house. When I became pregnant again, my mother cried. I heard her telling my aunt that she could not believe that a child of hers could be so foolish and I took off again to live with Boyfriend No. 2.

You could guess what happened. He found a job and a woman. Before my second son was born, he was finished with me. I am living with a friend but I can't stay here indefinitely. I don't know how to go back to my mother, although I am in contact with my aunt and she tells me my mother is always asking how I am.

I just want other young girls to see how easy it is to go down the drain and hurt people who love you. I love my children but I have to say that life would be much easier for me if I had not had them so early for men who could not care less about them or their mother.

WA.

INSIDE WELFARE'S NEW WORLD
WATCHING REFORM AT WORK

WASHINGTON POST OCTOBER 19,1997,USA

"I try to think logically about what I should do," says Denise Jordan, whose 15-year-old daughter has had two children, "but what I end up with is panic."

Painful Choices

Denise Jordan Is Off Welfare and Loves Her Job. But What About Her Daughter?

Washington Post October 19, 1997

Another in a series of occasional articles

By Katherine Boo
Washington Post Staff Writer

"**N**ew Jersey prom mom held on suspicion of murder," the newscaster is saying. "Plus, newborn found dead in Prince George's County storeroom." Denise Jordan snaps off the Channel 9 news. This sweltering summer evening, in the shades-drawn dark of a Benning Road apartment, such stories are best avoided. Tonight, 34-year-old Jordan understands too well the urge to make a baby disappear.

Shuffling into the living room is the source of Jordan's despair: a girl with bow lips, almond eyes and a T-shirt that says "Major Attitude," a quality this child singularly lacks. Jordan's 15-year-old daughter, Kyisha Whittico, holds in her arms her sickly 9-month-old son, Keon. In her belly, Jordan has just discovered, Kyisha holds five months' worth of another life.

There were clues, yes, Jordan can see that now: the Kotex box grown dusty, the T-shirts too big to pass as urban style: But some truths are too grim to accept until they literally protrude before your eyes.

You desk-jockeyed by day, french-fried by night. You sprayed a "Money House Blessing" potion around the apartment, knelt on linoleum to pray. And finally you achieved what the federal government would consider a social policy triumph: You got off welfare, stayed off, *and* inched up the socioeconomic ladder. Just in time to see your own teenage mistakes rematerialize in the convex silhouette of your child, to see your whole family—including your youngest, the bright 7-year-old girl

See WELFARE, A16, Col. 1

Jordan's daughter Kyisha Whittico watches a rerun of "The Cosby Show" while she cares for her son Keon in their Benning Road apartment in Southeast Washington.

Mother Struggles Off Welfare Saddled With Daughter's Troubles

THE WASHINGTON POST

INSIDE WELFARE'S NEW WORLD

WASHINGTON POST OCTOBER 19, 1997, USA

Kyisha Whittico, 15, plays with her son, Keon, while her mother, Denise Jordan, holds Kyisha's new baby, Marques, at Kyisha's grandmother's house in Mount Pleasant.

NEWSDAY JANUARY 6, 2000, p 8

From a love affair at age 13 to years of domestic abuse

IF I HAD TO LIVE MY LIFE OVER, I WOULD LISTEN TO MY PARENTS

BY HERMAN ROOP DASS

WHEN ANGELA MAHARAJ (whose home name is Angelie) fell in love with her neighbour, Stanley Harewood, at 13 years of age, and went across to his home to begin a common-law relationship, little did she know that it would end as a sordid domestic violence story.

It began in 1982 while she was living at Rivulet Road, Brechin Castle, California, and came to a disastrous end on Monday night at Paradise Avenue, 9th Street, New Settlement, Dow Village, California, when two of their three children perished in a fire which the husband started.

According to Angela, "Life with him was good at first, but as time went and children came, living with him was hell at times.

In relating her life with Stanley, Angela said that her parents, three brothers and two sisters "never approved of the relationship, especially at so young an age. Some of them even stopped speaking with me, but I was in love and I thought what I was doing was right.

"If I had to live over my life I would listen to my parents and older relatives, and by so doing this might help me to make a better decision when it comes to having a relationship with someone else," she said.

The two children who died in the fire at a

pound cylinder and lit a match caused the death of the two children who were tied to the bed and locked in the bedroom, according to reports reaching the Couva Police.

From Rivulet Road the couple moved to the Squatters Settlement in 1985 and the husband, who was a skilful mason, never liked to work, Angela said.

He successfully applied for Public Assistance and with that cash helped to run the home but at the same time he developed a love for the bottle and drank heavily with friends, Angela said.

It was when he came home after drinking that trouble always took place, she said.

"He would pounce on the children, beat me up and mash up things in the house. Once just after Christopher was born he asked me for money and when he did not receive any he cut me on the right arm and I received six stitches," she related.

"I really had a terrifying relationship with Stanley. It was in 1996 that I was badly beaten and had to spend three months at the Pundit Rambachan's Home for Battered Women at St James," she said.

A follower of the Nazarene Church, Angela used to get regular visits from Stanley when she was recovering at the Home and he promised faithfully "that he would never again be violent

143

Destitute mother of 7 cries out for help

NEWSDAY AUGUST 15,1999,p 20

MARIA, stands with her seven boys, Clarence, Terrence, Lawrence, Tarrance, Torrance, Torance and Jim Davis.
PHOTOS RALPH BANWARIE

By NEWSDAY REPORTER

A 27-YEAR-OLD mother of seven children of Jubilee Trace, Tamana, is crying out for help for her children and herself. Maria Jadoo, mother of seven boys — Clarence 13, Terrence 11, Tarrance 10, Lawrence 8, Torrance 4, Torence 2, and Jim Davis 11 months — is desperate for help for her children.

She said she would accept clothes, food, mattresses, bedsheets so as to make her children a little comfortable.

The family of eight lives with their grandmother Margaret Jadoo in an old boxboard one-room dwelling house on an estate in Tamana.

Maria said she seldom has food to feed her children and most of the time they go to bed hungry. Most of her children remain naked as she cannot afford to buy clothing for them. With tears in her eyes, Maria said that when night comes the seven children sleep on burst up mattresses, some sleep on the floor.

Poverty, she acclaims, is really a crime and believes that her experience proves the point. She admits that she was at fault in bearing so many children, but her poverty and poor educational background are also to blame for her unfortunate situation.

The distressed Tamana mother said she is not employed and depends on the provision that is grown on the estate to feed her children.

Newsday visited the Jadoo family one morning last week and what was seen tells a sad story.

Maria was about to prepare breakfast for her family and she was found peeling four potatoes. Most of her children were cuddled up on the bare floor of their one room home.

Most of the children had no clothing and those who had were still half naked.

When questioned how this would feed her children she said in a sad tone of voice "we make do".

Maria is appealing to members of the public to "have a heart" and assist her destitute children.

The mother of seven said she thought of committing suicide but could not go through with it when she considered the suffering her children would have to bear.

She said she had made numerous attempts to have social welfare assistance but she was turned down on several occasions.

One officer of Social Welfare told her bluntly that she is not qualified for social welfare assistance, but Maria said would continue to seek assistance.

medical attention. Maria said it cost about $100 to take Clarence for treatment at the Port-of-Spain Hospital. This, she claimed, they cannot afford hence the reason why Clarence's condition continues to deteriorate.

In spite of bad times Maria's 11-year-old son Terrence was able to complete a computer course and was awarded a certificate.

"Things are really rough," Maria says. They have no electricity and depend on flambeaux for light at night. With the opening of school she was unable to purchase any books for her children.

Also visiting the Jadoo family was Insp Errol Mitchell who promised to seek help for them.

A family in need

Ramphals struggle to cross hurdles of poverty

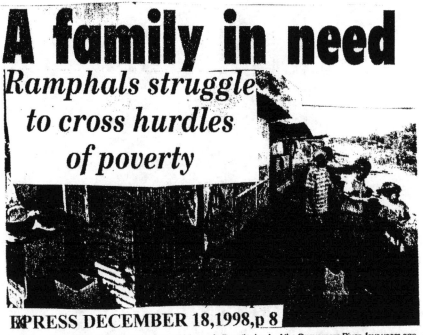

EXPRESS DECEMBER 18,1998, p 8

THE Ramphal family outside their tiny shack which was built on the bank of the Guayamare River four years ago.
Photos: STEPHEN DOOBAY

By SUSAN GOSINE

SHOMA RAMPHAL, 13, curls her body into a ball and goes to sleep on a discarded Datsun 120Y car seat. Her sisters, Siscila, 11, Neela, ten, and brother Sean, nine, huddle together on a tattered piece of foam on the cold, uneven ground in a cramped kitchen.

Parents, Seenath and Sandra Ramphal, and the other siblings, twins Darian and Daren, four, and Stacey, three, sleep on a bed nearby, in a tiny shack on the bank of the Guayamare River.

They have been living in the dilapidated shack for the past four years. The family moved to the river bank when Seenath lost his job and could not afford to rent a place.

Ramphal, a strong-willed woman, has always been content to live one day at a time and has learned to "pinch and squeeze" from the $200 a week salary her husband earns at a fowl farm to keep her family from starvation. Now she needs help fast "or I feel I will lose one of my children", she cried.

She needs $1,100 for Siscila to have a CAT scan. Doctors believe she may have a brain tumour but cannot make a more accurate diagnosis until the scan is done.

Siscila got a high fever last October, and developed seizures twice. She was warded at the Paediatric Unit at the Eric Williams Medical Sciences Complex for three days where a number of tests were conducted. When she was sent home the doctors said she would need a

CAT scan. Since then, she has been getting severe headaches almost daily. "I take Panadol but sometimes I cannot stand the headache. It makes me feel sick and dizzy," she said softly. She needs the money "urgently" for the CAT scan.

While homes are buzzing with Christmas preparations, Ramphal worries about where she will get the money for the medical test.

Poverty has made her a hard woman. Her cheek bones are prominent and her eyes, which twinkle when she laughs, are sunken. The children, she said, are quiet and obedient. Seenath stood quietly while she spoke. A shy man, with an easy smile, he declined to have his picture taken.

The children have not asked for anything special for Christmas. "They don't ask because they know we cannot afford anything. When we ask them what they want for Christmas, they don't answer," she said, and quietly added: "We really cyar buy anything for them because we trying to save the money for Siscila. I worry about her. They (doctors) think she may have a brain tumour. They said they saw something at the back of the brain."

A distant look filled her eyes as she looked at the children. Though 29, she looks much older. The painful struggle to stay alive has taken its toll. She yearns for a better home and improved conditions for her children. "I hope we don't have to live like this for the rest of our lives. They deserve something better," she said, sadly.

The children have not asked for anything special for Christmas. "They don't ask because they know we cannot afford anything. When we ask them what they want for Christmas, they don't answer."

Ramphal is a thin, tall woman with the stamina of an ox. She has gone from a "comfortable" life to one of poverty, with nothing but a bed, an old four-burner stove and a battery operated 12-inch black and white television given to her by a friend.

The home is a tiny shack, built from used plywood and galvanise. It is surrounded by mangrove with the dirty river flowing at one side. At night, they don't go outdoors, because the mangrove is eerie. During the day they are plagued by house flies, mosquitoes and sand flies.

There is no pipe-borne water at the home. Ramphal and the children tug a barrel on a box cart about a mile from the home to fetch water. It lasts two days, she said.

Siscila, Neela and Sean attend the Charlieville Presbyterian School—they walk the near two miles back and forth each day.

145

NEWS

FROM A CATTLE SHED —

Mother of four cries for help

NEWSDAY Thursday December 16, 1999 Page 3

Newsday December 16, 1999

By SASCHA WILSON and
INNIS FRANCIS

PRISCILLA FRANCOIS and her four young children live in a cattle shed. It has been their home for the past three years.

The shed is situated on top of a steep hill at Union Village, Claxton Bay.

Every day Francois, 41, and her four children—Nikita, 15, Shanel, 10, Shanel, 7, and Kyle, 6, —have to trot one mile along a muddy trail from the main road to their home. The only furniture in the shed are two old mattresses. When *Newsday* visited the home, Shanel, dressed in a dirty vest, her hair uncombed, took *Newsday* to the back of the house where she pointed to an even smaller shed.

She said: "That is where mih father does stay. He doh give we nothing. He have potato and thing and he doh give we nothing," she lamented.

Her feet along with her mother's and siblings' were covered in mud. Little Kyle and his sister Shantel were fighting for a biscuit. Francois said that she was frustrated and fed up with the hardships the family endured on a daily basis.

"It hard, it really hard. I does watch mih children and they so thin. Sometimes days pass and we have nothing to eat", she sobbed. Seven-year-old Shanel said all she wanted for Christmas "is an apple".

Her nightmare began not long after her mother died.

Francois said she had a dispute with her brother and was thrown out of the house. With no one to turn to for help, a man offered them his cattle shed to live in until they could find a better place.

A foul, stifling stench was emanating from inside the shack.

There are no street lights or houses nearby. Therefore at night the area is very dark, except for a kerosene lamp. She said about ten cattle were tied around the shed at nights which explained the awful smell.

Her common-law-husband was not at home when *Newsday* visited. Francois said, "He gone. I doh know way, sometimes he gone for days and I doh know way he gone." The family survives on Francois' infrequent days of work. the neighbours have also tried to help her over the years, but they can only do so much.

Asked what she wanted for the new year Francois said, "All I want is for my children to be happy and to have clothes and food."

146

Oh happy one! Jacqueline, 37-year-old mother of 12

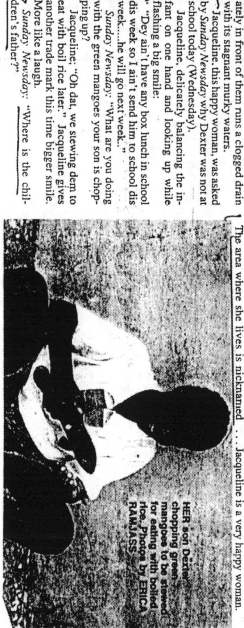

JACQUELINE happily feeding her newly-born grandchild.

DON'T for one moment let Jacqueline Hackett's station in life give you an emotional low.

She is a happy woman.

The 37-year-old mother of 12 was sitting at the entrance of her humble abode at Phase Four Beetham Estate, cuddling her grandson, recently born to her 15-year-old daughter.

One of her sons Dexter, was a little distance away chopping up green mangoes in a small area which passes for a yard. Immediately in front of them runs a clogged drain with its stagnant murky waters.

Jacqueline, this happy woman, was asked by *Sunday Newsday* why Dexter was not at school today (Wednesday).

Jacqueline, delicately balancing the infant on one hand and looking up while flashing a big smile:

"Dey ain't have any box lunch in school dis week so I ain't send him to school dis week....he will go next week."

Sunday Newsday: "What are you doing with the green mangoes your son is chopping up?

Jacqueline: "Oh dat, we stewing dem to eat with boil rice later." Jacqueline gives another trade mark this time bigger smile. More like a laugh.

Sunday Newsday: "Where is the children's father?"

Laughing again, Jacqueline: "Oh, the last gentleman I lived with left me in 1985 and he took all the things from the house. My other husband was in condemned row but they recently take him out and he now serving 75 years in jail."

Sunday Newsday: "So how do you take care of your children?

Jacqueline: "I used to get welfare from government but only one child is eligible to receive. I used to iron for a lady but she dead. I am hoping to get a job."

The area where she lives is nicknamed "Hell Hole" but as far as she is concerned she could be living in heaven.

Asked if she always displayed that jolly disposition she replied yes, and to support this she shouted across to her neighbour:

"Carol! en I always smiling, always happy?"

Carol: "Yes, Yes."

Jacqueline: "Yuh see me I always happy. Why should I take on my problems . . . I leave them with the good Lord. Again with that signature broad smile. "Me, why worry."

. . . Jacqueline is a very happy woman.

HER son Dexter chopping green mangoes to be stewed for eating with boiled rice. Photos by ERICA RAMJASS

The Independent   THURSDAY DECEMBER 4, 1997   PAGE 7

THE GASPARILLO MURDERS

Mother: Kenrick changed our world

WHEN DHANWATEE SOOKDEO'S husband died, she vowed to take care of her four children, determined to see them prosper by getting jobs to help themselves. She harboured this hope through the most difficult times, but over the last few days she says she knows that not even she could predict the horrible fate that would befall her still poor, family.

Yesterday the grieving mother from her Sookoo Trace, Esperanza, California, home related the hardships and the nightmare she has had to endure since her husband's death, a period made worse when Kenrick London entered their lives.

Her younger daughter, Meena Sookdeo, was found murdered last Thursday, and her entire world crumbled when she learnt that her bigger girl had been charged for having a part in Meena's killing.

DHANWATEE SOOKDEO,
mother of Chandroutie

"They came back and began living next door to us, but when she came by me she could never speak," the mother related. "From the time she go to say something he would call her, or he would begin to talk. It was like she was under his control."

Despite the unanswered questions and strange activities surrounding her elder daughter, Dhanawatee said, "I could never ask her to leave him. My world was never the same though. People tell me he use to read a bad book on obeah and he was a Spritual Baptist."

The mother recalled that one neighbour had informed her that she saw the couple going to the beach and recalled Chandroutie's husband cutting off piece of her hair and tossing it into the sea.

"They told me that make him get ah grip on her and she would roam from shore to shore with him.

Dhanwatee, between sobs, described her loving younger daughter.

"When she got the work she tell me, mammy we go build over the home and fix it up, nice."

THE LONDONS' crude shack in Sookoo Trace, Esperanza , in the middle of surroundings that have become the setting of one of the country's most bizarre murder investigations

CECIL LONDON, father of kenrick

Heroine in need

TRINIDAD GUARDIAN OCTOBER 27, 1998

Woman who saved brothers and sisters turns to the President for help

By PRIOR BEHARRY

AGAINST THE ODDS

SANDRA GRANT was once hailed as a heroine who saved the lives of her brothers and sisters when their Tobago home was destroyed by fire.

Today, she is an unemployed woman desperately trying to save her sons and daughters from an uncertain future.

Twenty-three years after being presented an award for bravery by then-Tobago politician ANR Robinson, Grant is facing financial hardship and has turned to Mr Robinson for help.

"Many years have passed and my life has been difficult," says Grant in a letter to the President. "What I need is a job of some kind so that I can try to be self-sufficient and set an example to my children."

At age 35, Grant is a single parent to six children: Keshawn, 19, Leon, 7, Mhoein, 6, Maria, 5, Asha, 3, Tafari, 1.

Five of them are still in her care, Keshawn having left home to stay with one of his friends. But, deprived of finances, she cannot afford to send the children to school.

"I don't want them to go to school and beg anybody," she said in an interview with the *Guardian* on Wednesday.

However, she admitted that there have been days when she has had to go begging for food for her children.

"I'm having some real problems making ends meet," Grant cried, noting that her monthly Public Assis-

tance cheque of $632.60 is not been enough to take care of her family's needs.

"Welfare assistance just pays the bills," she said.

The bills include a monthly rental of $75 for a house "made with river sand" on Laventille Road in Port-of-Spain's East Dry River district.

Unable to purchase beds, they sleep on the floor.

"One night I catch a scorpion crawling right where we sleep," said Grant.

It is the same house she had shared with the father of the five children. But, when he left her last March, life took a turn for the worst.

As she told it, his legacy was failure as an itinerant vendor and a financial debt to a neighbourhood benefactor. The friend had stood as guarantor for a loan which the couple had secured from FundAid to purchase a vendor's pushcart. The business venture failed and, according to Grant, her neighbour is demanding that she pay back the money.

Grant's life has been required visits to the Samaan House Shelter for Battered and Abused Women and Children in St Clair.

Such visits have put her in touch with some good samaritans, including Independent Senator Diana Mahabir-Wyatt.

"God bless that woman," she said, "for all the times she has helped put food in the mouths of my hungry children."

But, Grant is determined to avoid the dependency syndrome and rid herself of the cycle of poverty.

Though living life against the odds she made it clear that she was not asking for money, donations or charity. What she wants is employment. "I want a cleaning work," she declared.

In desperation, Grant has taken her plight to President Arthur NR Robinson.

In her letter, dated August 19, she reminds the President about the award for bravery which he had presented her.

"Twenty-three years ago, Mr President, you presented me with an award for bravery in Tobago at the Roxborough Composite School for saving my four brothers and sisters from our burning house. I felt very honoured and proud when I received this award and I remember the experience very fondly."

And, in making her case for help, she pleads for the President's support of her efforts:

"I appeal to you to help me by writing a letter to support me in my attempt to seek employment with the Service Commission or MTS.

"I want to get out of the circle of poverty. Please help me sir."

SANDRA GRANT... a brave woman struggling to get out of the circle of poverty

149

One month after rescue from squalid shack...

Neglected Marabella youngsters still at hospital

NEWSDAY Tuesday December 26, 2000 Page 7

Tuesday December 26, 2000

By SASCHA WILSON

ONE MONTH after police rescued four malnourished youngsters from their dilapidated Marabella home they are still warded at the San Fernando General Hospital in stable condition.

The children were discovered naked, their abdomens swollen from malnutrition. The police were informed of the unhealthy and unsafe conditions under which the children lived by the local government representative, Councillor Jennifer Marryshaw.

The infants — Daniel, three; Reshma, two; Jason one and David, one month and three weeks — lived with their parents Dandy Ganga, 41, and Pulmatie Sunny, 26 in a one-room wooden house at

Bayshore, Marabella.

Their mother reportedly suffers from epilepsy and appears to be mentally unstable.

Recalling how she found out about the disturbing situation Councillor Marryshaw said she was walking through the neighbourhood when a resident informed her of the family's predicament.

"When I went down to the house I saw the baby wrapped in a wet jersey and two bigger children rocking naked in the corner," she said. "Apparently the one-year old could not even walk. He was crouched in a foetal position. They had big bellies and heads."

The councillor said she noticed the three-year-old boy drinking a bottle of watery milk. His mother grabbed the bot-

tle from him and gave it to the baby.

There is no pipe-borne water supply or electricity in the house. Only two buckets are used to store water obtained from neighbours.

Marryshaw made a report to the Marabella Police Station and accompanied by the police and the City Medical Doctor of Health, Dr Krishna Kumar the four children were rescued from the home.

A neighbour indicated that the children were not allowed to leave the house.

"She does not let the children outside. The children does be naked. She does take the children clothes and burn it in the heap outside the house."

When *Newsday* visited the dilapidated wooden house there were two old mattresses lying on the floor, a broken bed frame and a small fire cracker connected to a gas tank. The only food items were rice, dhal and black eye peas.

150

EXPRESS Thursday, November 12, 1998

•TL.104   64 PAGES   THURSDAY, NOVEMBER 12, 1998   •$1.50

Sugar water for baby

EXPRESS November 12, 1998

SARAH CAMPBELL, an URP employee, holds up a bottle of "sugar water" which is all she can afford to feed her child, she says.

Campbell was among several URP workers taking part in a protest demonstration outside The Tunapuna Regional Corporation yesterday. Campbell, along

with other protesting workers have not been paid for Protests about URP workers have been a regular feature year.

The protests have been by charges that there are the URP.

Photo: ST

Runaway mom speaks of hard life

By PHOOLO DANNY
South/Central Bureau

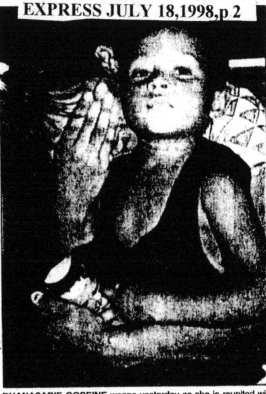

EXPRESS JULY 18,1998,p 2

DHANASARIE GOSEINE weeps yesterday as she is reunited with her son, three-year-old Aneil, whom she left with her step-brother seven weeks ago. **Photo: KRISHNA MAHARAJ**

SHE ran away from home at the age of 12, and by 14 she had her first child.

Today at 25, Dhanasarie Lisa Goseine, mother of Aneil Goseine, believes she lived a hopeless life.

But as she clutched, her hands protectively around him yesterday, she swore: "His longing for me, his love for me give me new life. I would never leave him alone for so long again, honest to God."

It was Aneil's plea for his mother to come back for him that brought them back together.

Goseine had left him at the home of her stepbrother and his wife. But after she disappeared for seven weeks and they could no longer afford to take care of him, the Singhs went to the police and then came to the *Express.*

Recounting her life, Goseine said she was forced from a tender age to sell channa to make a living. She ran away from home when the going got too tough.

After having her first child at 14, she returned home but "was disowned by my family. Nobody wanted to see me. Some of them don't call me a sister, they say I am a cousin, all because I had a dougla child".

Her second child was born the next year, when she was 15. She had hoped and prayed for a family life, but when physical abuse became the order of the day she left to return to her family.

"That was the turning point in my life. None of my family accepted me, so I drifted," said Dhanasarie.

Those two children, a 12-year-old boy and a girl, 11,

are with their father.

Later, Goseine said, she met another man with whom she felt "things would have worked out". She had three children with him, including Aneil.

The other children, an eight-year-old boy and a five-year-old girl, are also with their father, she said. But she said she left him when she was pregnant with Aneil.

Also known as "Channa Girl", Goseine has a brother, two step-sisters and a step-brother.

She said: "My brother and I used to leave home about 6 a.m. every day to go to sell channa. Sometimes we would come home early and sometimes late. We would not go home until we finish sell the channa."

She was a pupil of the Tunapuna Hindu School, but never attended classes regularly, and when she failed the CE examination, she stopped school altogether.

"When I could not take the hard life anymore, I ran away from home, with some friends," she said.

The young mother, who admitted that she had left Aneil at her step-brother's home in Debe seven weeks ago, swore: "I had no intention of leaving him there forever. I had no telephone to call them and I had no money to travel there."

Aneil was also said to have been found on a garbage heap in Tunapuna by passers-by who took him to an aunt who carried him to the police.

Aneil was asked yesterday if he wanted to stay with his aunt at Debe.

"No, I want to stay with my mommy," he replied.

Goseine swore she never dumped Aneil in "any garbage heap".

"I was the one who was

dumped in a garbage heap by my father. I used to beg him for a dollar. But he used to pass by our house and pretend he did not see us after he left my mother," said Goseine.

She said one of her relatives had taken her in, "give me room and work, but I never had time for my son. I used to look at her (the relative) playing with her daughter and I did not have time to play with my Aneil".

Now Goseine is making doubles from 1 a.m. to 8.30 a.m. for a living. She earns almost $300 a week and thinks she has enough time during the day to look after Aneil.

She is currently staying

in Aranjuez, with a "lady who accepted me as a mother. I met her when I was pregnant with Aneil. I call her 'mum'."

A neighbour, Vidya Reds, who accompanied Goseine to San Fernando, promised to assist in caring for Aneil when his mother goes to work.

Asked if she did not want the other children with her, Goseine said: "They are well taken care of and loved by their fathers. I get to see them when I want, so I have no problem."

As for Aneil, she plans to send him to school come September, and "let him enjoy life as a child should".

152

NEWSDAY Tuesday May 29, 2001 Page 9

MOTHER OF CHILDREN BURNT IN FIRE PREGNANT: 'I am asking anyone to assist'

Newsday May 29, 2001

By SASCHA WILSON

IN THE blink of an eye, Magdalin Lezama lost two of the most precious things in her life — her babies. She also lost her home.

Although she is still grieving and in a lot of pieces and move on, not so much for herself but for the unborn baby she is carrying in her womb.

Spain, Lezama, 18, has decided to pick up the Madras Public Cemetery.

She wants to rebuild her home but is unable to do so as she comes from a poverty-stricken family.

Over a week ago her two babies, Afisha, 22 months and Denzl Nelson, nine months, were burnt to death in a fire which destroyed her home, at Kernahan Road, Cunupia. On Saturday they were laid to rest in a single white tiny casket at

The children's deaths added fuel to an already shaky relationship between the families of their parents. Except for the support of few relatives,

who do not have the financial resources to assist her.

Lezama has been left to fend for herself. She has sought refuge with relatives at Edward Street, Princes Town, but they cannot afford to purchase clothes or other personal items for her.

Wearing a borrowed jersey, jeans and a pair of sandals, Lezama bowed her head as she spoke to *Newsday* about the deaths of her babies.

"If my daughter did light matches we would ah reach home in time before the house burn down. It would have never burn down so fast. I believe in my God and He will give me justice for my two innocent babies," she said.

The unemployed teenager has been living with the children's father, Pete Nelson, for almost two years. Nelson, who is staying with Lezama's grandmother, is also unemployed.

"This child needs help," said Lezama's aunt Merle Clarke. Clarke said she is willing to assist but does not have the financial means to support Lezama who is due to have a baby in six months.

Lezama said: "I want to build a

little place in the back of my grandmother's home at David Toby Road, Chin Chin, but I don't know where to start. I am asking anyone to assist in buying materials to build my home and also some clothes because I have lost everything. After I build my house I want to try my best to get a work to provide for my baby and myself."

MAGDALIN LEZAMA

COPS SEIZE BABY FROM MOTHER

By AZARD ALI

NEWSDAY Thursday August 5, 1999 Page

POLICE OFFICERS have taken away a one-month-old baby from her mother, claiming that young Melise Bellile had not been fed, and was living in unsanitary conditions.

But Cassina Bellile, 28, the baby's mother, is so traumatised by the loss, she intends to sue the State to retrieve her toddler from a children's home where police have lodged the child.

On Sunday, three policemen delivered a baby at the St Margaret's Police Station, an act which earned them a commendation from Police Commissioner Hilton Guy for dedication beyond the call of duty.

Yesterday, WPC Richardson Torab, of the Chaguanas Community Police Division, said that she and her colleagues had been moved to tears by the filthy condition of Melise and the house she had been living in at Gordon Village, Tortuga.

When the cops took the child to a doctor, the baby was found to be malnourished, with a skin rash from sleep-

ing on dirty linens on the floor.

"But this is not true. Other people living in worse conditions," sobbed Bellile yesterday, "I want back my baby."

Admitting she is poor and lives in humble dwellings, Bellile, who has two other children, contended that no mother deserved to be separated from her child. "Regardless what is the state of my place," Bellile cried, "at least they could tell me where my child is."

Community police officers declined to reveal at which of the children's homes the baby was staying, insisting that Melise was still recuperating from malnourishment.

They commented that while they were distraught by Bellile's longing for her child, they had to act on what was described as a crisis, in the baby's best interest.

Bellile has two other children who live with relatives and her woes began three weeks ago when police officers visited her home. Following that, Annette Bryce, a social worker in the

ramily Services Division, intervened.

Bellile received a message to take her baby to the Freeport station. She complied and, after questioning, the mother was asked to hand over Melise. "I refused and walked out the station. A police vehicle pulled up beside me, and a policewoman snatched the baby and shove me in the vehicle," Bellile said.

The mother said that she and her baby were first taken to a children's home in Couva and it was there her baby was finally taken away from her.

The Community police seized the baby, acting under the Children's Act, which does not require a court order for 21 days. However, after that period, the police must seek a renewal of the order, and *Newsday* learned that was done last week Tuesday.

"But if there was a court order, at least I should've known." Bellile said.

She claimed she has not seen nor been told how her baby was faring. "It's my child, if I'm poor, that's not a sin. Is the police going around snatching people's children simply because they can't mind them," she enquired.

Mohan is like the old woman who lived in a shoe

... he has so many children (14), he doesn't know what to do

HE reminded me of the nursery rhyme of yore:

"There was an old woman who lived in a shoe, she had so many children, she didn't know what to do ..."

Unemployed father of 14, Mohan Bittan, lives a similar life to the old woman in the popular pre-school poem ... he has so many children he doesn't know what to do.

Mohan, who lives in a ramshackle hut at Tabaquite Road, Rio Claro, has been struggling to feed his 10 girls and four boys. The children range between the ages of 21 years to two and half.

"Putting food on the table for all those empty stomachs is my biggest problem at present," the 43-year-old man complained last week.

The distressed father told *Tn.T Mirror* that, with each passing day, the pressure, stress and worries keep mounting.

"I just can't seem to land myself a permanent job, to ease the burden off my shoulders," Mohan said with a sigh.

as he looked at his offspring playing merrily in the parched and cracked dirt yard.

Mohan paints the interior and exterior of houses for people in the sleepy district, but seldom rakes in a substantial figure doing the laborious task.

"Besides, this job is seasonal ... is only Christmas time business does boom," he pointed out, sadly.

He also revealed that he had been offered a permanent painting job in Port-of-Spain by a home construction firm, but had to turn it down.

"The firm wanted me to stay with them during the week, and go home on weekends.

"But I didn't want to leave my 10 young girls and wife for such a long time, alone, so I declined the job.

"That would be putting their lives at risk ... anybody could do them anything when I am not there," he reasoned.

To supplement the family's income, Mohan would plant short-term crops to sell in the market.

When things get rough, he

would cut the grass around his neighbour's yard for a small fee.

And on the days he comes home empty-handed, Mohan would go begging in the remote village.

"Sometimes people would send a little flour or rice for the kids to eat," he disclosed, with a hint of embarrassment in his dull eyes.

When dusk falls, Mohan would pull out five mattresses from a corner of the shack, and place it on the ground for the kids to sleep on.

"There is no partition or rooms in the house.

"Everyone sleeps in one area, because space is limited as it is," he revealed.

At the break of dawn, the mattresses are put back into their respective areas so that the family can go about their chores during the course of the day.

The family uses a fully-charged car battery to generate electricity, and is given pipe-borne water from kind-hearted neighbours.

Mohan's aim is to construct a concrete house on the land can't

TT MIRROR MARCH 24, 2002, p 17

MOHAN BITTAN (second from left) with 10 of his kids and wife SAMDAYE.

seem to materialise, however.

He managed to save $1,300 toward building the house off the ground.

"I wanted to build a room for the girls, so that they could have their privacy. But Samdaye's health comes first," he pointed out, touching his pale-looking wife, who was resting in a fam-

"All this set meh back in getting the house off the ground.

He managed to save $1,300 to buy foundation and building blocks, but then had to spend it on his 42-year-old wife, Samdaye, who became anaemic after battling with a low blood count for months.

155

Newsday

NEWSDAY AUGUST 25, 2000, p 10

Life with Jango

ANY OTHER decision, of course, would have been an outrage as it is clear that Shelly-Ann des Vignes' killing of her common-law husband was an act of self defence against the onslaught a man who had made her life a living hell by his constant and merciless battering. *Newsday* is pleased that Director of Public Prosecutions Mark Homammed has recognised the desperate plight of the 19-year-old woman and has decided not to prefer any charges against her. In his own words, it was "a clear case of self defence based on domestic violence."

While no one will rejoice in the stabbing death of 22-year-old Sebastien "Jango" White, it seems almost inevitable that the reign of terror he imposed on his teenaged lover would one day end disastrously. His friends and neighbours where they lived at Hell Yard, Beetham Estate, have given graphic accounts of the callous and gratuitous beatings which "Jango" inflicted on Des Vignes almost as a matter of ritual during their four-year relationship.

They have described him as "the beast of Hell Yard", a coke addict who always appeared in a violent mood, taking out his rage also on his four-year-old daughter of a previous relationship. On several occasions, the neighbours told *Newsday*, they had to intervene to save Des Vignes from being killed.

White's neighbour Darren Joseph recalled: "I see Shelly-Ann get licks one time with a piece of iron and she had to get 13 stitches on her head. You just don't treat a woman like that."

He added: "I sorry my friend dead, but he used to beat Shelly-Ann too much. She couldn't take it any more."

Last Monday night this horror story came to a tragic end when Des Vignes, eight months pregnant, was again set upon by her brutal husband. She sought refuge at the home of a neighbour but was advised to return home. To defend herself, the pregnant mother of one armed herself with a knife and as "Jango" attacked again she plunged the weapon into the left side of his chest.

The terrible ordeal of this 19-year-old mother gives us another and perhaps different insight into the problem of domestic violence in our country. Indeed it has serious lessons for young women who leave school poorly educated with no job skills and are tempted to get into liaisons with men as their only means of survival. The circumstances of such relationships are invariably miserable and often produce disadvantaged offspring and tragic endings.

Des Vignes told this newspaper that she loved "Jango", but what did that love bring her? What future, what kind of life did she expect to have with a violence-prone cocaine addict?

Teenaged girls leaving school, regardless of the level of their education, must first seek to become employable and productive adults, to acquire vocational skills in whatever areas, to develop some kind of financial self-support instead of thinking of going off to live in a dependent and chancy common-law relationship with a man.

Even before entering full adulthood, Shelly-Ann des Vignes has lived through a nightmare that may echo through the rest of her life. Joined to the "beast of Hell Yard", she has had to defend herself in an ultimate and bloody way. We can only hope that the teenaged mother will emerge stronger and more sensible from the experience. And that other girls her age will gain from her ordeal a life saving lesson.

Page 10 NEWSDAY Saturday December 19, 199

1998

Published by Daily News Ltd.

Young criminals: a sign of society in decay

THE SUDDEN rash of senseless and brutal murders in Trinidad and Tobago today defies understanding and merely serves to demonstrate how cheaply human life is held by all too many persons.

The drug culture has largely determined that — and the value of the life of a man reneging on an agreement to pay for illegal drugs taken on credit and sold, appears equal, merely, to the money owed. Then, too, his murder is seen by those who order his killing as a lesson to others. Pay up or else.

What is perhaps equally disturbing is that the age of suspected killers along with that of persons held for other serious crimes seems to be getting younger and younger, reaching even into the classroom and/or the school compound.

Teenagers are being inveigled into crime by much older adults and, almost as if to convince their criminally-minded elders that they are capable of "doing a man's job", they are committing serious crimes, even murder, in the belief that the law will be lenient.

One of the problems facing the society today is that children are being born of mere children who are ill-equipped to deal with both providing an adequate living for themselves and for the challenge of rearing their sons and daughters and are, unwittingly, unleashing in all too many cases criminals on the rest of Trinidad and Tobago.

Many of the young parents are school dropouts, unable to cope, because of their lack of training and skills development, with almost any job a cut above the menial. In this setting they are easy prey to drug traffickers and/or other evil men wishing a youngster "to put down a wuk".

They place great store by expensive sneakers and brand-name clothes and are prepared in so many instances to rob, maim and even kill for them.

This week's murders of a good

Advice from Carlos

THE MOST irresponsible advice we have heard so far from the election platform came from Infrastructure Minister Carlos John who told a crowd of UNC supporters at St Augustine on Wednesday night to "go ahead and multiply". Can you believe this? Just go ahead and multiply!

Instead of elevating the minds of his listeners, the Minister proceeds to appeal to their basest instincts. Don't worry, go ahead and copulate as much as you want and have as many children as possible. Mr John's advice, of course, is a recipe for social and economic disaster but, in his desperate quest to win votes, this calamity is clearly of no concern to him.

Mr John's justification for urging such procreative activity among the population is the UNC boast to educate whatever children they produce. Specifically, he referred to the UNC promise to provide every secondary school student with a yearly $1,000 book grant and primary pupils with free school books. The Minister, who is contesting the St Joseph seat in Monday's election, told his audience that these grants would make the "fear and trauma" of not having enough money to send their children to school a thing of the past. "As I was telling my very productive constituents in Bamboo last night, go ahead and multiply. We go educate them for you. No problem."

It is amazing to us that a Minister of government could be so oblivious to the serious moral and social problems of our country that he would publicly encourage its citizenry to go ahead and multiply. One of the most critical needs of our people now is for them to exercise restraint, moderation and good sense in sexual matters, not only in the planning of families but also in pre-marital relations. The frightening statistics of the incidence of AIDS in TT underscore this imperative. Mr John should also know the burden that overpopulation in TT, particularly among the poor, would place on government facilities and the inevitable impact it would have on crime.

In any case, it is quite absurd for any Minister to invite the population to multiply on the basis that school books and book grants will be provided for their children. The Minister indulges in an expansive fallacy by assuming that education is based simply on the provision of school books. Imagine the scenario a few years from now if, acting on Mr John's advice, the population multiplies and grows producing an extraordinary increase in the number of school-age children who have their school books but there has been no simultaneous expansion in school places or in the establishment of teachers.

In such a situation, what would Mr John tell parents? "Yes, I told you to multiply but, good heavens, I didn't mean for you to multiply so much"? But the provision of school books, no matter how helpful this may be, is certainly no guarantee that the "fear and trauma" experienced by poor families in sending their children to school would become a thing of the past. There are other necessary expenses such as clothing or uniforms and transport. When the population multiplies as Mr John urges, would the UNC government meet these costs as well? It is unfortunate that the quest for votes could produce such silliness from campaigning politicians.

Police make breakthrough in baby kidnapping

BY PHOOLO DANN
South/Central Bureau

POLICE believe they have made a breakthrough in the kidnapping of a new-born baby from the San Fernando General Hospital.

Last night they had a woman in custody. And, a new-born baby which she had at her home, was in the hospital under police guard.

Birth marks that resemble a dasheen leaf and a curled bodi will determine whether the baby belongs to teenage mother Ann Thomas.

Police said they were waiting on Thomas to make a positive identification.

Thomas's unnamed baby girl was kidnapped at the San Fernando General Hospital last Friday, three days after her birth.

Yesterday investigators found a new-born baby girl in a house in Rio Claro.

A 40-year-old woman of the district was up to late last night assisting police in their inquiries.

Thomas, who yesterday winced in pain as she attempted to get up from a bed, said she would be able to identify her baby by two birthmarks on the upper arms.

Thomas, 18, of Webber Trace,

Palo Seco said: "When I was cleaning her on Friday, I noticed one birth mark like a dasheen leaf, and the other was like a curled up bodi."

The first-time mother, who had a Caesarean delivery, said: "I talked with the lady (kidnapper) because my mother was talking with her. So when she told me my mother said to start walking down the stairs, I believed her. She offered to help me with the baby and I allowed her."

Lynette, Thomas's mother, had gone to get medicine for her.

Thomas said she took about half an hour to walk down the stairs at the hospital because she could not get a wheelchair or use the elevator.

When Thomas reached the end of the stairway, neither her baby nor the woman could be found.

When the *Express* visited Thomas at her home yesterday, she could barely get up from the bed. She said she was in extreme pain and was coughing. She received 36 stitches.

"The poverty stricken family lives in a one-room shack with barely anything visible to eat, and nothing to sit on. Thomas lives with her mother and eight-year-old sister Keisha.

She said she and the baby's

EXPRESS JULY 21, 1998, p 3

WITH a Bible in hand, **Ann Thomas** (right), says a prayer for the safe return of her baby girl while being comforted by her mother **Lynette** at their home on Webber Trace, Palo Seco, yesterday.
Photo: KRISHNA MAHARAJ

father "broke up" before the baby was born. Her mother is unemployed.

Hospital authorities said they

could not be blamed for the kidnap since the baby's mother willingly sought the kidnapper's assistance.

EXPRESS DECEMBER 28,1997

Abandoned children placed with aunt

Community Police, Partap to the rescue

BY PHOOLO DANNY
South/Central Bureau

Express December 28, 1997

SIX CHILDREN who have been living in a squalid one-room apartment since they were abandoned by their parents five months ago were rescued yesterday by community police in collaboration with Labour Minister Harry Partap.

The children, Bryan Arosco, 16, Renee, 14, Afisha, 11, Jonathan, eight, Dillon, five, and Maureen, two were all abandoned by their mother and father. The eldest child, Nigel, 18, stays with an aunt.

The children's mother, who is living in a common-law relationship quarter of a mile away, has been questioned by the police. The woman, according to police, would "drop in now and again to check on the children". But she could not take them to live with her because her common-law husband did not want them. Police say she could be charged with abandoning the children.

Partap, MP for the area, learned of the children's plight from councillor Zephyrine Bissessarsingh and formed a "social act committee" to look after the children's welfare.

The committee includes Partap, his wife Nazra, councillor Bissessarsingh, the Minister's personal assistant Tahir Hosein, villagers Nehru Rattan, Kumar Singh and James Ramnath.

The committee was formed to monitor the situation and look after the children's interests.

When they arrived at the Nester Village home yesterday, Partap said, they found the year-old Afisha mothering" the other children. Afisha told Partap that they managed to survive for the last five months by eating whatever pittance they received from well-wishers. She said her mother came "now and again" to bring some food.

The newly formed committee contacted the children's aunt Sybil, who lives about one mile away, and asked her to keep them at her home. The committee members also committed themselves to ensure that she had enough food and clothes for the children. They also plan to get the children enrolled in school as early as possible.

However, before the children were handed over to Sybil, community officer PC Baptiste took the children to the Sangre Grande Police Station to "formalise things". The children were to be examined by a doctor to ensure that they had not been physically or sexually abused.

Partap said when he discovered the children they were staying in one room that was apparently not cleaned for years.

He appealed to the police to ensure that the children were not traumatised any further during the investigations by the officers.

The children were taken to the station in an unmarked police vehicle.

Partap said: "It was a rather sad situation, seeing the children huddled in that room. We have given our word to ensure that their aunt Sybil has ample food and clothes for them. And I want to ensure that those of school age get into schools, while the police are continuing their investigations."

NEWSDAY SEPTEMBER 27, 1999

Help me build back my home, man pleads

By ALLISON ALI

JASON DAVE CHARLES, a 22-year-old man of Upper Bell Eau Road, Belmont is in desperate need of materials to build a new house, or at least fix the old one in which he currently resides.

Charles, who lives with his seven months pregnant sister Melinda, is unemployed and lives in a house that is "falling down".

He explained that the house which he lives in belonged to his grandmother and was left for his family when she died.

Charles said that he would usually get "PIs" like cutting grass and mowing lawn but lamented that this money was not enough to even buy food.

He said that there will be days when he and his sister will go without food and drink water "to keep up".

He added that there is no electricity in the house and that they depend on the rain for their water supply.

Charles pointed out that he has been desperately trying to find a "permanent work" but noted that even if he were to get a steady income, it still will not be enough to fix the house and buy food.

He said that he has completely given up on life, and that he has left everything in God's hands.

PREGNANT Melinda, in front of the rotting building she calls home.
PHOTO BY ENRICO MATTHEWS.

Husband commits suicide —
Financially insecure wife refuses 5 children

Newsday December 23, 1997

By RICHARD CHARAN

TWO WEEKS after a couple abandoned their five children at the homes of relatives and a neighbour, never to return, the decomposed body of the husband, Mungroo Harry, 37, was found in a forested area in Penal, the victim of suicide, police say.

Up until yesterday, the children, aged between 3 and 10, were still at the neighbour's home, being cared for on a temporary basis, while Community Policing Officers, and Social Welfare Officers tried to find a home for them.

Two other children of the Harry's, 11 and 12 years old, are being taken care of by relatives.

According to police, Harry, who did odd jobs in his village, left his small wooden house on December 6, in company with his wife of 13 years, leaving the three children at the home of Wilberforce Bharose, a

neighbour. The couple promised to return later that day, but never did.

Last Monday, Bharose went to the Penal Police Station and reported the situation.

Efforts by police to locate Harry proved futile. However, the wife was found at her new home, but refused to return to the matrimonial home and take custody of the children.

She expressed the fear that her husband, a violent man, would kill her.

The case became even more bizarre when Harry reportedly was seen in the Mulchan Trace area telling his friends that his wife's adulterous ways had driven him insane, and that he was going to kill himself.

Over the weekend, a search team was organised by Harry's relatives and they combed the forested area close to his home.

On Sunday evening, the decomposed body of the man was found in dense bushes off Sirju Trace, Penal, not far from

where he had lived with his wife and three of his five children. Harry's body was clad in a pair of pants, lying face up, with an empty bottle containing traces of a greenish substance discarded nearby.

The body was viewed by DMO, Dr Furlonge, who ordered its removal to the Forensic Science Centre.

Harry's wife was contacted at her new home, and told of the discovery.

In an autopsy conducted yesterday confirmed that death was due to the ingestion of a poisonous substance.

Meanwhile, Community Policing officers told *Newsday* that the fate of the five children looked grim for the Christmas, since a lenghty investigation would have to be made as to whether, if the mother wanted, the children could return to her care, since she is financially insecure.

A decision will only be made, *Newsday* was told, after social workers submit a report of their findings.

161

Mothers forget their children

EXPRESS JANUARY 1,1998, p 3

By PHOOLO DANNY
South/Central Bureau

The BIG story

FOR NEARLY a dozen children their New Year's wish will be the same as it has been for the past few years — a new home or to be reunited with the parents they never knew.

The only home they know is the San Fernando General Hospital. They have been there since birth-abandoned by their mothers.

Their case is a worry and a costly burden to hospital authorities. A home which was promised by the Government last year for the children has not materialised.

Their ward is still brightly decorated with paintings and Yuletide ornaments. Santa Claus brought them a Christmas tree and sackfuls of toys and eats. There is a television set and the nurses act as their mothers and guardians.

Their ages range from three months to 17 years and they all appear to be happy.

But if only their biological mothers were around to cuddle them close to their breasts, stroke their hair, hands and little feet and whisper sweet nothings in their ears...

Or wipe tears away from their innocent faces and most of all love them as only a mother could it would be the best New Year's gift they could ever get, hospital officials say almost hopelessly.

They have known nothing else all their lives other than a hospital room, a crib-like bed which looks too small for the elder ones. And their only playmates have been each other and the doctors and nurses who look after them.

Service and community groups drop in at times with food, clothes and toys.

There are three girls and seven boys at the ward for the abandoned children. The eldest, Brent Jennings, 14, and Sookdeo Mungroo, 17, cannot walk. All day and all night long, day after day, month after month, they are forced to remain in the crib with limited body movements for their own safety. Jennings and Mungroo, like all but two of the children, were born with serious birth defects.

The youngest — five-month old Dodi and Evelyn, who was born three months ago — are "normal", said Medical Chief of Staff, Dr Austin Trinidade.

He said they were all abandoned by their mothers immediately after birth. "Their mothers just walked out of the hospital, leaving the babies here," said Dr Trinidade. And in most cases, "they do not ever return to look for the children". Some of the mothers do return but refuse to take them home, he said.

Dr Trinidade said the hospital authorities could not monitor all the movements of the mothers "so they quietly slip out of the hospital, leaving their children at the mercy of the hospital staff".

Most of the time the mothers give incorrect names and addresses, said a nurse. "It's as if throughout their pregnancy they planned to abandon their children," she added.

Dr Trinidade lamented the lack of special homes for the children, but noted that social workers were always on the look-out for people who express an interest in adopting the children.

Every year, Dr Trinidade said, about five or six children are rejected by their mothers and left on the wards.

It costs the hospital $500 a day to look after one child or anyone who occupies a bed at the hospital, said Dr Trinidade.

He said the nurses, who are not specially trained "must love children to be able to deal with them".

"We maintain the ward with love and teamwork," said one nurse.

Hospital authorites have been appealing year after year for special homes for the children.

Dr Trinidade, who referred to the abandoned children's ward as his "pet ward" said although the children were pampered and loved by the nurses, "they still need homes, toys and clothes, pampers, baby formula and people to take time to teach them to read and write".

He hoped that some retired workers would offer their services in the new year.

Trinidade said promises were made in 1996 to ensure a special home for the children, but so far nothing had materialised. The children are usually referred to the Social Work Department who assist in finding homes for those born without defects.

Dr Trinidade said the children who suffer from Downs Syndrome needed to go to a special school. One such child, eight-year old Aaron Peters, gladly accepted a pen and note pad from the *Express* team that visited. And although he could not write, he attempted to draw.

Dr Trinidade noted that the Adoption Board had been giving support in getting homes for the normal children at the hospital. "We prefer when the children are adopted early, because its better for the process of bonding with the new parents," he said. However, in most cases, the parents must give permission for the adoption, and that can sometimes be a tedious process, said Dr Trinidade.

Police rescue sisters
Child minding child

EXPRESS Thursday, September 19, 1996

By SUSAN GOSINE

POLICE yesterday rescued a six-year-old girl who had been forced to take care of her 18-month-old sister in a squalid shack with neither lights, furniture nor water, but overrun with rats, cockroaches, mosquitoes and flies.

Hours after the children's mother was admitted to hospital, suffering from a cocaine overdose, police rushed to a squatter's settlement in Mon Repos and removed the girls from what they called "home".

Krystle, six, and Kerry Ann Brown, had been left to themselves, naked and without food one week ago. But that has been their state for weeks in the past and neighbours told police that they were used to the sight of Krystle going to neighbours' homes with empty soft drink bottles begging for sugar and water to feed herself and Kerry Ann.

"I am not afraid to stay in the house alone. When Kerry wake up and cry in the night I pat her until she fall asleep," Krystle told an *Express* team that met them lying on a dirty piece of foam surrounded by empty soft drink bottles and other kinds of garbage.

Their grand-mother Patsy Young, 51, had appealed to authorities to "take charge" of the children. "I cannot afford to take care of them. I am not able. I have other children to look after," exclaimed Young.

Police took the children to the San Fernando General Hospital where they were medically examined and from where

they will be take morning to a ma who will determi immediate welfa

Young said h year-old daughte "desperately help", had on s occasions left th dren alone for and, in one in more than a m the "unsafe shac out food".

She said when Ann was just months old s taken away by th and sent to an o age. The moth placed on a six bond and told help for an add Young said.

"She behaved and the chil returned to h But she did n the drug. She s clothes neig bought for the cl to get money drugs. Wheneve at home she sle day and the childr left unsupervise grandmother disc

Young, a wid does domestic said she was un look after the ch because of her job.

"They need s sion, care and att but I cannot giv that," she lament

Waiting in v

ABANDONED CHILDR Krystle Brown (right), wh six, and her little sister K Ann, 18 months, were cued by San Ferna police yesterday from a room shack filled with r flies, cockroaches and m quitoes at Mon Repos terday.

Photo: TREVOR HACK

Breakdown of family blamed for child poverty

Toronto Star March 23, 1999

Liberal MP urges return to traditional values

By WILLIAM WALKER
OTTAWA BUREAU CHIEF

OTTAWA — Canada needs to attack the "national disgrace" of marital breakdown before it can begin to reduce child poverty, a Liberal MP says.

In a 120-page report to be released today entitled "The Child Poverty Solution," Mississauga South Liberal Paul Szabo argues that Canada's divorce rate is a root cause of child poverty.

Szabo authored the report on his own initiative at a time when child poverty is rapidly becoming the major political issue in Ottawa. But the MP notes that his views on reducing marital breakups may not be considered "politically correct."

"Family breakdown is by far the single largest cause of poverty in Canada," he says, noting that although single parent families comprise only 12 per cent of Canadian households, they produce 46 per cent of all children living in poverty.

PAUL SZABO: MP says his views may not be politically correct.

mentary committee is conducting hearings on children at risk and will report this summer.

Szabo's report is based on previous parliamentary studies, reports by Canadian anti-poverty groups and social activists, work by academics, United Nations reports and U.S. government policy.

In his most controversial recommendation, he calls for a renewed commitment to families and efforts to reduce Canada's 40 per cent divorce rate (70 per cent among common-law couples) as the best means to attack the problem.

"Since the real victims of family breakdown are the children, we cannot ignore this national disgrace," he says in the report, to be released today at a press conference.

"Strong families make a strong country and we need to invest in our family relationships each and every day," said Szabo, who has been married 25 years and has three children.

A battle against marital breakdown could be conducted through tougher measures against domestic violence, Szabo recommends, including mandatory counselling for anyone convicted of spousal assault.

Infidelity, alcohol and drug abuse and immaturity are also major factors in marital breakdown, but "governments cannot legislate moral and social values," he says.

But governments could begin to teach children at a younger age about the importance of fidelity and marriage, Szabo recommends.

"We need to teach our children at school and at home how to nurture relationships, what it means to make a life-long commitment to a partner and how to deal with problems without walking away from them," his report says.

As a result of breakups, Statistics Canada reports that 25 per cent of Canadian children enter adult life "with significant emotional, behavioural, academic or social problems," he says.

The emphasis in any attack on child poverty needs to be on prevention against such factors and a return to "family values," the MP concluded.

"If we were to raise one healthy, well-adjusted generation of children with sound social, moral and family values, we will have taken the first meaningful step towards eliminating poverty in Canada."

> **'Strong families make a strong country and we need to invest in our family relationships each and every day.'**
>
> PAUL SZABO
> Liberal MP for Mississauga South

Child poverty has increased by more than 50 per cent since the House of Commons voted in 1989 to eradicate it by 2000. Only nine months before the deadline, one-in-five Canadian children live in poverty, or about 1.5 million kids.

The Liberal government of Prime Minister Jean Chrétien has already begun to hold caucus meetings to discuss how to address the problem. A parlia-

Page 14 NEWSDAY Wednesday November 18, 1998

NEWS

Over 2,000 teens gave birth

TEENAGE pregnancies accounted for 14 percent of the total number of births in this country in 1996. Minister of Social and Community Development, Manohar Ramsaran, made the announcement yesterday as he opened a Caribbean Sub-regional Meeting for the Mid Term Review of the International Conference on Population and Development, Programme of Action.

"Here in Trinidad and Tobago teenage pregnancy accounted for 2,513 births in 1996, or 14 percent of the total number of births," the Minister stated. Pointing out that Government's

population policy was being implemented in several stages, he stated that part of the first phase was to develop and support programmes aimed at reducing the rate of teenage pregnancy. A reduction of the poverty rate by 20 percent by the year 2010, re-examination of the education system, training of educators, and the analysis of living conditions and needs of older persons were also among the stated objectives of the policy.

Yesterday's meeting focussed on the integration of population and development concerns into the national planning process; gender equality and the empowerment of women;

reproductive health care and reproductive rights; and partnerships in civil society.

Ramasaran gave a brief report on Government's progress in these areas, claiming that this country had done well. Representatives from Caribbean countries were present at the meeting, including CARICOM, United Nations and Latin American organisations. Towards the end of the meeting, a workshop was held during which participants collaborated to decide the major issues of concern with respect to population development. These issues are intended to be presented at the general summit of the United Nations in May 1999.

PAGE 6A

THE GLEANER, MONDAY, JULY 10, 1995

St. Lucia population affecting social and health

CASTRIES, St. Lucia (CANA) – St. Lucia, which has the second highest birth rate in the Western hemisphere, celebrated World Population Day Sunday, amid concern about the burden this trend is placing on health and social services.

"The population size in St.

Lucia has been rapidly increasing and that continues to put a strain on the limited resources in St. Lucia," chief social planning officer, Ezra Jn Baptiste said.

"Our resources cannot sustain a large population and some effort must be made to control its size and growth.

Jn Baptiste said the island was having "less and less" control over its ability to provide school places, medical care, housing, recreational facilities and police protection.

He said the teenage birthrate among women between 15-19 was very high

and accounted for 20 per cent of all births which occur in any one year in St. Lucia.

"This situation gives rise to a very young population. In the long run a large percentage of our population will be very young for a long time, and will have to depend on the ability of the work force to produce for them," he warned.

Government, Jn Baptiste

said, may eventually have to cut back on its capital expenditure to provide social services for its growing population.

The seriousness of St. Lucia's predicament will be highlighted during a week of activities from July 9-15, under the theme "Population Issues, Our Concerns, Our Responsibility".

The chief social planning

TEENAGE PREGNANCY WORRIES JAMAICA

KINGSTON, JAMAICA: Family planning officials in Jamaica are grappling with a problem of teenage girls becoming mothers.

The country's statistics on children born to teenage mothers has risen to 25 percent.

Martin Campbell, liaison officer of the St Ann Family Planning Board, told a recent public meeting that teen-

age pregnancy was a major problem.

He related a case in which a 25-year-old man got the 14-year-old twin daughters of a woman pregnant. She reportedly is not taking the matter any further because the man is expected to be a good father to his children.

Campbell said that the board knew of six girls in the parish, ages 13 and 14, who are pregnant. Most of them, he said,

got pregnant either because they were not told about sex and were experimenting or because of "an accident".

Campbell pointed to a cycle in which the daughters of teenage mothers also become single teenage mothers. In the cases mentioned, he said the pregnant teenagers were all from homes where there were no fathers.

(CANA)

NEWSDAY Friday February 19, 1999, Page 43

THE

CRITI

WASHINGTON POST AUGUST 21,1994,USA

AID Program [INDIA] to Lower Birthrate

By Molly Moore
Washington Post Foreign Service

NEW DELHI—Three years ago, the U.S. government approved the most expensive foreign population project in its history: $325 million to help curb the birthrate in India's most populous and impoverished state. Today, no program payments have been made, and the project has become mired in political squabbles, bureaucratic red tape and anti-American sentiment.

"It's been like two trains crashing," said one U.S. official, describing U.S.-Indian attempts to launch the project in the northern state of Uttar Pradesh.

Although the U.S. Agency for International Development (USAID), the World Bank, the United Nations and other organizations have offered India more than $1 billion in grants and loans in recent years, many of the programs have ended in failure. Tens of millions of dollars have been wasted, and millions more have gone unspent on some of the world's neediest recipients.

The last major USAID population project in India—$47 million for marketing contraceptives—ended in disaster in 1991 after seven years because U.S. and Indian government officials failed to resolve differences over how the program should be administered. In the process, $17 million in U.S. taxpayer money was spent on a program that never got off the ground.

The World Bank has withdrawn tens of millions of dollars worth of loans because the Indian government failed to initiate population programs with the money. States perpetually strapped for cash frequently diverted money from population projects to state employee payrolls or accounts, according to several World Bank officials.

"You want the country to spend the money," said one international aid donor. "But you're working with the weakest ministries—health, education, welfare. If you take it back, it's perceived that you're taking money away from starving women and children."

Officials involved in a wide range of Indian population programs agreed to be interviewed for this article only if their names were not used.

To many frustrated agency officials, the aid experiences in India reflect why this country has been unable to control its population—which is growing faster than any other in the world—while other developing nations, such as Bangladesh, have embraced outside assistance.

But Indian officials, echoing leaders of many other developing nations, point to the poor track records of international aid groups, which they say have imposed Western technologies and ideas that do not easily convert to Third World needs.

In years past, when U.S. agencies first encouraged the use of vasectomies for men and intrauterine devices for women, they did not consider that India's health infrastructure could not provide the trained medical officers, proper sanitary conditions or adequate follow-up care needed for successful programs, according to Indian government officials.

As a result, hundreds of men died from tetanus infections after having vasectomies, and a large percentage of

A18   WEDNESDAY, MAY 3, 2000   WASHINGTON POST MAY 3.2000,p A18,USA

One-Child Policy Faltering in Rural China

CHINA, *From A1*

China's family planning effort remains perhaps the most misunderstood, complex and varied of all the policies China has embraced in its race to become a modern nation. On one hand, the campaign has prompted intense criticism from the West. Human rights advocates have denounced forced abortions, the destruction of homes, coerced sterilizations and the killing of female babies that were triggered in part by strict population controls.

On the other, little mention has been made of the fact that the policy has been neglected more than it has been carried out, that many exceptions have been allowed and that, according to Chen Shengli, a senior official at the State Family Planning Commission, only 60 million of the 300 million children under 14 today are from single-child families. That means 80 percent of China's children have brothers or sisters, and many have both.

"If wasn't easy to have all those children, but it wasn't hard either," said farmer Huo, as he squatted near his one-third-acre field of winter wheat in this district 420 miles southwest of Beijing. "If things became tough in our village, my wife went to another township to have the child."

And so as census takers fan out across China this year for the fifth national census, they will find a country that has implemented the one-child policy in enormously varied ways. No cities so far have loosened the reins on 200 million urban dwellers, still limited to one child and held back by a system of fines and the reality of crowded city living. But some townships in the central province of Ningxia, China's poorest region, openly tolerate families with five or six children. Others, such as villages in mountainous Anhui province, have been mandating sterilizations after just one child.

Thus administered the one-child policy has created enormous demographic stresses and set the scene for severe social problems. In some areas, there are two boys for every girl, a product of the Chinese preference for male heirs combined with the restrictions on births. That in turn has spawned a growing industry in the trafficking of women.

In other areas, however, corruption has weakened population controls. Interviews throughout the perous cities and remote villages alike—is an attempt to make sense of the tangled web that China's family planning policies have become over the years.

In the early days of China's revolution, Mao Zedong, influenced by the Soviet Union, embraced the ideal of the "glorious mother" and called for Chinese babies, the more the merrier. The government began to rethink Mao's idea in 1971.

an open letter to all Communist officials ordering that they could have only one child. China's provinces and major cities passed laws and regulations limiting births. The one-child policy had begun.

The 1980s brought tough government campaigns involving forced abortions and heavy fines—giving the policy its notoriety abroad—but alternated with long periods of lax enforcement, something that was less well known abroad. The Huo family and their neighbors, for instance, had many children during the 1980s.

See CHINA, A19, Col. 1

In the 1990s, the family planning campaign was intensified but at the same time the government sought to move away from the erratic measures of the previous decade and toward some kind of comprehensive standard. Following the Cairo conference on population in 1994, Chinese officials made the link between population size and the economy. The central government started soft-pedaling coercion, emphasizing education and economic development. Couples in

The Barbados Advocate: March 29, 2003

Programme for teenaged mothers

THE Ministry of Social Transformation is continuing its drive to alleviate poverty by seeking to curb the high incidence of teenage pregnancy.

Minister of Social Transformation, Hamilton Lashley, made this declaration recently while at a graduation ceremony for participants of a Residential Housekeeping course at the Grand Salle, Tom Adams Financial Centre.

Lashley added that his Ministry had recognised that a significant number of families existing in poverty had at least one adolescent parent within the household. "That subsequently evolved into further births, often in quick succession, that exasperated the family's social and economic development and consequently, their standard of living," Lashley stated.

168

Page 20 NEWSDAY Wednesday February 20, 2002

NEWSDAY FEBRUARY 20, 2002, page 20

MONEY MATTERS

Tax breaks for two-parent families

By IAN GOODING

A BUSINESSMAN is suggesting that some sort of tax incentive be given to families with both parents taking care of their children.

Gregory Aboud of Jimmy Aboud textile company and president of DOMA put forward the idea recently at a Business Round Table Meeting at the Hilton, called to deal with the mounting problem of juvenile crime.

He feels that two-parent families who are trying their best to inculcate the much-needed family values should be rewarded for doing so.

While he could not say just how this should be done, he felt that this idea should be put out in the public domain for discussion.

"It is one way of encouraging the desired behaviour in the family," said Aboud.

"Just as Canada provides a tax incentive to encourage families to have more than three children, to encourage couples to have more children to populate that big country, a tax incentive would help to encourage parents to accept their responsibilities in the home.

"We are looking for suggestions to solve the problem of delinquent fathers. And this might be one that we could discuss."

Another businessman agreed with Aboud, and suggested that rather than put the emphasis on helping unwed mothers, it should be placed on helping mothers and fathers who are trying their best to bring up their children in the right way.

"It's about time we reward the hard work being done by thousands of 'good parents' and deal severely with the irresponsibility of 'bad fathers'," he said. "Parents must be held responsible for the unlawful acts of their children under the age of 18, even it means sending some of them to jail."

169

JENNIFER THOMAS with her hats and baskets.

'Poor women have too many kids'

TT MIRROR AUGUST 2, 2002, p 7

MOTHER of one and basket entrepreneur, Jennifer Thomas, who has risen from poverty, has hit out at poor, unemployed women who continue to have children.

"These women make too many children," said Thomas.

"They need to take stock of their lives.

"If they need to make children, then it should not be more than one, while they concentrate their efforts on getting skills that will make them employable.

"There are resources available and these women should use them instead of making plenty children."

Recalling her situation Jennifer explained: "12 years ago I was unem-

Cocoyea nats/ ployed and a mother of a four-year-old child.

"I saw an advertisement on the television by a foreigner inviting persons to learn to make baskets.

"I joined and now I am reaching for the stars.

"My daughter is now sixteen and I can give her everything she wants, all because of the skill I learnt.

"And I can concentrate my efforts on her."

Thomas is also employed at the Gems and Souvenir Gift Shop, at the Cruise Ship Complex, Port-of-Spain.

The confident mother said she also peddles her wares at Maracas Bay, Tobago and anywhere there are tourists.

CHILD IDENTIFICATIO

Fingerprint   Ame

DNA

PINE BLUFF POLICE DEPAR
PINE BLUFF, ARKANSAS, USA

CHILD'S FULL NAME

THIS KIT WAS COMPLETED ON _____/

KEEP IN A SAFE, ACCESSIBLE PLACE

FOR YOUR RECORDS ONLY

INSTRUCTIONS

1. Clearly print your child's full name and the date completed on the front cover. Due to changes in physical characteristics throughout your child's growth, we recommend updating kits annually.

2. Attach a recent photograph of your child, preferably a front shot of their head and shoulders.

3. Attach strands of your child's hair as a DNA sample.

4. Enter all applicable identification information into the spaces provided.

5. Fingerprint your child using the attached ink strip. *(See fingerprinting instructions underneath ink strip.)*

6. Allow ink to dry, taking caution not to smear.

7. Dental chart should be completed by your child's dentist at your next visit.

8. Store in a safe, accessible place for your records only.

9. Talk with your child about safety often. Make sure they know their complete name, address and telephone number including area code.

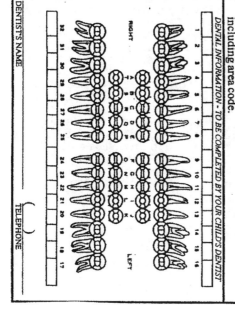

RIGHT

LEFT

DENTAL INFORMATION - TO BE COMPLETED BY YOUR CHILD'S DENTIST

DENTIST'S NAME

TELEPHONE

DAILY MAIL SEPTEMBER 13, 2002, ENGLAND

'All Britons should give DNA profiles'

Daily Mail September 13, 2002, LONDON

EVERY Briton should be compelled to give their genetic information to a national database, a leading scientist said yesterday.

Professor Sir Alec Jeffreys, who pioneered DNA fingerprinting, said it would be a great help to police investigations and better than the present 'discriminatory' system.

Britain's £187million criminal DNA database holds the genetic profiles of 1.5million people and is scheduled to have three million by April 2004.

'But recently it was extended to allow the inclusion of people who had been cleared of any criminal offence, and at that point I become very uncomfortable,' said Sir Alec.

'In my view that's very, very discriminatory,' he added.

The new powers were upheld by the Court of Appeal yesterday.

Lord Justice Sedley ruled that the keeping of DNA samples and fingerprints taken from unconvicted people did breach their right to respect for private life, but it was justified by the legitimate aim of preventing crime. At the British Association for the Advancement of Science's annual meeting in Leicester, Sir Alec said: 'The logic behind it is that if you have someone brought in under suspicion, okay they may not have committed that crime, but maybe they'll commit some crime in the future. I think that's a rather arguable proposition.'

There are also concerns that many law-abiding citizens give DNA samples in large-scale murder inquiries, and have little idea that their genetic information would be stored forever.

Sir Alec said there was now a 'very powerful argument' to extend that database so that the genetic profile of every British citizen was included.

'With the right very strong safeguards, I would probably be in favour of that genetic database.

'With a genetic national database it would be straightforward to identify a prime lead in an investigation.'

But it should be managed by an independent body, rather than the police or the Home Office, said Sir Alec, from the University of Leicester.

Taking Back Baltimore's Streets

WASHINGTON POST NOVEMBER 27 1993, USA

LOITERING

timore Mayor Kurt L. Schmoke is known for his unorthodox ideas about ting drug abuse, and his administration has experimented with native drug treatments, including acupuncture.

Mayor, Volunteers Demonstrate Against Drug Trafficking

By Paul Valentine
Washington Post Staff Writer

BALTIMORE Nov. 26.—Wearing a bulletproof vest, Mayor Kurt L. Schmoke joined hundreds of community volunteers and "occupied" 22 drug-infested street corners today, declaring symbolic war on drugs and briefly disrupting the cocaine and heroin trade in parts of the city.

Wearing bright orange armbands, activists waved anti-drug placards and staked out space on the sidewalks, as many street corner regulars appeared to back away, if only temporarily. Police, both uniformed and plainclothes officers, kept a watchful eye.

Most bystanders cheered. Others mocked the action, brazenly promising that drugs, momentarily off the street, would return. "Clear the streets. Clear the streets," taunted one west Baltimore youth, mimicking a police order. Some bystanders chortled at his sarcasm.

Tireless and wearing the bulletproof vest under a brown leather jacket, Schmoke stared at a cluster of youths at Wilkens Avenue and Payson Street. "There's the problem," he said, shaking his head. He said City Hall had received telephone threats from drug groups pledging to "take a stand" against him and others if they showed up for today's well-publicized action.

The "take-back-the-steets" demonstration was the latest gesture to come out of Schmoke's unorthodox approach to the drug epidemic plaguing Baltimore and other cities.

Already known for his controversial suggestions that drugs be decriminalized as part of a massive diversion of resources from law enforcement to drug treatment, he joined today's noon-to-midnight street action with unstinting enthusiasm. He crisscrossed the city, hopping out of his Lincoln Towncar, driven by a police officer, at street corner after street corner and mingling with pre-assembled groups. "This is just a first step, just a symbolic step," he said at Sixth Street and Patapsco Avenue in south Baltimore, where he and about 50 ministers and community leaders sang "We Shall Overcome."

Acknowledging that the 12-hour action by itself would have little or no lasting effect, Schmoke said he hoped it would encourage residents to exchange information about drug activity and report it to police. "People have already given us a couple of locations we didn't know about, a couple of stash houses," he said.

Md. Targets Crime 'HotSpots' For Aggressive Enforcement

Program to Coordinate Police, Volunteer Efforts

WASHINGTON POST JULY 1, 1997, USA

By Charles Babington
Washington Post Staff Writer

Maryland police officers, probation agents and others will focus on 35 high-crime areas, including a dozen in the Washington suburbs, as part of a nationwide trend to target trouble spots for more aggressive law enforcement.

The 35 "HotSpot" neighborhoods, announced yesterday, account for 11 percent of the state's violent crime, state officials said. The program will devote $10.5 million in state and federal money for new police officers, "nuisance abatement teams" and other efforts to reduce crime by 25 to 35 percent during the next three years.

The idea is to coordinate community volunteers and government agencies in targeting certain street corners, houses and even individuals who play disproportionate roles in triggering crime or police calls. The 35 sites also will get new after-school programs to keep teenagers busy and new pregnancy prevention efforts.

"HotSpots represents a dramatic change in the way state government fights crime," said Lt. Gov. Kathleen Kennedy Townsend, who heads anti-crime efforts for Gov. Parris N. Glendening (D). "Previously, our crime grants were scattered and uncoordinated."

The 35 areas include six in Baltimore, four in Prince George's County, three in Baltimore County and two each in Montgomery and Anne Arundel counties. All other counties have one HotSpot except Queen Anne's County, which did not apply, Townsend's office said.

David Kennedy, a criminal justice senior researcher at Harvard's John F. Kennedy School of Government, said the HotSpots strategy is spreading "all over the country" and is showing promise in reducing crime.

Instead of simply sending another patrol car to a trouble area, he said, "the new approach is to match the HotSpot with some of the possibilities we get from community and problem-solving policing." That can include using "reverse stings" that target drug buyers rather than drug

dealers and persuading landlords to screen tenants more diligently to drive away drug users, he said.

"With many Maryland communities competing for HotSpot designation, some local officials worry that non-HotSpot neighborhoods might lose out.

"One of my concerns is if you put

this much focus on say, Denton, would in fact the crime just move 15 miles down the road to Federalsburg?" said state Sen. Richard Colburn, a Republican who represents four Eastern Shore counties and is the town manager for Federalsburg, Kennedy said Colburn's fears may

See CRIME, B6, Col. 1

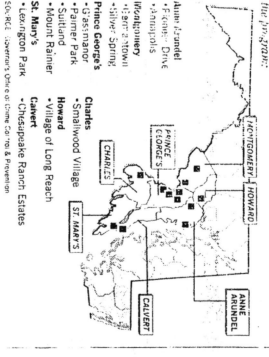

HOTSPOT BENEFICIARIES

Maryland's HotSpot Communities Initiative is a first-in-the-nation effort to combine a wide variety of grants and other state assistance to help specific neighborhood strategies to combat crime through the state. Here are the Washington area counties that will benefit from the program:

Anne Arundel
- Pioneer Drive
- Annapolis

Washington
- Germantown
- Silver Spring

Prince George's
- Glassmanor
- Palmer Park
- Suitland
- Mount Rainier

Charles
- Smallwood Village

Howard
- Village of Long Reach

St. Mary's
- Lexington Park

Calvert
- Chesapeake Ranch Estates

SOURCE: Governor's Office of Crime Control & Prevention

— THE WASHINGTON POST

LOITERING

WASHINGTON POST JANUARY 11,1999,USA

A4 MONDAY, JANUARY 11, 1999

Police, for Now, Hold the Power In the Liberty City Drug Wars

Miami Community Repeats a Pattern of Violence and Hope

By SUE ANNE PRESSLEY
Washington Post Staff Writer

MIAMI—The bicycles flit by the window of the Rev. Richard Bennett's office in Liberty City, one of Miami's most chronically troubled and violent neighborhoods. They are not ridden by children, but by young men who seem too big, too bulky, for the small, low-slung seats.

"If the police come to catch you on the corner loitering, as long as you're moving, well, you're not really loitering," explained Bennett, 42, executive director of the African American Council of Christian Clergy. "They're brilliant young men. They just need to get jobs."

The police have been a powerful presence here in recent days, questioning the young men on street corners, nosing their cruisers through the trash-strewn streets, watching the rhythms of life from unmarked cars. More than 200 city, state and federal officers, overseen by Miami Police Chief William O'Brien, have taken part in "Operation Draw the Line" to curb a drug war in Liberty City that has claimed a dozen lives in recent months, five in December alone.

"There are so many policemen around here, it's like the president is in town," Bennett said.

FILE PHOTO/BY JON KRAL—MIAMI HERALD
Miami officials and members of the African American Council of Christian Clergy prayed last month for peace in troubled Liberty City neighborhood.

175

LOITERING

NW Neighbors Gang Up to Roust Drug Dealers

WASHINGTON POST AUGUST 7, 1995, USA

By Bill Miller
Washington Post Staff Writer

The small group of neighbors didn't know what to expect that balmy night in October 1990 when they nervously put on bright orange hats and launched a patrol to rid their Northwest Washington neighborhood of drug dealers.

Alpha McPherson, Roger Conner and a few allies acted out of fear and frustration. They were hearing gunshots at night, seeing the open sale of crack cocaine along upper Georgia Avenue and finding syringes on their sidewalks. Night after night, police were in the area, but the drug trade kept thriving.

So they began patrolling. "Scared as the dickens," McPherson said.

Conner recalled: "The first thing that happened was the street just emptied. We looked up, and they were gone. That very first night, we saw them leave, and we had a real feeling of power. And a false sense of confidence."

As it turned out, the drug dealers were persistent. They moved from one block to another, changed their hours and kept on selling. But the community was persistent, too. And now a violent drug gang—the Fern Street Crew—has been forced out of business, law enforcement officials say, largely because of the neighborhood's resolve.

The residents walked, getting more neighbors to join them. They took pictures of loiterers, kept notes and wrote down vehicle tag numbers. They forced the closing of a neighborhood bar that police said was a hub of drug activity and gunplay. They recruited two of the city's top law firms to represent them free. They met with police and prosecutors.

The residents' willpower and work habits provide a model for people hoping to shut down street drug markets, according to U.S. Attorney Eric H. Holder Jr. and others. They say that the experience of these residents of Takoma, Shepherd Park and other neighborhoods along Georgia Avenue near the Walter Reed Army Medical

See FERN STREET, A6, Col 1

CHAPTER 6. LEGALIZATION OF ABORTION AND EUTHANASIA

I shall not dwell much on these two subjects, I shall make my position clear. I shall not quote any sources of materials on abortion nor euthanasia, but allow the reader to digest the original 12 information sources or articles on abortion to follow and original 16 information sources or articles on euthanasia allowing the reader to read and assess for themselves the contents. It is their option to be swayed for or against. The articles here will give a balance of opinions both for or against, although there is included a greater preponderance of articles for in the case of both subjects. There are some articles which are still weighing the pros and cons from lay to medical opinions. I concern myself with the rights of women.

I support the legality of both abortion and euthanasia. I support abortion except in late term or that period medically classed as 'late term.' In rape cases I support abortion,for nobody has the right to force a girl/woman to convey and deliver in her body an object from sperm to fertilization, that she did not consent to or was forced by way of sex. Any incestuous product by way of sexual coitus between: a father and daughter,mother and son,brother and sister, uncle and niece, aunt and nephew whether consented to or coerced is an abhorrence and abortion therefore is a must. In severe foetal abnormality, I support abortion, and where the mother's life is threatened I support abortion.

I support euthanasia where there is diagnosis of terminal illness or where there has existed a patient who for years has suffered excruciating,unbearable pain, having to live a life daily on pain killers and medical expenses have exhausted the family's financial assets or income. Where the immediate family or the individual patient if able to convey their right to die based on years of in-curable debilitating condition. When the patient is comatose, brain-dead or in a vegetable state of existence. I ask myself who pays the bills? Is a fertilised egg a human, is destroying a fetus a dead human?

Abortion allowed for incest victim

EXPRESS JULY 28, 1998

BROTHER & SISTER

THE parents of a 12-year-old girl allegedly made pregnant by her 17-year-old brother were granted permission on Friday to take the girl to another state for a late-term abortion.

An attorney for the girl, however, said she did not know if the abortion would be carried out.

"It's up to her family and I'm happy to leave it at that," said Elizabeth Gleicher, an attorney for the American Civil Liberties Union, which co-represented the family.

"There's nothing blocking her and her family from making whatever reasonable and rational medical decision they choose to make."

The legal decision came after the girl, now entering her 29th week of pregnancy, was evaluated by a psychologist.

Macomb County Prosecutor Karl Marlinga intervened last week as the girl's parents were making plans to take her to an abortion clinic in Kansas.

Prosecutors said they feared the parents, who learned of the pregnancy only on July 6, were making a snap decision that would endanger the girl's life.

Macomb County Probate Judge Pamela Gilbert O'Sullivan put the girl in temporary state custody so she could be evaluated by a psychologist, but on Friday, she dropped the order at Marlinga's request. Marlinga said he expected criminal sexual assault charges to be filed against the brother as early as next week.

The girl had been moved out of her parents' two-bedroom apartment in Sterling Heights, Michigan—where she shared a bedroom with her brother—and was living with an aunt. The boy still lives with his parents.

—**Reuters**
Mt Clemens,
Michigan

NEWSDAY Sunday October 17, 1999 Page 29

Abortion cuts crime says study

UP TO half the fall in the Untied States crime rate is due to abortions for teenagers, the poor and women from minority communities, according to research that gives a new twist to one of the most divisive issues in the country.

"No one will like it," said Steve Levitt, a University of Chicago economist. "I don't think it is our job as economists or scientists to withhold truth because some people are not going to like it."

Women whose children would have been most likely to commit crimes as young adults instead chose to have terminations after abortions was legalised in the early 1970s, says the report by Levitt and John Donohue, a law professor at Stanford university. "Abortions provides a way for the would-be mothers of those kids who are going to lead really tough lives to avoid bringing them into the world," said Levitt.

The paper, which has not been submitted for publication in any academic journal, says that states with high abortion rates in the 1970s had bigger drops in crime in the 1990s and that each 10 percent rise in terminations lead to a 1 percent drop in crimes years later.

Serious violent crimes by 12 to 17-year-olds dropped by 40 percent between 1993 and 1996, says the justice department's latest crime victimisation survey, and the number of youths arrested for murder fell 39 percent between 1993 and 1997, says the FBI.

But David O'Steen, executive director of the national right to life committee in Washington, said: "You mean killing babies in the 1970s led people in the 1990s to do less shoplifting? I can't believe that any significant percent of the population would argue that we should kill unborn babies to affect whatever they say is being affected."

The fall in crime this decade started about 20 years after abortion was legalised across the states in 1973. Previous theories for the decline included increased prison sentences, more effective policing policies, a slower crack cocaine trade and a strong economy.

Inclusion of abortion in the debate comes at a time when terminations are at a new low, about 1.2M a year, down from the 1990 peak of 1.4M. The latest poll on abortion shows that 42 percent describes themselves as pro-life, up from 36 percent

three years ago, and those who are pro-choice fell eight points over the same period to 48 percent.

During the 1990s doctors and abortion clinics have been the targets for at least 19 bombings, 100 arson attacks, seven murders and 621 death threats or stalking incidents. Ten months ago one doctor, Barnett Slepian, was shot in the head by a sniper at his home in Buffalo, New York.

Women aged under 25, separated, have never married, are poor or from minorities, are about twice as likely to have an abortion as others of child-bearing age, said the Alan Guttmacher institute, a New York-based research organisation. One in four pregnancies ends in abortion now compared to 20 years ago when the figure was one in three.

Cory Richards, the institute's vice-president of public policy, said of the Levitt-Donohue paper: "This is not an argument for abortion per se. This is an argument for women not being forced to have children they don't want. This is making the point that it's not only bad for the women, but for children and society."

LETTERS

Review of abortion law long overdue

179

WRITE TO:

*Newsday,
Chacon Street,
Port-of-Spain*

THE EDITOR: The abortion law is inequitable. The fact that after more than a generation of political independence we are still encumbered with a UK abortion law that had its origins in 1803, 200 years ago, and which the UK itself replaced 35 years ago (1967) is an indictment of us all.

The Offences Against the Person Act is not passive. Every week, it is actively the cause of harm to poor women's health — several dozens of them. The law is irrelevant to women of means who easily obtain safe abortions from medical doctors. That old, harmful abortion law persists today because those who have the voice to change it have no need, and because those who have the need, have no voice to change it. It is as simple as that.

We should all join together with health and legal professionals and resolve to provoke a sustained dialogue on this fundamental and gross inequity that persists in our midst. This is a dialogue that must transcend all boundaries of class, religion and ethnicity. For unwanted pregnancy does not discriminate in any of these. We should not allow this issue to become the province of any parochial, partisan interest.

Now, when every substantive issue of public policy has been displaced by the ruinous politics of politics, now is precisely the time to raise an issue that should unite us all. Here is a public health situation that screams for rational, courageous, informed leadership. We must do now what we should have done so many years ago — review this archaic law that ruins poor women's health. Even in the Caribbean, our law trails behind those in Guyana, Barbados, Belize and St Vincent. For those among us with any appetite for social justice, this review is long overdue.

LYNETTE SEEBARAN-SUITE
Attorney at Law

180

EXPRESS Saturda   23

Abortion
To legalise or not?

EXPRESS JUNE 19,1999

By DAVID NANTON
Features Desk

ABORTION is the second leading cause of maternal mortality in Trinidad and Tobago, according to a 1997 study by the Pan American Health Organisation (PAHO) on health conditions in the Caribbean.

Attorney-at-law and women's rights activist Roberta Clarke pointed this out as she sought to make a case for the legalisation of abortion, during an address to the Family Planning Association (FPA) at the Holiday Inn on Thursday evening.

Clarke is also an FPA board member.

While she acknowledged that making abortion legal would not dispose of the ethical issues surrounding the procedure, Clarke suggested that, in Trinidad and Tobago, the consensus "among a majority of women, whatever their views on abortion" would be that "there is no role for the coercive powers of the State in reproductive health".

The risks of abortion arise from its illegality and not from medical factors, she said, adding that complications arising from unsafe abortions represented an enormous cost to public health systems.

In some cases women resorted to extreme measures and put their lives at great risk, she said, citing the case of one woman who threw herself off a tree onto her stomach in an attempt to end her pregnancy.

She said during research at the University of the West Indies, she had spoken to women who said they attempted to induce abortions by stripping paint off the walls and swallowing it, thus putting themselves at risk of lead poisoning. Other women reported drinking what she described as "noxious" home-based remedies.

Clarke noted that Guyana and Barbados had already enacted legislation to facilitate the legal medical termination of pregnancy under specific conditions.

In Guyana, where the implementation of the law has been closely monitored, it has shifted abortion from a clandestine operation to a regulated, competitive professional service and given women legal access to, and choice of, medical practitioners, she said.

"Women are in a position to take legal or other action against medical practitioners whose services do not conform to acceptable, professional and medical standards," she said. "In other words, the balance of power has shifted towards greater equity and accountability between women making this difficult choice, and the service providers."

A study conducted in Guyana, before the new legislation was enacted, suggested that at least 30 per cent of all pregnancies there ended in abortion. It found that 51 per cent of women seeking abortions were married; 52 per cent had secondary school education; 74 per cent were between 20 and 34 years old; and only 22 per cent were not using any form of contraception when they became pregnant.

The Guyana study concludes, Clarke said, that induced abortion was not restricted to the common stereotype of unmarried adolescents, and that it was prevalent even where family planning services were available. Most importantly, she argued, it proved that the motivation to limit family size was high and that women would use any option if contraception failed and unwanted pregnancy occurred. This was the case throughout the Caribbean, Clarke said.

"It is because of the constancy of statistics such as these and the continued criminalisation of abortion that much of the debate, such as there has been, around reproductive rights, has focused on the abortion issue," she told the gathering.

There are two major arguments for abortion. One is the health rationale, which denounces the illegality of abortion as a significant contributing factor to women's mortality. On the other hand, human rights proponents argue that, independently of the public health issues involved, a woman's right to terminate a pregnancy is one protected by the fundamental principles of individual human rights. Advocates argue that the basic right of couples "to decide freely and responsibly on the number and spacing of their children" has been established by United Nations documents.

Clarke, a proponent of the latter arguments, said it was time for family planning policies to shift from being motivated by issues of demography and population control to empowering women to take control of their own fertility and reproductive health.

Doctors abort foetus in unconscious woman

By NALINEE SEELAL NEWSDAY JULY 28, 1998

A ST JOSEPH mother of three, whose sister and mother were beaten to death in last Friday's brutal attack at their home, had to abort a two-month-old foetus which she was carrying.

Contrary to previous reports, Anna Arjoon has not died as a result of the attack, but is hanging on to life at the Intensive Care Unit at the Eric Williams Medical Science Centre, Mt Hope.

Newsday learnt yesterday that Anna was two months pregnant when she arrived at hospital in an unconscious state on Friday, but the severity of her condition forced doctors to terminate her pregnancy.

Arjoon, has been unconscious since the attack.

Anna, her mother Sita and sister Asha, were beaten with a wooden plank at their in St Joseph home last Friday night.

Sita and Asha died as a result of the beating.

When *Newsday* visited the hospital yesterday, doctors described the condition of Anna as critical and could not speculate on her chances of survival at 'The young woman was being kept alive with the aid of a respirator, and several other machines.

The man detained by police in connection with the two murders was kept in an office at the La Horquetta Police Station yesterday

CHIEF INVESTIGATOR Inspector Nadir Khan at the Intensive Care Unit of the Eric Williams Medical Sciences Complex where Anna Arjoon is warded.

CHILDREN OF murder victim Asha Arjoon. Four-year-old Victoria hugs her 18-month-old brother Brandon and asked where are my mummy and daddy?

PHOTOS BY TERRENCE JARVIS

182

TEEN ABORTIONS UP
Schoolgirls terminating pregnancies daily

NATION
FRIDAY and **SATURDAY,**
OCTOBER 27 and OCTOBER 28, 1989

BARBADOS, W.I.
BDS. $1

ABORTIONS among schoolgirls are on the increase in Barbados. For $500 to $600, the operations can be obtained easily, three doctors told the WEEKEND NATION yesterday.

They also told of the frequency with which they are approached by these girls seeking the operations. And they all carry out the schoolgirls' wishes.

"If they come into my office, say they are pregnant and ask for an abortion, I give it to them," one doctor said.

Another said three or four teenagers from different schools come into his office every day to have abortions done.

Yet another doctor told of feeling sorry for the young girls,

---

A dozen chickens, please

Abortion

THE EDITOR: I imagine that those anti-choice persons who make no distinction between a zygote and a person, would be just as happy to insist that a dozen eggs is indeed a dozen chickens. When we eliminate the distinction between items we open ourselves to manipulation.

Language is important. The reduction of vocabulary is a dangerous practice. This was the message of Newspeak in George Orwell's classic novel, 1984. The fewer words the population has, the less they are able to think, the less they can think the easier it is to control them.

The anti-choice persons who equate a fertilised egg with a person are ignoring several distinctions in biology, law and theology. To begin with they ignore the fact that Mother Nature aborts more than 80 percent of fertilised eggs.

So in their language Mother Nature "murders" the vast majority of "innocent, unborn children." A zygote is not a child any more than an egg is a chicken. But let us not bother with these trivial distinctions.

When you are next shopping for groceries, ask for a dozen eggs, everyone will immediately know you really want chickens.

R JONES
Cascade

183
DAILY NATION FEBRUARY 25,1992,BARBADOS

Parents appeal ban on abortion

DUBLIN *Ireland* — The parents of a 14-year-old girl, made pregnant by an alleged rapist, asked Ireland's Supreme Court yesterday to overturn a lower court's ban and allow her to have an abortion in Britain.

Five judges in the Supreme Court, Ireland's highest legal authority, were to spend the next two days hearing the appeal that could plunge Roman Catholic Ireland back into another divisive referendum on abortion.

The schoolgirl, allegedly raped by the father of her best friend, flew to Britain for an abortion. But she returned home without having one after Attorney-General Harry Whelehan issued an injunction and the Dublin High Court backed his ruling.

In an emotionally charged case that has bitterly split Ireland and confronted its new government with a major crisis, the girl's lawyers are seeking to overturn the High Court's ban.

The media yesterday asked the Supreme Court to forego its usual practice of hearing such cases behind closed doors. But the judges turned the request down.

Prime Minister Albert Reynolds, battling to maintain all-party consensus in the explosive morality row, has said he is reluctant to stage another referendum to modify Ireland's blanket ban on abortion. (Reuter)

Nicaragua mulls abortion for nine-year-old

NEWSDAY FEBRUARY 19, 2003

MANAGUA, NICARAGUA: A government board was studying whether a nine-year-old girl could carry a baby to term safely while considering her family's request to have an abortion.

The girl's parents said she was raped in Costa Rica and have asked for the government's approval to give her an abortion.

Abortion is allowed in Nicaragua in cases of sexual abuse, when the mother's life is in danger, and when the foetus has severe deformities.

184

RELIGION

Pope urges legislators to give embryo legal rights

Page 38 NEWSDAY Monday February 4, 2002

VATICAN CITY: Pope John Paul, who is staunchly anti-abortion, called on legislators yesterday to recognise embryos legally as human persons.

"Every human must be guaranteed the right to develop himself according to his potential...

from conception to natural death," he told pilgrims and tourists in St Peter's square for his weekly address and prayer.

The Roman Catholic Church teaches that abortion at any stage of pregnancy is murder and has condemned such scientific develop-

ments as stem cell research using embryos.

In his address, he asserted that science had proved that an embryo was a human being from the moment of conception and therefore immediately had its own identity.

"It is therefore logical to demand that this identity should be juridically recognised, above all in its fundamental right to life," he said.

The 81-year-old Pope has often thundered against abortion, even calling on Catholic doctors to shun the practice, legal in many countries including Italy.

(REUTERS)

DAD FORCED TO RAPE TEEN DAUGHTER

By KEN CHEE HING — *Newsday* March 5, 2001 Trinidad

IN WHAT has been described by police as a most heinous sex crime, a D'abadie teenager was raped repeatedly by an armed, masked intruder who later ordered her own father to rape her. The brutal assault was committed during the pre-dawn hours on Saturday.

The incident has reportedly left the victim and her father emotionally shattered and in need of psychological counselling. After carrying out the attack, the rapist went to another house in the area and raped another teenager at gun-point. According to police sources, around 3.10 am the first victim's father was awakened from sleep by sounds coming from his 13-year-old daughter's bedroom.

When the man went to investigate, he was confronted by a masked intruder armed with a gun who ordered him to go back to his bedroom. The intruder later grabbed the sobbing teen and forced her into her father's bedroom. He then tied up the girl's father and ordered him to sit on the floor. He then flung the teen on a bed, ripped off her clothes and in front of her weeping, helpless father, raped her repeatedly on the bed.

After the assault, the rapist got dressed and rummaged through the bedroom, leaving the bleeding teenager lying on the bed. The intruder later seized a gold chain from a drawer.

Police told *Newsday*, the intruder who had gained entry into the house by smashing some glass louvres, united the victim's father and ordered him to have sex with his daughter. However, police said, the man repeatedly refused. The intruder later placed his gun to the man's head and threatened him saying, if he did not rape the teen, he would shoot them both. The weeping father was forced to comply. The intruder warned the man and his daughter not to call the police, or he would return to shoot them. He then left the house.

After some time passed, the man took his weeping daughter to the Maloney Police Station and made a report. The victim was taken to a health facility where she was medically examined by the District Medical Officer who confirmed to investigators that she had been assaulted.

Less than two hours after the first assault, a 19-year-old woman from the area was awakened by a masked, armed intruder and raped repeatedly. The rapist gained entry into the house by climbing through an open window. The second rape victim later made a report to the Maloney police. She was also taken to hospital where she was examined by the DMO. In a quick response to these two rapes, a team of officers coordinated by Ag ASP Gregory Correia and Sgt Philbert Pierre, including Cpl Louise Maloney, PC Dexter Bernard and others carried out a mobile search in the D'abadie and Maloney districts for the rapist. Lawmen are appealing to members of the public to properly secure their homes before they retire to bed and immediately report to police, any strangers seen lurking in their community.

"This is a most heinous crime and we are putting all our resources towards arresting the perpetrator. The public must have a right to a good night's sleep without being attacked in their own homes," a senior officer stated.

Lawmen also said night patrols would be increased and urged the public to cooperate with the police. Up to late yesterday no arrests had been made in the rapes and PC Dexter Bernard of the Maloney Police Station is continuing investigations.

NEWSDAY MARCH 5.2001

Mother loses baby after fight

NEWSDAY JULY 7, 2001

EVEN IF someone is reportedly responsible for the death of Natoya Fraser's unborn baby, no charge can be laid because the law does not recognise a foetus as a human being. The only charge that can be laid is wounding of the mother.

Police were yesterday attempting to establish whether Fraser's five-month-old foetus died as a result of a kick to her abdomen alleg- The 20-year-old woman, of Lorensotte Village, Palo Seco is detained at the San Fernando General Hospital. She told police she began bleeding after being kicked by a young woman during a dispute triggered by an alleged love triangle. Police intend to question a suspect after they get a medical report on Fraser's injuries.

FOETUS NOT RECOGNISED AS A HUMAN BEING

186

Archbishop says violence in womb like violence in the society

ANTI-ABORTION MARCH TODAY

ARCHBISHOP EDWARD GILBERT

A MASSIVE gathering of supporters is expected for today's march against abortion, which is intended to send a clear message to government that abortion should not be legalised in Trinidad and Tobago.

Initiated by the Catholic non-governmental organisation (NGO) — Emmanuel Community, the demonstration is open to all denominations.

It will begin at 2.30 pm from Morvant Junction, and the Audrey Jeffers Highway near the Jean Pierre Complex, and 3 pm from the Brian Lara Promenade. All groups merge for a rally at the Queen's Park Savannah.

The abortion debate was prompted by an appeal from Advocates for Safe Parenthood: Improving Reproductive Equity (ASPIRE) for abortion to be decriminalised.

ASPIRE has described the criminal abortion law which dates back to the early 19th Century as antiquated and "restrictive."

The group said it drove poor women to put their lives at risk as no service is available at public hospitals.

ASPIRE said in 1991/2 unsafe abortions were the leading cause of hospital admissions detrimental to the quality of life of an international society.

Globe + Mail April 3, 1996

MDs can aid suicides, U.S. court rules

Using drugs to hasten death no different from withdrawing life support, judges say

Reuters and Associated Press

NEW YORK — A U.S. federal appeal court ruled yesterday that New York State's ban on doctor-assisted suicide is unconstitutional, saying that prescribing drugs to hasten death is no different from withdrawing life-support systems.

The 2nd Circuit Court of Appeals found that New York statutes against assisted suicide violate the Equal Protection Clause of the 14th Amendment because "they are not rationally related to any legitimate state interest."

The court held that giving drugs to hasten death no different from withdrawing life support drugs to terminally ill patients is no different from the withdrawal of life-sustaining treatment, which is allowed by statute.

"Physicians do not fulfill the role of 'killer' by prescribing drugs to hasten death any more than they do by disconnecting life-support systems," the court said.

The 2nd Circuit encompasses New York, Vermont and Connecticut. New York Attorney-General Dennis Vacco said he strongly disagreed with the ruling and is prepared to appeal to the U.S. Supreme Court.

"The court's decision would give sweeping autonomy to doctors in making deeply personal decisions affecting the health care of individual patients," Mr. Vacco said. "By opening this door, the court has set us on a path which will lead to abuse that is virtually undetectable until it is too late."

New York is one of 30 states that have specific bans against doctor-assisted suicide.

The ruling by a three-member panel of the 2nd Circuit marks the second federal appellate victory for proponents of doctor-assisted suicide. On March 6, the 9th Circuit Court of Appeals upheld a district-court ruling throwing out a ban in the state of Washington.

Washington's attorney-general said she would ask the Supreme Court to review the decision. The 9th Circuit includes Washington, California, Alaska, Arizona, Hawaii, Idaho, Montana, Oregon and Nevada. Only days after the appeal court handed down its decision on Washington's ban, Jack Kevorkian was found not guilty in Michigan of assisting two suicides.

Please see Ban / A13

188

A16   THE TORONTO STAR Tuesday, February 15, 1994

THE TORONTO STAR

Give terminally ill the right to die

In the end, Sue Rodriguez had it her way. She died Saturday at home, never succumbing completely to the paralyzing effects of Lou Gehrig's disease. Only the federal government's persistent refusal to recognize the rights of the terminally ill marred her peaceful passage.

Equally unfortunate is the need for the investigation begun after MP Svend Robinson called the RCMP to her home in Victoria, B.C. He was with her at the time of her doctor-assisted suicide.

Although it is legal to commit suicide, it is a crime to counsel, aid or abet someone else. That means anyone too ill or disabled to perform the act has fewer rights than an able-bodied person.

It was this discrimination that Rodriguez devoted the last few years of her life to fighting. Her case — the first to challenge the issue of assisted suicide — sharply divided the Supreme Court of Canada. The court decided against her on the grounds that the law was needed to retain respect for life, to prevent Canada from sliding down a slippery slope to involuntary euthanasia, and to protect the vulnerable from abuse.

However, a new study from Simon Fraser University suggests that assisted suicide takes place anyway. Rather than prevent it, the absence of guidelines actually appears to have contributed to greater suffering at the hands of individuals who lack sufficient medical experience. A similar problem arose when women were forced to get illegal "back-alley" abortions.

Appropriate safeguards could easily be introduced. In a strong dissent in the Rodriguez case, Supreme Court Chief Justice Antonio Lamer outlined possible guidelines for legal assisted suicide, opening the door wide for Parliament to act.

To soften the federal law, B.C. recently passed new provincial guidelines giving the Crown the discretion to decide whether to lay charges in individual cases. But Rodriguez would never have been satisfied with such hit-and-miss justice, and neither should Canadians. Everyone — regardless of their physical ability — should have the right to die with dignity.

As Sue Rodriguez wrote to federal Justice Minister Alan Rock from her death bed: "I hope that my efforts will not have been in vain."

A14 · THE TORONTO STAR Monday, March 6, 1995

THE TORONTO STAR

End the hypocrisy on mercy killing

Can there be a fate more grim than stabbing to death a beloved husband of 45 years who begged to die?

Jean Brush, an 81-year-old model citizen, entered into a suicide-pact with husband Cecil, who was being ravaged by Alzheimer's disease. Frail and weak herself, Brush's self-inflicted wounds failed to carry her away. She awoke to first-degree murder charges and a society deeply divided over what she had done.

But crown attorneys and Judge Bernd Zabel of the Ontario Court's Provincial Division found themselves unable to treat her as a murderer. "She has already suffered a harsher sentence than could ever be imposed on her life — the loss of her loving husband," Zabel said in giving Brush a suspended sentence and 18 months' probation.

Brush's case has renewed calls for clearer guidelines on mercy killing, and awakened interest in the Senate committee currently struggling to find some consensus on voluntary euthanasia. The Liberals plan to use the Senate report, expected in May, to launch a national debate followed by a free vote.

Some are suggesting the federal government introduce a new crime of third-degree murder, one which would give courts the flexibility of convicting people like Brush without imposing harsh sentences. The idea is that the conviction registers society's condemnation of the crime, while the lenient sentence recognizes the unusual circumstances.

Such a step only would exacerbate the hypocrisy of our current conflicted approach to euthanasia and assisted suicide. If mercy killing is a crime, then sentencing should follow accordingly. But if mercy killing is not a crime in certain circumstances, then the state has an obligation to spell those out and erect appropriate safeguards.

By invoking the criminal law, then looking the other way, the government manages to avoid the critical questions of if, when and how the healthy may help the sick to die. Ignored, too, is Brush's complaint that she couldn't find satisfactory palliative care.

Before a doctor helped her take her own life, Sue Rodriguez begged the federal government to find the courage to legislate in these thorny areas. Supreme Court of Canada Chief Justice Antonio Lamer echoed that call, insisting that Parliament could develop clear rules for doctor-assisted suicide.

THE GLEANER, MONDAY, AUGUST 28, 1995

Should assisted suicide be permitted in Jamaica?

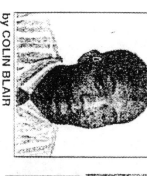

by COLIN BLAIR

PERSONAL freedom seems to be the prevailing ethos of this era. The current feeling is that there should be freedom to pursue one's chosen career regardless of gender; freedom to enjoy one's sexuality, so long as it is done with a consenting adult; freedom to change one's gender; freedom generally to do whatever one wants, as long as it does not infringe on the rights and freedom of others.

In cases where individual freedom impinges on the freedom of other members of society, it is judged as wrong because it impinges on other people's rights; thus highlighting the overall importance of and responsibility that goes with personal freedom in this era.

Thus, if personal freedom is the highest good, then it is only logical that an individual should have the freedom to end his existence, with or without assistance.

A pregnant woman in many parts of today's world has the choice to kill her foetus, generally with the assistance of others.

The question may therefore be asked, if the state can kill a member of society because it has been empowered to do so by its citizenry, why shouldn't individual members of the citizenry be allowed to exercise this power in deciding their own fate.

A defence often advanced for abortion is that the foetus is a part of the woman's body and the woman has a right to decide the fate of her body. The truth of this argument is not of importance here. What is important is that many states support the right of the woman to choose what is done with the foetus, and whether it is agreed that it is her body or a separate individual.

by MAIA CHUNG

THESE days one sentiment on the streets is that suicide is the coward's way out. Gone are the days when to die by one's own hand was considered a 'sadly romantic' way out of coping with a particularly 'bad scene'. Remember Romeo and Juliet?

These days, most people known to have committed suicide are viewed as wimps, idiots, etcetera. These are the times of the 'strong man'.

But though this view seems prevalent, I believe suicide is a personal option that cannot and should not be taken away from any person.

For those who hope suicide will die a natural death, dream on. If anything, people are finding new and improved ways to do the deed. And with these innovations comes the issue of assisted suicide or euthanasia, as it is termed in medical circles.

An individual who requests his own death, with the help of a consulting physician, is classified as being desirous of committing assisted suicide.

Not only do I feel assisted suicide should be made legal here in Jamaica and throughout the world, but I feel it should be the choice of whoever desires it.

To my mind this new option provides a cleaner, less violent and even safer approach to an age-old practice. Remember the man who leapt from a tall building to his death and landed on a woman seated below, killing her in the process.

In cases of severe illness, the idea of assisted suicide has gained minimal acceptance. In several European countries and the United States of America, cases where this is done are widely publicised, drawing mixed reaction.

Many feel those who request their own deaths and are assisted by their physicians, are playing and asking others to put a hand in playing God. But are they really?

Who in this country could stand to see their bodies crumbling, while their minds remain intact...

191

The Gleaner
Editorial

GLEANER MARCH 24, 1995, JAMAICA
THE EUTHANASIA DEBATE

THERE is at present a raging debate in the United States and parts of Europe on the issue of euthanasia, the practice of assisting terminally-ill patients to die peacefully.

The latest round of debate was sparked off by the recent screening in the Netherlands of a television documentary "Death on Request". The documentary shows Dr. Wilfred van Oyjen administering a lethal injection that would end the life of his patient suffering from an incurable, degenerative condition. Since its screening television stations all over the world have been toppling over each other to purchase the rights to the film.

Euthanasia has been tolerated in the Netherlands for the last 10 years, though it is illegal. In that country, there are clear codes of practice to which doctors strictly adhere. The guidelines require, among other things, that two doctors diagnose unbearable physical or mental suffering coupled with a voluntary, well-considered and lasting desire by the patient to die.

As reported in yesterday's **Gleaner**, euthanasia is an ethical issue that weighs heavily on any doctor's mind. Doctors also query the ability of a patient in pain to make rational decisions on his life. But what of the patient's rights when available medicine cannot save or improve his quality of life?

The present Medical Act makes no reference to the issue and the Medical Association of Jamaica has indicated that this is a subject that doctors are unwilling to consider. Indeed, many doctors say that assisting a patient to die is a decision a doctor should not have to make.

However, it may well have happened or could happen that a doctor makes this decision privately. Brain-dead patients cannot be kept alive forever on resuscitators. In a world which is now a global village, Jamaica can hardly avoid current trends that may be difficult to cope with. It would be useful for the medical fraternity to at least begin discussions on formulating suitable guidelines for doctors facing the dilemma euthanasia poses. The awful choice often involves family emotions as well as ethical and religious factors.

Opinions on this Page, except for the editorial above, do not necessarily reflect the views of The Gleaner.

192

Appeals Court in West Strikes Down Prohibition Against Doctor-Aided Suicides

WASHINGTON POST MARCH 7,1996,USA

By Henry Weinstein
Los Angeles Times

A federal appeals court ruled 8 to 3 yesterday that a mentally competent, terminally ill adult has a constitutional right to use a doctor's assistance in hastening death.

Stepping into "a controversy that may touch more people more profoundly than any other issue the courts will face in the foreseeable future," the 9th U.S. Circuit Court of Appeals in San Francisco held that the Washington state law that makes physician-assisted suicide a felony is a denial of due process of law under the 14th Amendment to the Constitution.

"There is a constitutionally protected liberty interest in determining the time and manner of one's own death," appellate Judge Stephen Reinhardt wrote in his majority opinion. "If broad general state policies can

be used to deprive a terminally ill individual of the right to make that choice, it is hard to envision where the exercise of arbitrary and intrusive power by the state can be halted."

Reinhardt's analysis relies heavily on language drawn from Supreme Court abortion cases because the issues have "compelling similarities," he wrote. "Like the decision of whether or not to have an abortion, the decision how and when to die is one of the most intimate and personal choices a person may make in a lifetime, a choice central to personal dignity and autonomy."

The decision, which may become the *Roe v. Wade* of "right to die" jurisprudence, is applicable in nine western states: Washington, Alaska, Arizona, California, Hawaii, Idaho, Montana, Nevada and Oregon, as well as the territories of Guam and the Northern Mariana Islands.

Although the decision has no immediate impact on the criminal trial of Jack Kevor-

kian in Michigan, its rationale would provide a strong defense for the conduct of Kevorkian, who has become a lightning rod nationally in the debate over the merits of physician-assisted suicide.

Yesterday's ruling states that in addition to doctors, others "whose services are essential to help the terminally ill patient obtain and take" medication that will hasten death are covered by the decision and thus are not to be prosecuted.

Washington officials said it was likely they would appeal to the Supreme Court.

The ruling reinstates a 1994 decision by U.S. District Judge Barbara J. Rothstein in Seattle. She agreed with the contentions of three terminally ill patients, five physicians who regularly treat such patients and Compassion in Dying, a nonprofit organization that provides support, counseling and assis-

tance to mentally competent, terminally ill adults considering suicide.

Rothstein found Washington's law violated due process and placed an undue burden on persons seeking to hasten their death with the help of a doctor. (The three patients died while the case was pending.)

Nearly a year later, Rothstein's ruling was overturned 2 to 1 by a panel of 9th Circuit judges, whose majority opinion stressed, "In the two hundred and five years of our existence no constitutional right to aid in killing oneself has ever been asserted and upheld by a court of final jurisdiction."

But the plaintiffs persuaded the 9th Circuit to grant a rehearing before a larger panel of judges, setting the stage for yesterday's ruling.

In the opinion, Reinhardt acknowledged that the liberty interest recognized by the majority "must be weighed against the state's legitimate and countervailing interests, especially those that relate to the preservation of human life. . . ."

Dutch Parliament Approves Law Permitting Euthanasia

By MARLISE SIMONS
Special to The New York Times

THE HAGUE, Feb. 9 — Herbert Cohen, who has a family practice, holds that doctors should be allowed to end the lives of their patients in certain cases. For more than 10 years in the village of Capelle, he said, he has brought on the end for some people and helped others kill themselves to relieve their suffering.

Dr. Karel Gunning, a family doctor in nearby Rotterdam, calls this murder. He did so again today after the Dutch Parliament approved by a 91 to 45 vote a law that sanctioned euthanasia under strict conditions, after two decades of tormented national debate.

"Today the Netherlands abolished the Hippocratic Oath," Dr. Gunning said. "Killing is not part of medicine. I regret to say that we are becoming a barbaric nation."

Growing Public Support

A Government-backed study says that Dr. Gunning belongs to the 11 percent of Dutch doctors who said they would refuse to practice euthanasia. Dr. Cohen is on the side of public and medical sentiment in the Netherlands and even lectures about euthanasia at police academies.

Both men have been very outspoken on the complex legal, ethical and moral questions of when and how doctors may actively bring on death.

Under the new law, euthanasia and help in suicide, by applying a lethal drug, while technically still illegal is permitted if doctors follow strict medical and ethical rules.

The rules, though not written into the law, state that the request for euthanasia and suicide must come from a patient who is doing so voluntarily, who is mentally competent, has a hopeless

'Today the Netherlands abolished the Hippocratic Oath.'

disease without prospect for improvement and is undergoing unbearable physical or mental suffering. The doctor may proceed only after consulting another experienced doctor and must then report the death and its circumstances to the city coroner.

Dr. Cohen says he has cooperated with his patients' request to die because "we need a counterweight for the enormous technology of present medicine."

"We are talking mostly about older people who in other times would have died from their condition," he said. "If we can keep people alive but give them a life that is no life, we must be consistent and give them the choice to end it."

The 62-year-old doctor said he was willing to discuss his actions in an interview because "I am used to reporting them" to the health authorities.

Openness, he said, is essential for him and for the patient. "I need to discuss the case with others," he said. "It gives the patient the chance to take leave openly of his children, his grandchildren, a nurse, a household help, perhaps neighbors, the people in his world."

Makes Mourning Easier

Saying goodbye is painful, but it can be of great benefit, the doctor said. "It is dignified to say, 'I'm leaving.' It creates moments of great intimacy between people." He has become convinced that it makes the mourning process easier.

Dr. Cohen said his views have have all been part of a learning process. "I've made all sorts of mistakes," he said. "Once I did not tell a nurse who came the next morning to find the patient dead. She came to me outraged. 'How could you not let me say goodbye,' she said. 'I cared for him for three months.' "

In his practice of 2,500 people, euthanasia does not happen often, he explained, because a request to die requires "an independent-minded person," someone who is willing to fight for that right.

194

Court rules woman be allowed to die

NEWSDAY Friday July 14, 2000 Page 17

LONDON: A British woman who has been in a permanent vegetative state (PVS) for more than 21 years should be allowed to die, the High Court ruled yesterday, after her family asked for her soul to be released from "limbo".

The 54-year-old woman has been in PVS since giving birth on New Year's Eve in 1978, when she suffered oxygen starvation during a Caesarian section procedure.

The High Court was told the woman's husband believed she would have wanted to be around for the child's 21st birthday last year.

But in a case which the High Court judge called one of the saddest ever likely to reach the courts, the woman's family including her husband said she should be allowed to die with dignity now the birthday had passed. (REUTERS)

Paralysed British woman wins right to die

Page 42 NEWSDAY Saturday March 23, 2002

LONDON: A British woman paralysed from the neck down on Friday won the right to die "peacefully and with dignity" in a landmark case that puts patients' wishes first.

The 43-year-old social worker, who can now effectively sign her own death sentence, was given the court decision by video link to her hospital bed.

High Court Judge Dame Elizabeth Butler-Sloss, clearly moved by a life-and-death ruling in one of Britain's most emotive court cases, praised the woman's "great courage, strength of will and determination she has shown in the last year".

Victory for "Miss B" - who cannot be named for legal reasons — follows a growing clamour by patients to elevate their own rights above the beliefs of doctors and decide when life is no longer tolerable. Doctors at the hospital treating her had said it was against their ethics to switch off the machine needed to keep Miss B alive.

A ruptured blood vessel in her neck a year ago left the woman paralysed and unable to breathe unaided.

The judge said Miss B was now "entitled to appropriate treatment including pain-relieving drugs and palliative care to ease her suffering and permit her life to end peacefully and with dignity."

The hospital said it would not appeal against the ruling.

It was the first time in Britain that someone considered to be in control of their full mental faculties had asked doctors to switch-off life support in this way.

In other cases, doctors have asked courts to sanction the switch-off for people in a permanent vegetative state.

Butler-Sloss ruled that the woman had the necessary mental capacity to ask for her equipment to be switched-off.

"Administration of ventilation by artificial means against the claimant's wishes since August 8, 2001, has been an unlawful trespass," the judge said in her historic ruling.

Miss B's lawyer, Frances Swaine, told reporters: "It is entirely up to her as to what choice she makes next. She has been given the authority to make the decision she wants."

The woman may now transfer to another hospital, she added.

The case began with high drama this month when the court was forced to gather at the woman's hospital bedside to hear her plead: "I want to be able to die."

Giving her final judgment, Butler-Sloss said: "She is clearly a splendid person and it is tragic that someone of her ability has been struck down so cruelly.

"I hope she will forgive me for saying, diffidently, that if she did reconsider her decision, she would have a lot to offer the community at large."

196

~~And~~ Tuesday, October 19, 1994 *Washington Post*

Parents Win Right to Let Son Die After 17-Year Coma

Knight-Ridder

ST. PAUL, Minn., Oct. 17—The get-well messages Jamie Butcher's high school friends wrote on his high-topped tennis shoes are barely readable now, faded and blurred by the passing of 17 years.

Brain-damaged and in a vegetative state since a 1977 car crash, their son has been "dead" ever since, say his parents, Jim and Pattie Butcher. Now they want to remove his feeding tube and "give him peace."

The White Bear Lake, Minn., couple got a judge's blessing for the second time today to make that life-or-death decision for their incompetent son. They have shown they have their son's best interests at heart, a judge ruled, and need no outside help to make decisions for him.

But members of right-to-life groups that lost the challenge say they won't walk away from a legal precedent they consider "very dangerous" to disabled adults. Jane Hoyt, who heads the Ethics and Advocacy Task Force of the Nursing Home Action Group, said her group planned an appeal.

"The law protecting rights of the severely disabled have been weakened," Hoyt said after the hearing. "We must ensure that people with severe disabilities get as much representation in court as able-bodied people get for themselves."

At issue is a Minnesota law that provides for disabled adults to have a court-appointed guardian who works with family members in making critical decisions.

the side of the Butchers, upholding an earlier court ruling that determined they are their son's sole and rightful guardians. The family waged a similar successful court battle earlier this year with Ramsey County's Human Services Department.

The Butchers say now they only want some time at home with Jamie before they say their last goodbye.

Earlier this month, they took him out of the White Bear Lake Care Center, where he had lived for 10 years. For seven years before that, they cared for him at home, hoping that one day he would wake up.

A high school senior and A student, he was driving a car when it went out of control and hit a tree. Though his visible injuries were minimal, the impact apparently triggered severe brain damage. A test a few years ago showed Jamie Butcher's brain was almost gone.

The Butchers brought their son home on the eve of the 17th anniversary of the tragic car wreck. He was 17 when it happened.

197

Battle over brain-damaged, deaf, mute

Page 4 **SUNDAY EXPRESS** July 30, 1995

Let our sons die

TWO British couples are battling, in separate but grimly similar cases, for the right to end the lives of their severely handicapped children.

Brain-damaged in the womb, Thomas Creedon, two, is deaf and mute, has no motor control, cannot nurse or swallow and is fed by tube through a hole in his abdomen.

His parents, Fiona, 31, and Con, 33, cannot even cuddle him because he suffers severe muscle spasms when touched.

He has been hospitalised at Hull Royal Infirmary in northern England since birth, and doctors say he will improve.

His parents believe the only thing they have to give their son is release from the wretched hand fate dealt him, and have asked the High Court for permission to withdraw his feeding tube and allow him to die.

"We love him more than anyone could ever know," Con Creedon said in an interview with the *Mail* last week. "But for him there is no comfort, no joy, no dignity.

"My son is forced to exist by a legal and medical establishment that says he must not be allowed to die," he said. "If our grief and pain stay private then this barbaric situation will never change."

In Sidmouth, Devon, western D...

NEW YORK TIMES MAY 26,1994.USA

Quinlan Case Is Revisited And Yields New Finding

Debate About Life Support

By LAWRENCE K. ALTMAN

Nearly 10 years after her death, Karen Ann Quinlan, who was the subject of a landmark court case on refusal of medical treatment, is the topic of an unusual scientific report today. Using laboratory techniques that were unavailable at the time of her death in 1985, scientists have performed an autopsy on her brain and come up with a surprising finding.

The researchers said they had expected to learn that the most severe damage was in the cortex of Ms. Quinlan's brain, the gray outer layer where many higher brain functions take place, because autopsies on others in this state had shown extensive damage in that area. But contrary to expectations, the new autopsy found that the major damage was to the thalamus, a structure that is deep in the brain and whose role is less well defined. There was no damage to the brain stem, which controls heartbeat, breathing and other vital functions.

The anatomical finding challenges scientific beliefs about the role of the thalamus in the persistent vegetative state, the new report says. Miss Quinlan fell into that condition at the age of 21 after ingesting a combination of prescription sedatives and alcohol, leading to cardiac arrest. She survived in a coma for 10 years after her family won a court battle to have the respirator removed.

Assisted Suicide Bill Passes

Oregon Law Puts State at Center of Ethical Debate

By Don Colburn
Washington Post Staff Writer

Oregon will soon become the first state where doctors can legally prescribe lethal drugs for terminally ill patients who request help in taking their own lives. The new Oregon law, known as the "Death With Dignity Act," was approved by voters in a ballot initiative last Tuesday, 52 percent to 48 percent. Similar measures were defeated in Washington state in 1991 and California in 1992.

The new law puts Oregon at the center of the growing controversy over when—or whether—hopelessly ill patients should be allowed to end their lives, and what the proper role is for doctors in such cases. Polls show that physicians are deeply divided over the issue, and the American Medical Association opposes the Oregon law.

The Oregon measure gives terminally ill adults the right in some cases to obtain a prescription for drugs that could be used to end their lives "in a humane and dignified manner." The law, which takes effect Dec. 8, imposes three main conditions on doctor-assisted suicide:

■ Two doctors must determine that the patient has a life expectancy of six months or less.

■ The patient must request a doctor's assistance ⁀ suicide three times, the last time in writing, ᵇᵉ statement signed and dated by the pa-
⁀resence of two witnesses.

thanasia, in which the doctor takes a more active role in administering the means of death.

"Nothing in this Act shall be construed to authorize a physician or any other person to end a patient's life by lethal injection, mercy killing or active euthanasia," the law states. Prescribing a lethal drug to a dying patient under the law's provisions, it adds, "shall not, for any purpose, constitute suicide, assisted suicide, mercy killing or homicide."

A major concern of those who oppose legalization of doctor-assisted suicide is that a request for help in suicide might "mask" a desperate plea for help by a distraught patient in physical or emotional pain.

"The fact that voters in Oregon passed the Death With Dignity Act reflects individuals' deep concern about what will happen to them when they are dying," said Karen O. Kaplan, executive director of Choice in Dying, a national group that counsels dying patients and their families. Choice in Dying distributes living wills and other documents that help patients declare in advance what kind of treatment they want—or don't want—in case they become incapacitated or terminally ill.

"Often, there are ways to address these fears other than to choose to ingest a fatal dose of pills," Kaplan said in response to the final vote tally in the hotly contested Oregon vote. "Clearly, we in this nation need to be taking better care of people who are dying."

Under the Oregon law, if either doctor—the at-

NEWSDAY Sunday March 7, 1999

What is brain death?

By ANNE HILTON

CONSULTANT JOHN SHAW

"DON'T take your organs to Heaven, Heaven knows we need them here!" is the campaign slogan transplant surgeons are hoping to spread throughout Trinidad and Tobago if the Tissue Transport Bill is passed in Parliament.

It was consultant surgeon Mr John Shaw of the UK (where specialist surgeons who become consultants drop the "Dr" and revert to being plain "Mr" — being relegated, in the dim and distant UK past, from the respectable profession of "physician" to the blood-letting trade of "barber-surgeon") — where were we? Oh yes. It was Mr Shaw who first uttered that slogan. And, having done so, he proceeded to define brain death in medical terms to his audience of doctors, nurses, patients, friends and the press in his speech after a dinner given in Singho Restaurant in May last year. The

No profound hypothermia

Absent cerebral function

No seizures or posturing

No response to pain in cranial nerve distribution

Absent brain stem function

Apnea in reponse (response — typo?) to acidosis or hypercarbia

No pupillary or corneal reflexes

No oculocephalic or vestibular reflexes

No tracheobronchial reflex"

The three criteria headed "Irreversibility."

200

Anaesthetists want national consultation on brain death

By LARA PICKFORD-GORDON

THE TT ANAESTHETISTS ASSOCIATION (TTAA) on Thursday advised Government to hold a national consultation on the issue of brain stem death.

It said the consultation should take place with a view to "formulating a policy which takes into account, among other things, the sensitivities of the grieving family, as well as the limited resources of the State".

In a release the TTAA said attempts were made in 1981 by some of its members to have the Law Commission deal with the matter. However, at the time the organisation was advised that the Ministry of Health was considering a draft policy on brain death.

"Obviously nothing came out of these attempts," TTAA declared.

Making reference to a publication by the United Kingdom Conference of the Medical Royal Colleges criteria for diagnosing brain death, the association maintained that "the concept of brain stem death as incompatible with recovery is now accepted. Brain stem death is now synonymous with death of the patient."

It added: "This has become the basis for the withdrawal of mechanical ventilation from patients in coma."

TTAA voiced support for doctors at San Fernando General Hospital's Intensive Care Unit (ICU) who took 55-year-old Joseph Dwarika off a ventilator last month.

"The decision of doctors at San Fernando is in keeping with acceptable clinical practice," it asserted.

However, the association cited the lack of protocol for dealing with patients who are brain stem dead as the reason for the present "furor".

"In the present circumstances it is left to the various ICUs to develop their own methods of dealing with this issue," the TTAA concluded.

NEWSDAY Saturday December 12, 1998 Page 19

Gov't to meet on 'brain dead' policy

EXPRESS JANUARY 10, 1999

By PHOOLO DANNY
South/Central Bureau

BRAIN DEATH will be the central topic of discussion at a high-powered meeting to be held on Monday at the offices of the Ministry of Health.

The meeting is expected to be attended by Health Minister Dr Hamza Rafeeq, neurosurgeon Rasheed Adam, anaesthetists Phyllis Pitt-Miller and Hamid Rajack, San Fernando General Hospital acting Medical Chief of Staff Dr Austin Trinidade, Chief Medical Officer Rawle Edwards and a State attorney.

The Express understands that the meeting will discuss the formulation of a policy on brain death in Trinidad and Tobago.

This has come about in the wake of the "pulling of the

HAMZA RAFEEQ

plug" controversy that surrounded the late Joseph Dwarika while he was a patient at the Intensive Care Unit of the San Fernando hospital in November last year.

It is understood discussions will centre around the following points:

• Clear areas on whether or not the family of a brain dead patient should be informed if the plug is to be pulled;

• If the family should say no to pulling the plug, the law should state clearly what to do;

• The law should also say which relatives should be informed of a decision to pull the plug and who should be present when the information is to be given;

• Should nurses' views be essential in the decision to pull the plug;

• What specific medical criteria should be followed if there is any doubt that a patient is brain dead.

Some doctors believe the policy should be clear that the family should not have the right to stop the authorities from pulling the plug after a patient is declared brain dead.

★ THE TORONTO STAR Saturday, July 6, 1996 **A13**

'Vegetative' patients really aware: Study

LONDON (Special) — A British study found that 17 of 40 patients diagnosed as being in a persistent vegetative state were later discovered to be alert, aware and often able to express a simple wish.

The study, published in today's *British Medical Journal*, is one of the largest, most sustained analyses yet of severely disabled people presumed to be incapable of thinking consciously, communicating or sensing their surroundings.

"It is disturbing to think that some patients who were aware had for several years been treated as being vegetative," said Dr. Keith Andrews, a neurologist at the Royal Hospital for Neurodisability in London who led the study.

The results raise the possibility that a significant number of the tens of thousands North American children and adults said to be in a vegetative state may not be so profoundly incapacitated after all.

Dr. Ronald Cranford, a neurologist at the Hennepin County Medical Centre in Minneapolis and a leading authority on the persistent vegetative state, praised the British researchers' detailed and careful effort to "unravel the mysteries of the vegetative state for the welfare of individual patients, their families and society."

However, he said he was skeptical of the high level of misdiagnosis. He speculated 2 per cent of such diagnoses by U.S. neurologists and other specialists might be wrong, along with 5 to 10 per cent of diagnoses by nonspecialists.

According to the American Neurological Association, people in a vegetative state betray no awareness of self or surroundings, do not respond to questions or physical stimuli except reflexively, but do open their eyes and appear to go through waking and sleeping periods.

Coma victims, by contrast, rarely if ever open their eyes and do not appear to have a sleep-wake cycle.

The study has major implications for the debate over prolonging the lives of terminally ill people, researchers said.

LOS ANGELES TIMES

CHAPTER 7. MAKING DELINQUENT PARENTS/ GUARDIANS PAY FOR THE CRIMES OF THEIR DELINQUENT CHILDREN.

Because of my personal interest in the fight against crime, I have developed over the years my own personal collection of resource materials: local, regional and international on as many subjects which I perceive bear a relationship to engendering crime or criminal activities.

One such factor in my perception was the delinquency of parents or guardians. The compilation of materials or articles either quoted or presented in original form for the reader to digest, have been extracted from years of putting together such sources that make up this and other chapters in this book and even those other areas which I have not included.

It is hoped that the extracts from these articles will lay the basis for a case against such unscrupulous parents/guardians, and will seek to establish a stronger law that will deal with such lawless parents. Bear in mind that there are good parents or guardians dedicated in the right up-bringing of their children, but it seems that such right instructions fell on "deft ears" or weak minds who choose to follow bad company.

Any law so proposed must take the efforts of good parents into consideration and absolve them from blame. It is the lawless parents/guardians that we are after, whose children are the lawless products which they have moulded into minds of criminality. If we can blame the juvenile delinquent child by law, then a punitive way must be found to punish the root or casual factor- the malefactor parents or guardians.

For too long they have been the cause but have escaped the net of culpable accusations and the penalties for such a callous and reckless office of parental ir-responsibility.

In the effort to search for solutions to the causes of crime, the focus has been at times to center on the perpetrators of crime. Much has been explored and written about the "juvenile delinquent" and "juvenile delinquency" so many in sociology, psychology, probation and law enforcement are well versed on the subject or may have had acquaintances with juvenile delinquents in court. This chapter is concerned with the delinquent parent/guardian as a cause of crime and thus the focus is from the juvenile to the adult.

The law has always sought to protect children from manipulation and abuse by mal-intention adults. There is a wide spectrum of writings on the subjects: from adoption to maintenance, sexuality to inheritance and a wide array of statutory provisions covering virtually every aspect of children.

I have looked diligently at the "Laws of Trinidad and Tobago and concentrated on the punitive measures of such laws as it applies to adults in relation to criminality of children: an itinerary List of such laws are as follows:Act 19 of 1994"Children Act(amend), Laws of Trinidad and Tobago(revised edition)1980 Cpt 46.02

"Infants Act relating to Guardianship,custody,property "

sections 7 and 10, Chapter 46.03 section 7 "Adoption of Children", Chapter 46 "Affiliation Act to provide for the Maintenance of children", Act 27 of 1986 "Sexual Offences"

Sections 7 to 16 and 21, Laws of Trinidad and Tobago 1980 revised) Cpt 11.08 "Offences against the person" sections 1, 32,33(1),33(3), 34 to 39, 43(3) 44. Laws of Trinidad and obago 1980(revised) Cpt 11.18 "Children and young Persons(Harmful Publications Act", "An Act to prevent the Disseminationof certrain pictorial publications harmful to children and young persons", Act 15 of 1981 "Family Law"

Sections 29,30, 31, Laws of Trinidad and Tobago 1950 and 1980(revised) Chapter 4. 17, Sections 5 and 70 of the Summary Offences Act."

But a new angle and a new law is necessary dealing with parental/guardianship contributors to juvenile crime.

The accusation against ir-responsible parenting has grown, so too literature on the subject is replete with data to cite in order to present a case to support the need for a law that will make that category of parent/guardian pay for the crimes of their children.

In tackling crime new and innovative ways must be found to deal with. I repeat again that some parents merely make children but neglect to provide the proper guidance and supervision of their children. That supervisory neglect is a breeding ground for development of the criminal mind. Eventually the juvenile pays for the crime in court while the erring parent goes free.In order to be absolved the parent must.

In any new law to be applied require that a concerned parent with an un-controllabe child must report the child to the police who ill be required to visit the home environment and speak cautionary to the child,the police will be required to further inquire from neighbours to attempt to get a clearer picture of what is happening(if there is a community police unit) This could be one of their assignmen ts.recommendation at end.

Let me show that in subsequent previous up-dating of the existing law cognisance of the vital role of the parent/guardian was taken into consideration, but merely removes the child from custody jurisdiction of the parent/guardian when the courts ascertain negelect(not abandonment). It is a non-punitive act by the court.

Act 19 of 1994 "An Act to amend the Children Act" or Chapter 46.01 Section 14 states (1) Where a child or young person is charged with an offence or brought before a magistrate under this act, his or her parent or guardian may in any case and if he can be found and resides within reasonable distance , be required to attend at the court before which the case is heard or determined..."

From here on I require the reader to delve and digest keenly the number of supporting documents which I have included on the subject and judge for yourself; are irresponsible parents/guardians liable for the crimes of their children?

TRINIDAD GUARDIAN SEPTEMBER 3.1997

Trinidad Guardian September 3, 1997

Deosaran: Blame parents for their children's crimes

By FRANCIS JOSEPH

PROFESSOR Ramesh Deosaran said yesterday the time had come for parents to be held accountable for the criminal actions of their children.

Parents should be responsible for their children and they must face the penalty of the actions of those children, he said. He found that the rest of the society must no longer carry that burden.

Speaking at a Rotary International luncheon at the Queen's Park Oval, Deosaran also recommended that managers of the country's juvenile homes play a more active role to ensure they were not producing more criminals.

Deosaran, who is the Director of the Centre for Criminology and Criminal Justice at the University of the West Indies, said that during visits to juvenile homes he found that the majority of the youths were interested in following the straight path.

"They feel that 10 years from now, they intend to make it better, be more educated and obtain viable employment. I found rays of optimism in those youths. They are remorseful for what they had done."

Deosaran said over 80 percent of the youths were showing a willingness to change. But he pointed out that they must never be allowed to go back onto the streets without supervision.

He suggested that the homes should play a more active role and supervise these youths. "They are just let out into society alone, without any supervision and support. How can we get these youths to go on a straight and narrow path?" the UWI criminologist asked.

Deosaran said the vast number of people in this country were law-abiding. He said although the statistics show that crime was increasing, he revealed that it was just a minor group which was responsible for the crime situation.

"We have the capacity to curb it," he said, adding the judiciary must play a more active role with expeditious hearings. A lot of good judges had gone in the 1970s, leaving the judiciary "watered down," he stated.

Deosaran said he believes Chief Justice Michael de la Bastide was the right person to bring the judiciary back to strength.

Kamal blames breakdown in family for 'hordes of criminals'

TRINIDAD GUARDIAN AUGUST 1 1996

By INGRID ISHMAEL

FORMER PNM Government Minister Kamaluddin Mohammed is concerned over the high incidence of crime and juvenile delinquency which he says directly impacts on the family unit.

Mohammed believed that "it is imperative that governments throughout the world move boldly to re-establish strong family units by providing the opportunity for members to be able to identify with the values that our fore-parents so painstakingly established."

Addressing foreign delegates at the inaugural World Convention of The Family Federation for World Peace' in Washington DC this week, Mohammed shared with

KAMALUDDIN
MOHAMMED

them "how we in Trinidad and Tobago, a small Caribbean Island Nation feel about family Life, an issue in Caribbean society."

He said that "The problems of crime and the sad reality of juvenile delinquency are signs of the breakdown of the family. The disintegration of the family has led to dysfunctional behaviours, thus creating hordes of criminals among us. Many of these are young.

They have adopted a criminal life-style because of low self-esteem and because they are angry with the impersonal aspects of a consumer-oriented society."

"Many are unemployed, limited by inadequate education or racist attitudes. They feel outside of the family unit and so they seek to destroy what to them are impersonal aspects of 'downpression'. But their anger causes massive disruption to the fabric of our society," he continued.

Mohammed then went on to give a gripping account of related murders which appear often in the newspapers and admitted that international crime has not escaped this small twin-island state. He said that "the growth of international crime with the attendant casual factors of drugs, prostitution and murder have not left our Caribbean enclaves untouched. Most heinous murders are today committed by men who have no respect for the sanctity of the family or for the fact that this unit needs to be preserved at all cost."

Mohammed felt that "Family ties, themselves, are no longer respected brother against brother against friends which end up in our courts of law. I do not wish to give the impression that this is all new, but the founding of well-structured families was expected to establish a well-ordered society."

Mohammed then asked, "Why is the family in such danger?"

tional crime with the answer lies in "the disillusionment of people with religions' failure to bring solutions and the lure of a purely materialistic life which are symptoms of an age that requires results 'now for now.'

Mohammed also stated that "today almost every society has to grapple with the question of vagrancy among all levels of the population. In most large cities of the Caribbean, street children have become the most important and worrying phenomenon in our societies.

Also a sign of the disintegrating family can be seen clearly in the large population of old people who also live on the streets, eat from dustbins and bathe in the street pools.

TORONTO STAR OCTOBER 3.1996, CANADA

Parents may pay for youths' crimes Harnick suggests

BY TANYA TALAGA
STAFF REPORTER

Ontario should be getting tougher on the parents of young offenders, Attorney-General Charles Harnick told a public forum on crime in Vaughan last night.

Harnick said he was taking "a very close look" at Manitoba's legislation, which would hold parents of young offenders responsible for their children's crimes.

In cases of vandalism and mischief, restitution should be examined as a possible strategy, he said.

"If the offender will admit guilt, we're looking at ways to get them to pay the victim back, pay the community back," he said.

Ontario has 43 per cent of the national total of youth offences, he said, a number he called far too high.

"It's no secret I've been one of the most severe critics when it comes with how we deal with youth crime. We should make some serious changes," Harnick said.

"We're not doing enough to deter young people from crime."

Turning toward youth crime committees for young offenders that commit minor offences should be examined as an alternate punishment program, Harnick said at the Vaughan Civic Centre. This could help alleviate some of the thousands of minor-crimes cases currently before the courts.

The province needs to allow the court system to concentrate more on serious crimes, he added.

Transportation Minister Al Palladini, the MPP for the area, and York Region Police chief Bryan Cousineau also were at the town hall meeting, which was attended by a couple of dozen citizens.

The town meeting provides them with a chance to talk to the people who uphold and administer the laws, Palladini said.

Vandalism, robberies and break-ins at homes and businesses continue to plague the area.

209

A8 THE TORONTO STAR Thursday, May 18, 2000

Parents pay for child's crimes

Toronto Star May 18, 2000

Law lets victims claim $6,000 for property damage

By CAROLINE MALLAN
QUEEN'S PARK BUREAU CHIEF

A bill that makes Ontario parents financially responsible for the crimes of their children passed into law yesterday.

The Parental Responsibility Act passed third and final reading in the Legislature by a vote of 52 to 32.

When it takes effect with royal assent, parents will have to prove in small claims court that they took reasonable measures to prevent their children from breaking the law.

The law lets victims of property crime sue parents of children under age 18 for up to $6,000 in damages.

No criminal conviction under the Young Offenders Act is required for a civil case against parents to proceed, Attorney General Jim Flaherty said in introducing the bill last month.

The law is modelled on similar legislation in Manitoba.

Unlike the Manitoba law, Flaherty said, Ontario's law applies reverse onus, meaning the burden will be on parents to prove they were not responsible for damages caused by their children.

Flaherty said property crimes by children in 1998 ac-

counted for almost 20,000 cases in Young Offenders court in Ontario.

> **'All this act did was in fact dilute victims' rights by giving parents a bunch of excuses their criminal lawyers can use'**
>
> MPP MICHAEL BRYANT
> Liberal justice critic

"The action of the young person will be deemed to be intentional; it will be deemed to have been due to the failure of the parents to supervise, so it will be much easier to prove," Flaherty said in first introducing the bill.

Liberal justice critic Michael Bryant (St. Paul's) said the leg-

islation is an attempt by the Conservatives to give the impression that they are battling youth crime.

"Yet again, this government is talking about the issue of crime and they're not doing anything about it," Bryant said yesterday. He warned that, in order to protect themselves from having to pay thousands of dollars under the law, parents might discourage their children from taking responsibility for their actions.

"All this act did was in fact dilute victims' rights by giving parents a bunch of excuses that their criminal lawyer's can use in the courts and that's not going to help parental responsibility or youth crime at all."

NEWSDAY JANURARY 24,1999

Co-charge parents for their children's crimes

ALLEYNE

GEORGE

TOO MANY parents today are afraid to question their children's choice of friends, their staying out late, not advising of where they planned going out and with whom, their children's possession of unaccountable sums of money and their ability to "acquire" brand sneakers, watches and/or clothes.

They never seem to be aware that their children possess guns and other dangerous weapons; are more often than not engaged in gun talk and in gun play, hustle drugs for drug middlemen and, cynically, help warp and sully scores of young minds.

And in all too many of these homes the children, some of them still in school, but clearly not working toward either "O" or "A" levels, except perhaps the unlisted subject of crimes of commission, appear to be effectively in control and can do as they please.

The parents are working at Walkers and getting paid at the family."

Idle Hall and as long as their children's illegal efforts provide them with "creature comforts" and/or food on the table they are prepared to turn the proverbial blind eye. Laws should be framed and placed on the statute books under which these parents could be co-charged along with their children for any serious crimes that their children commit.

Good Heavens, only a few decades ago most parents, even those of the humblest of circumstances, were uncomfortable if their daughters were referred to as loose, and their sons as wayward. Invariably, depending on the children's ages, the parents would set out to remedy this through medicinal use of the strap, a carefully selected piece of "pessie" or hurriedly dispensed clouts.

They would do this as the late hard. Lord Melody, has told and left us in song: "To prevent shame and scandal in the family."

Admittedly, the methods would not be considered orthodox today by the bleeding heart, collective M'ss Goody Two Shoes, but they had a way of working. And, of course, there would be the constantly repeated lagniappe: "Hard ears, you won't hear. Hard ears you goin' feel."

I have taken a break from politics today to seek to drive home the important point that critical to any development of Trinidad and Tobago is the development of its young

ple and the family unit.

We must set acceptable limits of behaviour for our children. We must give them the right to make choices, or perhaps opportunity may be the better term than right, and point out to them that they must be prepared to take responsibility for their actions.

But in order to optimise the effectiveness of parental discipline, parents themselves have to be consistent in their dealings with their children. This must be demonstrated in the identifying of and sticking to limits and in pulling into effect "the consequences of inappropriate behaviour".

Parents should not threaten their children, but rather be consistent in their methods of handling them.

Effective parenting demands a direct and positive approach to discipline and children understand that this must be put in place almost immediately after birth — love, caring, consistency and a willingness to

INDEPENDENT · WEDNESDAY, SEPTEMBER 3, 1997 · PAGE 5

Delinquency factories in some TT homes

SOME homes in Trinidad and Tobago are virtual factories for delinquency, according to Professor Ramesh Deosaran, Head of the McAl Psychological Research Centre on the UWI St Augustine campus.

Addressing a Port-of-Spain Rotary Club luncheon Dr Deosaran also reiterated his contention that parents should be held legally accountable 'for the delinquent actions of their offsprings.

He told his audience at the Queen's Park Oval yesterday:

"I do not think that the rest of the society should carry a burden like this any longer. It isn't a matter of fathers and sense. It is a matter of serious deleterious repercussions on the rest of a society that is trying to be law-abiding and peaceful."

These young offenders break into people's homes, cars and harass people at the malls and other places throughout the country.

"We really are facing a crisis of sorts."

Deosaran added, noting that life family breakdown was quite obvious. So too the lack of proper education, all of which were quite frightening.

"This meant that the circumstances into which these youths were born were real factories for delinquency and a productive base for producing delinquency. Deosaran said he was in possession of a preliminary report on young offenders at institutions like St Michael Home for Boys, the Youth Training Centre and the St Jude's Home for Girls.

"The data was very frightening and that 70 percent of the youths at those institutions have not lived with both mother and father. "I think that is a very serious commentary on family structure in this country and the potential for producing alienated criminal behaviour."

He said most of the delinquent youths are from parents with low income jobs. The data also revealed that 70 percent

of those youths who are in those homes were of African origin, 12 percent, Indian and mixed - 18 percent.

Most of the youths were those who did not attain secondary education; 51 percent reached primary schools, 21 percent reached Junior Secondary, 11 percent went to Senior Comprehensive, 3 percent went to Composite School, 4 percent to Government Secondary School and less than 1 percent went to colleges and convents.

Deosaran was very critical of those in authority for not providing some mechanism for the delinquent youths to receive additional assistance when they leave the homes. He added that this situation "would aggravate their disposition, it would lead to further broken expectation."

Deosaran said the homes provide a mediation role and stressed that the Police and the Judiciary have special roles to play in tackling the problem of delinquent youths in the society.

Professor Ramesh Deosaran, Head of the McAl Psychological Research Centre on the UWI St Augustine Campus, in conversation with Rotarians, Dr David Quamina and Frank Moutet before his address yesterday to the Port of Spain Rotary Club at the Queen's Park Oval on some aspects of delinquency in Trinidad and Tobago.

INDEPENDENT/BARRY JAMESON

Page 6, TRINIDAD GUARDIAN, Wednesday, April 16, 1997

national news

Bad family life breeding criminals says Minister

By PETER RICHARDS

A GOVERNMENT Minister yesterday attributed the social conditions existing in some homes as a major factor in the rise of criminal activities in Trinidad and Tobago.

Dr Daphne Phillip was at the time making her contribution to the debate on the Community Services Order Bill in the Senate.

Dr Phillip said that the Government was not "pussyfooting and playing daily house with crime," but was seeking to deal with the matter in a holistic manner and at various levels.

She saw the proposed legislation as fitting into that category noting the other part has to do with understanding the social conditions around us."

Dr Phillip, a sociologist, made reference to a number of cases involving young persons within the 14-18 age group who had run afoul of the law and had been subse-

IN THE SENATE

quently jailed, either awaiting trial or as their conviction.

She said an examination of most, if not all of the cases, would show there were problems existing in the homes where the offenders grew up, including cases of

sexual harassment and the father being on a murder charge.

She said sending these young offenders to jail, in fact, worsens the situation and appealed to fellow legislators to see the merit in implementing some form of community service arrangement for them.

"These are some of the social circumstances of these young persons who are being put in jail and that is the beginning of their crime life," she added.

"We need to take account of what is happening in the homes, conditions to which they (the young offenders) had no control over," she said, noting that community service will help reduce crime and the burden on society.

Page 10 NEWSDAY Monday May 24, 1999

PARENTS HAVE DUTY TO DISCIPLINE CHILDREN

THE BATTLE against growing indiscipline and violence in many of our schools today must begin with the parents and in the process shared by teachers and the community.

Parents must accept the responsibility for controlling their children, for their upbringing and for their actions. Teachers can then run with the baton. But it is the parents who must set acceptable standards of behaviour in the home, not simply by laying down the law, but by themselves setting proper examples.

Children watch their parents more closely than many parents are prepared to admit and are guided, accordingly, not only by what their parents say, but by what their parents do.

Two or three generations aback took care in the upbringing of their children and took pride in their deportment, their manners and their positive work in the classroom as judged by examination results. Today all too many boast of the amount of pocket change they can give them, and some actually advise that if another child should hit them they should hit the child back.

Values were the principal factor back then; today it is money.

In many homes that seem to produce the violent schoolchildren, who bedevil our schools, the problem is not one of poverty. Indeed, many of the "spoilt brats", the violent children come from middle and upper income homes.

You see it not only in Trinidad and Tobago, but in the United States of America and the United Kingdom. In the US, the two boys who massacred 13 schoolchildren and teacher in Colorado came from affluent homes.

In the United Kingdom has come the news that some of the students of upper crust Eton, are on cocaine and cannabis. Clearly, poverty is not the reason here. It may be boredom, just being plain old fashioned spoilt and/or devilish peer pressure. But whatever the reason or combination of reasons the fact is that poverty cannot be considered the determining factor. The child on cocaine or cannabis is very often likely to be more violent than one who is not.

Teachers can and should contribute on an ongoing basis to the disciplining and upbringing on the children within their charge. Admittedly, however, they are constrained by the overall hours the children are in the school and in their care, and the fact that, specifically in secondary schools they, the teachers, move from form to form depending on how they are rostered.

The community, particularly the elders in the community, can effect a change, but with the active cooperation of parents.

NEWSDAY Thursday May 16, 2002 Page 7

NEWS

Auntie running scared of jail for crime nephew committed

By AZARD ALI

CAN the parent or guardian of a child serve a jail sentence for failing to pay a fine imposed on a child under his or her care?

This is the question a 58-year-old woman of Chaguanas is seeking to have answered in the High Court. Hopefully, before the having filed a constitutional motion questioning the power of the magistrate to have her sent to jail on behalf of the nephew — Travis Alexis.

Newsday learned yesterday that a warrant has already been issued for Blair's arrest to have her begin serving the jail term. Attorneys yesterday expressed alarm at the decision. A motion has been filed questioning the magistrate's power and the pending warrant.

Jannice Blair, of Branch Street, Enterprise Village, Chaguanas, is running scared these days, despite

Alexis was charged with several offences of house-breaking and larceny. He was taken before Magistrate Annette Mc Kenzie in the Chaguanas Magistrate's Court in May last year.

Aunt Blair's name was also called in court and she appeared before the magistrate. Alexis, who was 17-years-old at the time, pleaded guilty to the charges.

The magistrate then ordered Blair, as the guardian of the youth, to pay fines and compensation of $15,092.50, in accordance with the Children's Act. The Act states that the parent or guardian of a child below the age of 16 shall be ordered to pay the fine or compensation on behalf of the child imposed on a court.

The sentence imposed on Alexis carried, an alternative of six weeks simple imprisonment.

Blair, in a motion filed by attorney Sunil Gopaul-Gosine, stated that she paid only $40.00. And after the 14-day period that was given by the court to pay had expired, Blair stated she went

before the said magistrate.

The magistrate extended the time period to six months.

Still unable to pay up, Blair, in February this year, returned to the court where she learnt that a warrant was out for her arrest. Blair is pleading that she cannot be sent to jail for a crime her nephew, and not she, committed.

She is contending that while she is answerable to the court for the fine imposed on her nephew under the Act, she cannot be made to serve a jail term. The magistrate, the motion stated, has no power to deprive her of her liberty because she was not the defendant in the matter.

But Blair is also contending that the magistrate is in breach of procedure in making such an order under the Children's Act. She stated that the Act specifically states that a parent or guardian is only responsible for a child below the age of 16. Alexis, she stated, was 17 years old at the time when he appeared before the magistrate. Yesterday, when *Newsday* tried to contact Blair at home, a relative said she had gone to Guyana.

The motion has been set for hearing next month in the San Fernando High Court.

THE SUNDAY TIMES · 14 APRIL 1996

It's a life sentence for little criminals

SUNDAY TIMES AUGUST 18,1996.ENGLAND

Those who deal with juvenile crime believe the roots of anti-social behaviour lie with parents who don't know how to be parents, and pass nothing on to the next generation, write **Jason Burke** and **Penny Wark**

I t was one of those incidents that shocked yet somehow failed to surprise. "Lucky to be alive — man clubbed by a boy of 12", the headline read last week after Bob Williams, a retired bricklayer, tried to catch two boys in his garden.

The younger, just 4ft 10in tall, hit Williams's head with an iron bar. He lost two pints of blood and needed 10 stitches. "It is silly and pointless," he commented sadly.

If government statistics on juvenile crime are to be believed, such incidents are in decline. The Home Office reports that in 1994 39,900 10- to 13-year-olds were' found guilty or cautioned for indictable or summary offences compared with 70,000 in 1981. Yet while the statistical drop is trumpeted as evidence that the problem is going away, prominent academics and senior police officers are uneasy about the claim. The figures are an "illusion", says Professor David Farrington, of Cambridge University's Institute of Criminology. As evidence he points to rises in burglary and motor offences, crimes popular with juveniles, and to the recent police practice of issuing "unrecorded warnings" that do not show up in Home Office figures.

Alan Brown, Northumbria's assistant chief constable, is equally certain that juvenile crime is rising,

that have become prevalent over the past 20 years, particularly the fact that more mothers now work.

What everyone agrees is that children do not suddenly become difficult when they are old enough to show up on crime statistics. It is no coincidence that teachers at their conference last week spoke of expelling uncontrollable three-year-olds from nursery classes. There are those who dispute the remedy but nobody denies the problem.

One nursery head teacher of more than 20 years' experience spoke of how the most difficult four-year-old she had ever encountered burnt down the school at 16. She also recalled how a three-year-old who reacted to any local difficulty by swearing and screaming had a mother with similar habits.

These stories highlight two widely accepted theories: that sad children can grow into bad children and that all too often there is a horrifying gap between a child's needs and its parents' ability to provide. Too many parents do not know *how* to parent, says the developmental psychologist Professor Elizabeth Newson.

"There is going to have to be an enormous salvage operation on young children because there is so much neglect. A lot of parents are leaving their children to bring themselves up, I have treated a six-year-

Sunday Times England AUGUST 18, 1996

Forcing parents to compensate the victims of their children's crimes would restore discipline and save a fortune, says the Audit Commission.
By David Leppard, Ciaran Byrne and Richard Woods

Fearful of where Brook's petty crime might lead, his parents sought help from social services and the police.

Under controversial proposals contained in a leaked official report, Andrea and her husband would be held responsible for their son, his 18.

The prospect horrifies the Saunderses. It could cost them thousands of pounds when

draft report from the Audit commission, the watchdog of government spending, proposes that parents be forced to compensate the victims of their children's crimes and contribute to the costs they impose on the state. Teenage tearaways would remain their responsibility until the age of 18.

committed by children — estimated by the Audit Commission at between £5 billion and £10 billion a year to their victims and a further £1 billion to the police and other

ACCORDING to the commission, a disturbing trend in criminality has been obscured by official figures suggesting that the number of children convicted of serious offences has fallen. It says young males are no longer growing out of criminal behaviour as they mature. "More of today's young people will grow up to be adult offenders unless action is taken to change their behaviour," it concludes.

The Conservatives and Labour both speak of a crisis. Michael Howard, the home secretary, has doubled the maximum sentence for juvenile offenders imprisoned in young offenders' institutions. He is also committed to setting up American-style "boot camps" to administer short, sharp punishments to persistent young offenders.

Ann Upstall and her husband Neil, a computer programmer, from Basingstoke,

public services — should such think it would make a lot of young people think twice about vandalising cars or whatever."

Professor David Smith of Edinburgh University, who studies crime trends among young people, also favours the spirit of compensation. But he foresees many obstacles in implementing the idea.

For a start, most perpetrators are not caught, so how could their parents be identified. Young male offenders commit crimes each year; only one in 40 ends up facing a caution or a court case.

Partly for that reason, the Audit Commission's leaked report suggests an even more radical approach, not so much punishing parents as training them. It proposes that they should attend courses on how to be good mothers and fathers — even before they have children.

not have done it," she said. "I knew had to pay hundreds of

If someone I knew had to pay hundreds of

Truants' parents face arrest

TORONTO STAR SEPTEMBER 30,1999, CANADA

Britain plans to fine each mother, father up to $6,000 for students playing hooky

By HELEN BRANSWELL
CANADIAN PRESS

LONDON — The British government wants to make parents take responsibility for their truant schoolchildren.

Education Minister David Blunkett announced yesterday parents will be liable for fines of up to £2,500 pounds (roughly $6,000) per parent if their children persistently skip classes.

Truancy in Britain accounts for eight million lost school days a year.

Blunkett called it getting "tough with those who get tough with our teachers.

"A child that isn't in lessons is a child that doesn't learn. It's a truism but it disables them for the rest of their lives," he told the annual Labour party congress where he announced the new policy.

Parents of persistent truants are now liable for maximum fines of £1,000 (about $2,400). That level of offence does not require parents charged to appear in court. So 80 per cent of them don't bother, Blunkett admitted. By increasing the severity of the charge, the government will make this an arrestable offence. Parents charged will have to go before the courts to explain themselves.

"There are far too many par-
ents who simply don't get up themselves in the morning, so no wonder the kids don't go to school," the education minister said. "I intend that many more people will get up in the morning and make sure that their child gets to school."

Surveys have shown that 44 per cent of parents whose children regularly cut classes know their children are playing hooky.

"The government hopes to cut truancy by a third in two years.

"The announcement drew mixed reactions from educators.

"We already know from the
education welfare service that they've got dozens of these cases which they could, in theory, take to court here and now," said Nigel de Gruchy, general secretary of the National Association of Schoolmasters and Union of Women Teachers.

But he said there's the risk of making a difficult situation even worse. "There's huge problems about finding the parents, let alone fining them."

Joyce Gordon, principal of a school in Prime Minister Tony Blair's riding, questioned the size of the proposed penalties, saying current fines are beyond the means of families her school serves. "For my parents, the £1,000 pounds is equally difficult to find."

CHAPTER 8.   ALCOHOL AS A CAUSAL FACTOR IN CRIME

This chapter's primary objective is for the banning of higher alcoholic content in beverage drinks with above two percent alcohol (2 % alc) as specified on bottle labels. I make this assertion on the basis of the definition of alcohol as so defined in "Oxford Dictionary (a reproduction of the page for the reader to observe is included further in this chapter).

The Oxford Dictionary states "Alcohol... is the intoxicating principle" so that is one of its primary principle or characteristics- it has the potential capacity to intoxicate. When an individual looks at the label of a bottle of beer, gin, rum, vodka, whisky or wine or whatever other titles,you will note it says "2 % alc" to as high as 75 % alc" which is the highest that I have seen. The higher the alcohol or alc percentage content, the greater its potent and intoxicating potential. This is very serious and must be taken into consideration, hence it is part of my recommendation at the end of this book. Beer and wine are most likely to have the least percentage of higher alcohol.

Here are four examples of varied sources that allude to higher alcohol contents:

(1) "Underage alcopop buyers beat stores safety checks" SUNDAY TIMES JUNE 22,1997, LONDON, ENGLAND "Children as young as 15 years are being sold alcopop in supermarkets...Sunday Times investigation found that pupils from school can walk into supermarkets which will SELL THEM THE HIGH ALCOHOL FRUIT DRINKS.

(2) "School dinner? Make mine a lager" GUARDIAN JUNE 21, 2001, LONDON, ENGLAND "A Flemish beer lovers club has approached 30 schools and suggested that they substitute LOW ALCOHOL BEER called tatelbier, for sugary drinks such as lemonade or coca cola. According to Chairman Bieryrienden,of the beer club behind the scheme,lager or bitter will not be stronger than 2.5 % alc.
He dismiss the idea that pupils may become too intoxicated, YOU WILL HAVE TO DRINK FIVE OR SIX LITERS OF THIS STUFF TO GET DRUNK..."

(3) "Impaired driving charges up 39% higher alcohol beer may be a factor police say" TORONTO STAR DECEMBER 13,1993, CANADA
"...But one factor may be THAT MORE PEOPLE ARE DRINKING HOME BREW AND NEW BRANDS OF BEER WITH HIGHER ALCOHOL CONTENT said metro constable Kealey. Right now they are going to parties and drinking what they think is a safe limit, but they are getting quite a bit more alcohol..."

(4) "Why this beer is strong" EXPRESS JANUARY 2, 1996
"Three years ago Carib Brewery asked its research department TO COME UP WITH A BEER OF HIGHER ALCOHOL CONTENT than Carib Beer. Main man behind the new beer was Research Technician and brewer Richard Clarke. CLARKE TOLD THE EXPRESS THAT THE NEW BEER WAS 7.6 PERCENT ALCOHOL AS AGAINST THE REGULAR CARIB 5.2 PERCENT, A WHOPPING 2.4 PERCENT MORE. BUT THE DIFFERENCE GOES BEYOND MERE ALCOHOL CONTENT.

Carib beer is more bitter, the sweetness comes not from sugar but from what clarke calls "ESTERS" BY-PRODUCTS OF FERMENTATION ALSO KNOWN AS HIGHER ALCOHOLS..."

Because the new beer was named "Carib Strong Beer" and the promotional advertising of the beer on television depict native indians dancing and drinking beer, these indians resented and were opposed to the beer.I shall not reproduce the article with their criticisms here, but ask the reader to look for the article"Caribs against carib strong beer"NEWSDAY DECEMBER 23, 1995 which is included further in this chapter.

Have you ever asked yourself, why is it that alcohol drinks are the only drinks for which there is a warning included in "learner drivers' manuals?" and the only drink for which the measurement of blood/alcohol level and the breathalyser is used by police. Following later in this chapter please read the contents of these "learner driver manuals" about alcohol drinks:

"HIGHWAY CODE FOR DRIVER,ENGLAND" pages 87 to 89

"MASSACHUSETTS,USA DRIVER MANUAL"pages 48 to 52

"MARYLAND,USA DRIVER MANUAL" pages 16 to 21

In this chapter alcohol, the concept must be that alcohol is a mind-altering substance. This chapter will be concern with presenting documents that will show alcohol in a negative light in the following manner (a)alcohol, violence and sexual assaults (b)alcohol and vehicular accidents(c)alcohol mental and psychological effects(d)alcohol and birth defects.

The materials presented relating to sections (a) to (d) will reinforce the definition of alcohol from the Oxford Dictionary quoted at the beginning of this chapter and also my claim that alcohol affect psychological and physiological changes that precipitate crime. That is to say that there is a strong relationship between alcohol and crime. Alcohol tend to spur, influence some intoxicated persons to act criminally and to make susceptible victims of crime as for example rape,where in many rape cases reported women drunk or highly intoxicated have low resistance,lower memory and may have even pass-out.

My rationale in this chapter is that crime can be reduced if one of its contributory agents "alcohol" is reduced in content. The manufacturer's mysterious substance must not be higher but lowered. The intoxicant must not have the power to create a state of stupor or irrationality to the mind and therefore this mysterious substance known to manufacturers' must be extracted sufficiently to limit the percentage of alcohol in all drinks to no more than two percent (2 % alc).

This is a manufacturers' problem, they have the technical know-how and must act now or face the consequences like that of a liability challenge by consumers. What the chemistry of such an extraction or reduction in higher alcohol is not my concern but that of the brewers.Their claims of pleasant or un-pleasant taste, mellow or aged,matters not in those advertised gimmicks, those adjectives are not for sobriety or temperance. It is imperative that the ingredient that creates euphoric high sprits which the imbibe crave and indulge must be removed from its gradated high level to a low level for that is the problem.

The only alternative from lowering to (2 % alc) is to produce or manufacture non-alcoholic products as there do exist on the market non-alcoholic beers and wines,so why not non-alcoholic brandy,gin, rum,vodka, whishy etc.

This chapter is not for the banning of alcohol,not for prohibition nor putting manufacturers out of business nor workers out of employment, it is about removing an offending ingredient which gives the high,tipsy,addicting effect in alcoholic drinks.Alcohol certainly is more potent than marijuana, you don't see marijuana smokers staggering in gait when they walk or have withdrawal effects as cocaine and other drugs; yet marijuana is illegal but alcohol legal, why? This is a dichotomous sense of double standards. No drug that contain mind altering substances should be legalised for pleasure purposes and that goes for marijuana and it must be applied also to alcohol unless safe levels can be determined scientifically. Anyhow what are the merits of smoking? Tobacco or otherwise.

The tobacco industry has been challenged and blame has been applied to the nicotine in tobacco cigarettes and the danger it has posed medically, and laws have been implemented even banning smoking in public places including transportation. The coffee industry has been challenged about the dangers of caffeine as it applies to health and coffee manufacturers have been required to de-caffeine,so why is the alcohol industry the last bastion unchallenged?

The modus operandi, means of achieving this challenge-and this chapter and its recommendation is a challenge- is to lobby governments,support and solicit organisations in the fight against drug abuse, mobilise concern citizens, the medical profession and urge the United Nations and its agency the World Health Oganisation(WHO) to establish a treaty banning the manufacture and international trade in alcoholic products above (2 % alc) for consumption, this is the second part of the recommendation at the end of this book as it applies to this chapter.

It is a fact that all alcohol drinkers will get drunk depending upon the level of continuous consumption at differential levels of enormity and high level of alcohol content. This is not a generalisation but a reality as to the capacity and capability of alcohol to do just that. But it can be said that not all alcohol drinkers commit crimes under intoxication. Facts have shown that there is a propensity to act in a derelict behaviour as inhibitions and scruples fall apart while under the influence of alcohol; in other words "things seem to fall apart."

It is said too that "prevention is better than cure" well here is one way that the city of Washington DC, USA at one time took in front, in advance before individuals got worsen coditions during the festive season so prone to indulgences and this was during the "old year" celebrations.City officials decided on the thinkable, to act as a preventor before catastrophe: in this article

"FREE TAXI SERVICE IF YOU ARE NOT ABLE TO DRIVE" WASHINGTON POST DECEMBER 21, 1995, USA

"NEW YEARS REVELERS WHO HAVE HAD TOO MUCH TO DRINK, CAN MAKE THEIR WAY HOME SAFELY, EVEN IF THEY DON'T HAVE THE MONEY TO HIRE A CAB. THEY CAN ARRANGE A FREE TAXI RIDE BY CALLING 800-200-TAXI, THIS FREE SERVICE WAS TOO KEEP DRUNKEN DRIVERS OFF THE ROAD."

This is how serious and destructive alcohol is and why a stop must be put on higher alcohol. It is so serious that countries are realising that they have to spend millions of taxpayers money on rehabilitative services and units at mental institutions on recovering addicted alcoholics, and too that many of the admissions to hospitals for violence and wounds of that nature including domestic violence and vehicular accidents has been persons under the influence of alcohol. You will read later in this chapter from original documents from governments and organisations around the world the nature of this statistical and financial problem, while the alcohol manufacturers go free, counting their profits.

You will note in other readings police chiefs, mayors of cities, hospital administrators, non-governmental organisations, UN World Health Organisations, ethnic groups such as African Americans, American Indians,corporations. All of these you will read in documents included later in this chapter.

Something is wrong really with alcohol and it is its stupefying residual effect it has on the brain and ultimately on the entire body. Here is this quotation from the Washington Post Newspaper:

"Why things are, drink to me only" WASAHINGTON POST MARCH 19, 1993, USA

"Why do a couple of alcoholic drinks give you a lift, a high even though everyone knows that alcohol is a depressent? Our own scientific investigations over the years indicate that the first two or three beers make the subject more talkative, expansive, uninhibited and sometimes euphoric-stimulated. But the next two or three beers propel the subject into a different phase... a willingness to dance in a ridiculous fashion, after a few more beers the subject looses motor control and uncounsciousness finally.

Why does alcohol seem to have this contradictory effect? Walter Hunt a neuro-phamarmacologist at the NATIONAL INSTITUTE ON ALCOHOL ABUSE AND ALCOHOLISM gave us this answer: he said ' there are two things happening at once: First, the alcohol triggers the release of dopamine in the brain-- it is some kind of brain dope that makes you feel good. With drugs like alcohol and cocaine, the feel good response is artificially triggered. Second, the alcohol increases the effectiveness of a neuro-transmitter called gamma-aminobutyric acid known as GABA. This GABA stuff is an inhibitory which makes you think less not more, as alcohol makes your brain slow down...a beer or two will sweep that stuff away so at that point you are feeling high."

IT IS NOT THE CONSUMER WHO DRINKS ALCOHOL AND GET HIGH TO BE BLAMED FOR ABUSING THE DRINK BUT THE MANUFACTURER WHO ABUSES THE RIGHT TO FOIST ON CONSUMERS A HIGHLY POTENT DRINK WITHOUT CHECKS.

OXFORD
ILLUSTRATED
DICTIONARY

TEXT EDITED BY

J. COULSON   C. T. CARR
LUCY HUTCHINSON   DOROTHY EAGLE

ILLUSTRATIONS EDITED BY
HELEN MARY PETTER

OXFORD
AT THE CLARENDON PRESS

ALCOHOL

made first non-stop flight across the Atlantic, 1919 (Newfoundland to Ireland, 16 hrs 12 m.).

✓ ăl'cohŏl *n.* 1. Colourless volatile inflammable liquid, also called *ethyl* ~ (C_2H_5OH), formed by fermentation of sugars and contained in wine ('spirit of wine'), beer, whisky, etc., of which it is the intoxicating principle; also used in medicine and industry as a solvent for fats, oils, etc., and as a fuel. 2. Any liquor containing alcohol. 3. (chem.) Any of a class of compounds analogous to alcohol in constitution and derived from hydrocarbons by the replacement of hydrogen atoms by hydroxyl groups. ălcohŏl'ic *adj.* Pertaining to, containing, alcohol. ~ *n.* Person addicted to alcoholism. [Arab. *al* the, *koh'l* powder (for staining eyelids)]

✓ ăl'coholism *n.* Action of alcohol on the human system; continual heavy drinking of alcoholic liquors.

✓ ălcoholŏm'ĕter *n.* Instrument for measuring alcoholic content of liquids.

225

(A) ALCOHOL VIOLENCE AND SEXUAL ASSAULTS:

CANADA

An Act to amend the Criminal Code (self-induced intoxication)

[Assented to 13th July, 1995]

Preamble

WHEREAS the Parliament of Canada is gravely concerned about the incidence of violence in Canadian society;

WHEREAS the Parliament of Canada recognizes that violence has a particularly disadvantaging impact on the equal participation of women and children in society and on the rights of women and children to security of the person and to the equal protection and benefit of the law as guaranteed by sections 7, 15 and 28 of the *Canadian Charter of Rights and Freedoms*;

WHEREAS the Parliament of Canada recognizes that there is a close association between violence and intoxication and is concerned that self-induced intoxication may be used socially and legally to excuse violence, particularly violence against women and children;

WHEREAS the Parliament of Canada recognizes that the potential effects of alcohol and certain drugs on human behaviour are well known to Canadians and is aware of scientific evidence that most intoxicants, including alcohol, by themselves, will not cause a person to act involuntarily;

WHEREAS the Parliament of Canada shares with Canadians the moral view that people who, while in a state of self-induced intoxication, violate the physical integrity of others are blameworthy in relation to their harmful conduct and should be held criminally accountable for it;

WHEREAS the Parliament of Canada desires to promote and help to ensure the full protection of the rights guaranteed under sections 7, 11, 15 and 28 of the *Canadian Charter of Rights and Freedoms* for all Canadians, including those who are or may be victims of violence;

WHEREAS the Parliament of Canada considers it necessary to legislate a basis of criminal fault in relation to self-induced intoxication and general intent offences involving violence;

WHEREAS the Parliament of Canada recognizes the continuing existence of a common law principle that intoxication to an extent that is less than that which would cause a person to lack the ability to form the basic intent or to have the voluntariness required to commit a criminal offence of general intent is never a defence at law;

AND WHEREAS the Parliament of Canada considers it necessary and desirable to legislate a standard of care, in order to make it clear that a person who, while in a state of incapacity by reason of self-induced intoxication, commits an offence involving violence against another person, departs markedly from the standard of reasonable care that Canadians owe to each other and is thereby criminally at fault;

R.S., c. C-46; R.S., cc. 2, 11, 27, 31, 47, 51, 52 (1st Supp.), cc. 1, 24, 27, 35 (2nd Supp.), cc. 10, 19, 30, 34 (3rd Supp.), cc. 1, 23, 29, 30, 31, 32, 40, 42, 50 (4th Supp.); 1989, c. 2; 1990, cc. 15, 16, 17, 44; 1991, cc. 1, 4, 28, 40, 43; 1992, cc. 1, 11, 20, 21, 22, 27, 38, 41, 47, 51; 1993, cc. 7, 25, 28, 34, 37, 40, 45, 46; 1994, cc. 12, 13, 38, 44

NOW, THEREFORE, Her Majesty, by and with the advice and consent of the Senate and House

Commons gets bill attacking drunk defence

TORONTO STAR FEBRUARY 25,1995,CANADA

Legislation reply to anger over rape, abuse acquittals

BY DAVID VIENNEAU
OTTAWA BUREAU CHIEF

OTTAWA — Canada's moral outrage at drunks and drug addicts getting away with rape and child abuse is spelled out in a new law unveiled by Justice Minister Allan Rock.

Bill C-72, tabled in the House of Commons yesterday, would for the first time specify in law that drunkenness cannot be a defence against serious offences such as sexual assault, assault and manslaughter.

The bill would also create an unprecedented "standard of care" that would apply to anyone who becomes extremely intoxicated and harms another person.

A person departing from that standard would be unable to use the defence of extreme intoxication.

"This measure will ensure that intoxication will not be used to excuse violence, particularly violence against women," Rock told a news conference.

"People who cause harm to others while in a state of extreme intoxication should be held criminally responsible for their behavior."

A preamble to the bill says Parliament "recognizes that there is a close association between violence and intoxication and is concerned that self-induced intoxication may be used socially and legally to excuse violence, particularly against women and children."

The government may refer the law — immediately after it is approved by Parliament, but before it comes into force — directly to the Supreme Court of Canada.

"I am confident it is constitutional, but I am not the sole voice," Rock said. "We'll make our decision in the public interest."

The legislation is the government's response to a highly controversial Supreme Court decision, the so-called Daviault ruling last Sept. 30.

The court set off a firestorm of anger among Canadians when it set aside the sexual assault conviction of Henri Daviault, 72, of Montreal. It ruled extreme drunkenness can be a defence against rape and other crimes, provided the accused could provide in-court confirmation from medical experts.

Daviault will get a new trial at which he will try to convince a jury he was too drunk to know he had raped a 65-year-old woman confined to wheelchair.

EXPRESS NOVEMBER 4, 1999

No to happy hour

LONDON (Reuters)—The traditional British "happy hour" — when pubs slash their prices— encourages drinkers to binge and boosts crime, according to a government report published yesterday.

"Discounted alcoholic drink promotions and 'happy hours' should be avoided," the report 'Alcohol and Crime—taking stock' said, denouncing alcohol-linked crimes as a major social problem in Britain.

"Alcohol-related crime is a significant problem in society — a problem which has no single cause and no magic solution," said Home Office Minister Charles Clarke.

Call for ban on alcohol

GUARDIAN | Monday, March 10, 2003

ATTORNEY Asaf Hosein's call for a total ban on alcoholic beverages fell on stony ground on February 27, even though he was speaking at a meeting on the negative effects of alcoholism.

Hosein, a criminal lawyer, was a guest speaker at a meeting of the Association of Psychiatrists of Trinidad and Tobago. It took place at Botticelli's restaurant at the Grand Bazaar.

In spite of this, however, Hosein's call for a ban got less than a warm reception. "The law has failed outright to curb the problem" of alcohol abuse and its effects, including road carnage, Hosein said. "There is but one cure for this. All we need to do is simply ban alcohol. That's the long and short of it.

"Let us be strong enough to come together and say to Parliament, pass one piece of legislation and end it all."

Alcohol-linked attacks cause most UK face injuries

EXPRESS FEBRUARY 1,1998,page 9

ALCOHOL-RELATED assaults are the major cause of serious facial injuries in young adults, British surgeons said on Thursday.

A national study showed that 15- to 25-year-olds had the highest rate of injuries to the face and most of them were caused by alcohol-related attacks.

"Abuse of alcohol is implicated in half of these assaults," Ian Hutchison, a surgeon at the Royal London Hospital, told a news conference.

Assaults accounted for 24 per cent of the injuries while road traffic accidents were linked to just five per cent. Falls, particularly among pre-school children, caused 40 per cent of the facial injuries but they were usually minor.

The study, which involved more than 6,000 patients in

emergency wards throughout Britain over one week in September 1997, was the first to record the number and cause of facial injuries on a national level.

Hutchison said Britain's Association of Oral and Maxillofacial Surgeons, which conducted the research, is planning a European Union study to compare results across nations.

The research showed that most the serious injuries

resulted from attacks on the street or in a bar and 80 per cent of the assaults were with bottles or glasses and related to alcohol consumption.

"Nearly 90 per cent of the facial injuries occurring in public bars, just under one half of those occurring in the street and one quarter of facial injuries in the home were associated with alcohol in the over-15 age group," the report said.

Men were four times more likely to be victims of assault, unless the attack was in the home where 44 per cent of all assaults on women occurred.

The study warned that facial injuries can be life-threatening and can cause permanent physical and psychological damage.

—**Reuters** London

Early alcohol use linked to fighting in adulthood

NEWSDAY SECTION 2 Wednesday October 31, 2001 Page 15

NEW YORK: Adults who began drinking alcohol in their teens may be more prone to alcohol-related violence, study findings suggest.

According to interviews with more than 42,000 US residents aged 18 and older, those who started drinking before age 17 were three to four times more likely to have been in a fight after consuming alcohol at some time in their lives, compared with adults who began drinking after age 21.

Individuals who drank alcohol at an early age were also three times more likely to have been in a fight after drinking in the past year regardless of their history of alcohol dependence, the number of years they had been drinking, how often they drank heavily or whether they smoked or used drugs.

The study, which is published in the October issue of *Pediatrics*, highlights pediatricians' responsibility to find out whether their adolescent patients drink alcohol and to discuss the risks of alcohol with those who do, the researchers report. The findings also underscore the need for policies such as a minimum legal drinking age and community-based programmes that aim to reduce adolescent drinking, they add.

"The good news is that there are things that can be done," Dr Ralph Hingson, the study's lead author and a researcher from Boston University in Massachusetts, said in an interview.

Alcohol treatment programmes, for instance, have been shown to lower the incidence of violent behav-

iour among people who have already developed drinking problems, while policies that restrict young people's access to alcohol can prevent them from drinking in the first place. Additionally, brief counseling sessions by healthcare workers have been shown to reduce drinking and related violence, Hingson explained.

It is not clear why adults who began drinking at younger ages are more likely to fight. It may be that they are more likely to engage in risky behaviours and therefore were more apt to get into fights before they started drinking alcohol, Hingson told

Reuters Health. Alternatively, they may be more likely to find themselves in situations or in places where fights occur, such as bars, he noted.

In other findings, 65 percent of adults reported that they ever drunk alcohol, of which nearly half said they began drinking before age 21 and three percent said they began drinking before age 14.

Those who began drinking before age 14 were 11 times more likely to have ever been in a fight while or after drinking and 14 times more likely to have been in a fight in the past year than adults who began drink-

ing later, the report indicates. Men, smokers, adults who did not graduate from high school, single people and those who used illicit drugs were significantly more likely to have begun drinking earlier in life.

One of the study's limitations, the authors note, is that the results are based on self-reported behaviour, which is always subject to difficulty remembering and a lack of willingness to acknowledge certain behaviours. "Whether there is a direct causal relation between alcohol use and violence is still a subject of investigation," Hingson and colleagues write.

230

Seetahal: Alcohol abuse common in reports of killings

NEWSDAY JULY 22,2001

By THERON BOODAN

Newsday July 22, 2001

ALTHOUGH alcohol use was not factored as a variable in several of the murders so far this year, it should come as no surprise that alcohol abuse is common in reports of killings where the parties know each other. The same is true of other crimes of violence such as wounding and assaults. Despite the lack of scientific studies in this regard in Trinidad and Tobago, anecdotal evidence of those in the criminal justice system support this view. This was the opinion of senior lecturer of Hugh Wooding Law School, Dana Seetahal, expressed during her recent address at the 2001 National Convention of Alcoholics Anonymous (AA), held at Valsayn Teachers College.

Obscene language in public places, she stated, more often than not results from drunkenness as does disorderly behaviour. The calypso "Drunk and Disorderly" speaks for itself in this regard, she said. Seetahal told AA members and guests that she highlighted the facts relating to crimes to emphasize matters that some of them have already realised. "In fact these concerns may have resulted in many of you joining the fellowship because of your desire to stop drinking.

"You are the ones who have taken the responsibility for your lives and together with over two million other recovering alcoholics worldwide have admitted your powerlessness over alcohol. And you have either turned your lives around or are in the process of doing so." She also noted that while most alcoholics are men 35 percent are women.

Seetahal said she was a child of an alcoholic, and although her father at the time of his death had celebrated 25 years of being alcohol free, the effects of his alcoholism had far reaching effects. "I know he would have liked to erase those years when the family suffered from his addiction. This was impossible although it became better as time passed." She went on to list several consequences of a family affected by an alcoholic parent. Consequences such as domestic violence, breakdown in family (divorce), unemployment etc.

LONDON, ENGLAND

HOME OFFICE

Produced by the Research, Development and Statistics Directorate

Further copies are available from:

Policing and Reducing Crime Unit
Room 415
Clive House
Petty France
London
SW1H 9HD

Tel: 020 7271 8225
Fax: 020 7271 8344

This publication is available on the RDS website:
http:/www.homeoffice.gov.uk/rds/index.htm

Alcohol and Crime:

Taking stock

Ann Deehan

Policing and Reducing Crime Unit
Crime Reduction Research Series Paper 3

Foreword

The need for effective action against alcohol-related crime was highlighted at the Association of Chief Police Officers (ACPO) liquor licensing conference in November 1998. Some areas have already begun to identify the need for a local alcohol strategy.

This review draws on information from the academic, health and policing fields to explore the links between alcohol and crime, and to suggest methods which might reduce alcohol-related crime and disorder. No one single measure is likely to be enough but the potential value of local partnerships in any strategy is underlined. This report will provide an evidence base that should aid the development of such local policies and strategies.

Ken Pease
Acting Head of Policing and Reducing Crime Unit
Research Development and Statistics Directorate
Home Office
November 1999

232

Britian plans curb on teenage boozers

EXPRESS SEPTEMBER 11,1996

BRITAIN launched plans on Saturday to curb Britain's growing "yob culture" by giving police new powers to stop young teenagers from drinking in public.

A Home Office (Interior Ministry) consultation paper said police should be allowed to confiscate alcohol from anyone under 18 seen drinking in public and take their names and addresses.

"Action is needed to stop drunken people vandalising property and causing mischief in public places," said Home Office minister Timothy Kirkhope.

"I know that some people find it very distressing and disturbing to see young people drunk in public, especially when they cause trouble," he added.

The proposals were welcomed by police and are expected to win the support of the opposition Labour Party which is keen to be seen as strong on law-and-order issues in the run-up to next year's general election.

The law currently prohibits the sale of alcohol to anyone under the age of 18, but drinking by teenagers younger than that is not illegal.

—**Reuter** London

233

Drinking age law may vary across country

SUNDAY TIMES APRIL 12,2001,ENGLAND

James Clark
Home Affairs Correspondent

THE minimum age for drinking in pubs and clubs could vary across the country under an American-style system being considered by ministers.

If Labour wins the election, the Home Office will consider a proposal to allow local councils to set minimum ages. It would be similar to America, where some states allow drinking at 18, others at 21. They can also impose bylaws about public and private consumption.

The controversial suggestion has been greeted warily by councils, which fear the possibility of hundreds of youths crossing the "county line" at night. It is one of a number of topics that will be put out for discussion in a green paper during any Labour second term as ministers launch a crackdown on alcohol-related crime.

Drink is the largest "driver" of crime in Britain and Jack Straw, the home secretary, wants to examine ways of reducing the problem, which is partly responsible for the 13% rise in violent crime under Labour. The health department, which bears the cost of alcohol-related crime in accident and emergency departments across the country, also backs action.

the move. They face stiff penalties for selling to anyone aged under 18, but complain that it can be impossible to tell.

The proposed crackdown is likely to see heavier penalties for pubs and clubs that breach licensing laws, while at the same time seeing an end to the 11pm "chucking out" time that sends thousands of youths on to the streets at exactly the same time. A new, more continental system would "ration" the numbers leaving bars.

Other suggestions will include making alcohol an aggravating factor in crimes, as well as educational campaigns about the dangers of alcohol.

The reaction among councils was varied. Tom Franklin, leader of Lambeth council, south London, said: "We would welcome greater flexibility."

Paul O'Grady, of Bournemouth council in Dorset, said: "If such legislation becomes law, we probably wouldn't change the current age range for alcohol purchase or consumption, as Bournemouth has a lot of pubs and nightclubs that cater for different age groups."

Terry James, leader of Herefordshire council, said: "I think it's absolutely barmy — a complete nanny state. We can't control the use of drugs, let alone the age at which children drink."

World Health Organization Press Office

FACT SHEET

1211 Geneva 27 Switzerland • Telephone: 791 2111 • Cables: UNISANTE-GENEVA • Telex: 415 416 • Fax: 791 0746

Fact Sheet N° 127
August 1996

TRENDS IN SUBSTANCE USE AND ASSOCIATED HEALTH PROBLEMS
FACTS ABOUT ALCOHOL

■ Alcohol is consumed in most, although not all, countries. However, drinking habits vary in different cultures. In some, traditional patterns of drinking are occasional and celebratory, while in others, alcohol plays a role as part of the diet.

■ Alcohol can bring both benefit and harm to the individual. Most of the scientific evidence about the benefit as well as the harm derives from industrialized countries and cultures where alcohol consumption is largely accepted and where diet and lifestyles lend themselves to heart problems. Any possible benefit from alcohol should therefore be considered in its socio-cultural context and cannot be generalized to those cultures and societies where drinking is not acceptable and abstention is the norm.

■ Alcohol consumption has been found to reduce, in certain age groups, the risk of coronary heart disease and ischaemic stroke. Despite this individual benefit, the harm associated with the misuse of alcohol constitutes a major public health problem in both developed and developing countries. According to statistics available to WHO, there are around three quarters of a million alcohol-related deaths each year. Alcohol-related diseases and injuries account for between three to four per cent of the annual global burden of disease and injury. Alcohol is a significant factor in hospital admissions, road traffic deaths, industrial accidents, accidental drowning, homicide and suicide.

■ The morbidity and disability resulting from alcohol misuse represent a major burden to nearly all countries in the world. Quite apart from the problems affecting individuals, alcohol is implicated in a range of social problems including domestic violence, marital breakdown, absenteeism from work, and child abuse.

■ Young people can be particularly vulnerable to acute alcohol effects because of their lower tolerance to alcohol, their lack of experience with drinking, and their more hazardous patterns of drinking which include episodic drinking in high risk situations.

■ Women are also at higher risk of alcohol-related harm than men because of their physical differences related to body weight and composition of fatty tissue. Women reach a higher blood alcohol concentration than men for the same amount of alcohol consumed. Drinking during pregnancy has been linked with a higher risk of miscarriage, still birth and premature births, and foetal alcohol syndrome.

■ The World Health Organization strives to reduce the morbidity and mortality caused by the use of alcohol. However, there is no single solution to reducing alcohol related harm. What is required is a comprehensive range of strategies which can address the many causes and dimensions of alcohol problems. Such strategies may include:

- controls on price and availability;
- minimum age for purchase of alcohol;
- legislative measures to curb driving while under the influence of alcohol;

235

WHO

Press Release EURO 2/01
Copenhagen & Stockholm

19 February 2001

Alcohol – number-one killer of young men in Europe

Health ministers gather to review new evidence and take action to save young people's lives

One in four deaths of European men in the group aged 15–29 years is related to alcohol. In parts of eastern Europe, the figure is as high as one in three. All in all, 55 000 young people in the WHO European Region died from causes related to alcohol use in 1999.

These shocking new data from the WHO Global Burden of Disease 2000 Study set the scene today, as health ministers, other high-ranking decision-makers and young people from the 51 countries in the European Region gathered in Stockholm for the WHO European Ministerial Conference on Young People and Alcohol. The Conference aims to agree on Region-wide action to reverse harmful trends related to changing patterns of alcohol consumption by young people and aggressive marketing by the drinks industry.

"Over the past 10–15 years, we have seen that the young have become an important target for marketing of alcoholic products. When large marketing resources are directed towards influencing youth behaviour, creating a balanced and healthy attitude to alcohol becomes increasingly difficult," stated Dr Gro Harlem Brundtland, WHO Director-General, in her opening remarks. "Based on these concerns, I am calling for a concerted review by international experts of this issue of marketing and promotion of alcohol to young people."

WHO will host a meeting on the impact of global marketing and promotion of alcohol, in collaboration with the Government of Valencia, in Spain later this year. WHO will also establish a strategy advisory committee on alcohol to address this serious public health problem.

In his address to the delegates, Dr Marc Danzon, WHO Regional Director for Europe, said "I understand that progress is not easily made in this area. Alcohol is deeply embedded in the culture and social activities of many societies. Health policies must have popular support based on an understanding of their importance. To help countries gain this support, the Regional Office is launching a new European alcohol monitoring system. This will provide on-going information on consumption, harm, drinks marketing and country experience in protecting public health."

As part of the programme for the Swedish presidency of the European Union (EU), the Conference agenda includes a special working-group session on future EU action on alcohol.

Page 42 NEWSDAY Tuesday February 20, 2001

WHO warns of youth alcohol danger

STOCKHOLM: Aggressive alcohol marketing endangers young people's lives and governments must work across borders to protect children in the Internet age, the World Health Organisation (WHO) said yesterday.

Opening a conference on youth and alcohol, WHO officials said drinks makers were cynically targeting impressionable young people, who were increasingly using alcohol like a drug.

"Young people are vulnerable. They need to be protected. They need to grow up without being drawn into something

that can ruin their life, change their future and lead to alcohol dependence", WHO Director-General Gro Harlem Brundtland told a news conference.

"Someone has to take a stand."

WHO Regional Director Marc Danzon said policy-makers must counteract the glamorous image of alcohol peddled by multinational drinks companies.

"We need to raise understanding among young people that consuming alcohol is no different to consuming a drug," he said. "More and more it is seeming that as a product alcohol is being used like a

drug." Governments must pay attention to worrying trends in alcohol usage and put alcohol policy back at the top of their health agenda, Brundtland said, calling for an international review of the marketing and promotion of alcohol to young people.

"In these times of globalisation what used to be national decisions now have to be taken across borders," she said, citing new data showing alcohol accounted for one in four deaths among young men in Europe.

"By mixing alcohol with fruit juices,

energy drinks and premixed 'alcopops', and by using advertising that focuses on a youth lifestyle, sex, sports and fun, the large alcohol manufacturers are trying to establish a habit of drinking alcohol at a very young age," she said.

Alcohol was involved in the deaths of 55,000 Europeans aged between 15 and 29 years in 1999, many through accidents, fires, drownings, suicides and violent crimes.

Liquor taking its toll here

by **JENNI CAMPBELL**
Sunday Gleaner Staff
Reporter

VOLUME XLX   NO. 36   KINGSTON   JAMAICA   SEPTEMBER 3, 1995

THE SOBERING FACTS
percentage who have used alcohol

MALES 45%   **FEMALES** 21%   **STUDENTS** 75%

THE island's hospitals are burdened by mounting costs to treat patients of alcoholism and alcohol-related medical and psychological illnesses.

Doctors estimate that a quarter of all medical cases are alcohol-related, accounting for J$215.7 million of hospital costs.

"The use of alcohol is often at the root of liver conditions, renal failure, domestic violence, auto crashes, injuries due to falls and many other cases, drug abuse epidemiologist Dr. Wendel Abel said.

Dr. George Leveridge, who works at the St. Ann's Bay Hospital in St. Ann, says one in every four admissions has some bearing on alcohol use.

"Alcohol is socially acceptable and persons who would satisfy the criteria for alcoholism do not think that they have a problem; nobody, including the users, take the effects seriously," Dr.

to check through our files," works in western Jamaica, females and 75 per cent of students ... causes of accidental death. Dr.

Many victims of falls, drownings, fires and burns were found with substantial levels of alcohol in their bodies, when they turned up at hospitals for treatment. Alcohol addiction is also a prime factor in on-the-job accidents, as 40 per cent of industrial fatalities and 47 per cent of industrial injuries could be linked to alcohol use, Dr. Abel said.

"It affects the level of production," Dr. Abel said. "Approximately J$29, 240,000 in wages is lost annually owing to excessive alcohol consumption."

He said that of 150 persons interviewed in a study, he found that each spent an average of four months away from work annually due to alcohol-related conditions (such as hang-overs and illnesses).

Jamaica, which in 1994 produced over 93 million litres of alcoholic beverages, ranks among the highest in alcohol consumption, a World Health Organisation survey claims.

White rum, Dr. Leveridge says, is the most popularly-consumed

The Washington Post

120TH YEAR .... No. 82

TUESDAY, FEBRUARY 25, 1997

Don't BYOB, Park Service Says

Outside Alcohol to Be Banned on Mall and Other U.S. Parkland Downtown

By Linda Wheeler
Washington Post Staff Writer

Forget the keg of beer or the bottle of fine wine to celebrate the Fourth of July on the Mall this year. As of Saturday, the National Park Service will ban people from bringing alcoholic drinks to downtown federal parks and will limit sales by vendors, too.

The prohibition affects popular downtown lunchtime spots at Lafayette, Farragut and McPherson squares and the monumental core that stretches from the Lincoln Memorial to the Capitol. The order expands a ban already in effect at Hains Point, Dupont Circle and Logan Circle.

Park officials say the action responds to complaints about drunken behavior at neighborhood parks, as well as alcohol-related unruliness and crimes during the annual Independence Day celebration on the Mall and Washington Monument grounds.

"The Fourth is a unique animal," said Arnold Goldstein, superintendent of the downtown parks. "I have firsthand observations from the past several years: underage kids getting sick from drinking, people getting hit in the head with bottles, several dozen fights breaking out."

Goldstein said U.S. Park Police estimated that 100 kegs of

See ALCOHOL, A7, Col. 6

Road to Lapeyrouse paved with rum

Page 10 NEWSDAY Sunday May 2, 1999

GEORGE ALLEYNE

WHEN WE speak of alcoholism and drug abuse we very often dwell simply on wasted lives and moralise on aborted promise.

Officialdom may go yet further and total the man hours lost and the cost to Trinidad and Tobago in medical and rehabilitative care, as well as in industrial accidents, many of which result in uncomfortable downtime and lost profits.

But there is another aspect that we, generally, affect to ignore — that of the effect on the children of alcoholics and drug abusers.

Apart from the exposure of the children to the way of life of their parents, while they are hurt and annoyed by criticism of their parents' moral slide, they all too often feel themselves placed on the defensive and in resenting the harsh comments, come to the defence of their parents, both consciously and unconsciously.

They indulge in a mental somersault and see in the criticism and dismissal of their parents a criticism and dismissal of themselves.

And in too many instances, sadly, they would take defensive action, not in seeking to orally stand up for their alcohol and/or drug abusing parents, but in drinking and/or the use of drugs.

And as many of them grew older they were inclined not to continue rejecting their parents' lifestyles and abusive environment, but to take refuge in the very substance of abuse of their fathers and/or mothers. Was it that, unconsciously, they were seeking in some odd way to convince themselves that their parents were right and the critics of the community were wrong?

They identified with their parents' tragedy and became drinkers or other forms of abusers. In far, far too many cases the children of alcoholics, in particular, have become alcoholics themselves.

We tend to copy or mimic our parents, the way they speak, and in the case of sons, the way their fathers walk, the way their fathers talk.

But because drinking is socially acceptable we tend, for the most part, if we are weak and insecure to hold high the man who can drink extensively, yet hold his liquor.

The fact that he may be doing irreparable damage to his liver and may not be able to function 100 percent is of little concern. Admittedly, he is not as great a problem and indeed embarrassment to his family as the man who after a relatively few drinks is "high" and badly affected by the liquor. But his liver may go faster.

Alcohol and other forms of substance abuse may be the greatest contributory factors to road accidents. Alcohol dulls the senses and the reflexes of a man who has had a few are slower than before the start of drinking.

Yet the alcohol freak may, indeed very often does, believe that he can drive better after a few drinks. The roads to Lapeyrouse and Paradise are proof that this is fallacious thinking.

The damage is repeated, as I stated earlier, in children who follow their parents into drinking. Perhaps the day will come when the society will demand of its Government that positive action be taken to discourage the use of alcohol. The United States tried it once and failed. Perhaps we can find a middle road.

Police Take Anti-Alcohol Stand in D.C.

Department to Oppose Fests That Sell Spirits

washington post september ...

By Linda Wheeler
Washington Post Staff Writer

WASHINGTON POST SEPTEMBER 28,1997,USA

The D.C. police department says it will oppose alcohol sales at festivals held in city parks and on District streets, following the lead of a similar ban in federal parks.

The decision, which is not binding on other city agencies, was prompted by a religious coalition's unsuccessful protest of a festival permit granted to the Mid-Atlantic Beer and Food Festival. Police said no problems were reported at the festival, which was held this month on four blocks in downtown Washington.

Terry Lynch, executive director of the Downtown Cluster of Congregations, had argued that the city should not promote alcohol consumption by closing streets and supplying police security.

D.C. Police Chief Larry D. Soulsby sided with Lynch at the urging of Capt. Michael Radzilowski, commander of the Special Events Branch, who sits on the city's task force that monitors festival permits. Radzilowski cited the department's recent emphasis on community involvement, neighborhood patrols and other quality-of-life issues.

"Keeping with the new mission of the police department to eliminate crime and the fear of crime and general disorder, while establishing the trust and respect of the community, we have decided to go in front of the mayor's task force and say we prefer alcohol not be permitted or sold on public space," Radzilowski said.

City Considers Alcohol Ban At Street Fairs

New York Times July 21, 2000

By C. J. CHIVERS p3 B1;B6

NEW YORK TIMES JULY 21,2000,USA

Glasses of white wine and cups of ice-cold draft beer, two thirst-quenching staples of summer festivals, could soon become memories of days gone by on the streets of New York, as the Giuliani administration is considering banning the sale of alcohol at outdoor street parties.

If the administration follows through with its plan, the ban would turn all manner of outdoor feasts — from the Feast of San Gennaro in Little Italy to the Ninth Avenue Food Festival in Clinton — into nonalcoholic affairs, parties at which sausage-and-pepper sandwiches and clams on the half shell would be washed down with soda, lemonade or bottled water. Violators would be ticketed under the city's open container law.

"This is under consideration," said Marilyn Mode, spokeswoman for the Police Department, who said the proposal was being reviewed with hopes of ensuring that the 400 open-air festivals held in the city each year provide "a peaceful and family-oriented atmosphere", for all who attend.

The plan has been met with surprise and consternation by organizers of festivals, some of whom said the city had recently notified them of its intentions to make the prohibition on alcohol sales a condition of street activity permits, which are required for all legal fairs and festivals.

"This could have a devastating impact on our feast and on the vendors who participate in it," said Arnold N. Kriss, general counsel for Figlia di San Gennaro Inc., the nonprofit group that is organizing the street fair for Sept. 14 to 24.

Publicly, city officials said the proposal is an extension of the city's quality-of-life campaign, from the crackdown of squeegee men at the beginning of Mayor Rudolph W. Giuliani's first term to the more recent enforcement of open-container violations during tailgate parties at Shea Stadium.

Privately, however, the authorities said the plan was a response to the events after the National Puerto Rican Day Parade on June 11, when scores of young men attacked at least 59 women in or near Central Park. After the attacks, witnesses said many of the assailants had been drinking or smoking marijuana

241

Surgeon General Links Teen Drinking to Crime, Injuries, Unsafe Sex

By Paul Taylor
Washington Post Staff Writer

WASHINGTON POST APRIL 14,1992,USA

The more teenagers drink, the likelier they are to be perpetrators and victims of crime, to suffer injuries and to practice unsafe sex, according to the latest in a series of reports on underage drinking released yesterday by Surgeon General Antonia C. Novello.

Novello cited Justice Department figures showing that alcohol consumption is associated with 27 percent of all murders, 31 percent of all rapes, 33 percent of all property offenses and 37 percent of all robberies committed by youths.

In addition to giving adolescents the "false courage" to commit crimes, Novello said, drinking makes them more likely victims of violence because intoxicated youths tend to "provoke assailants, act vulnerable and fail to take normal common-sensical precautions."

Among college students and teenagers, alcohol use is associated with one-third to two-thirds of all cases of acquaintance or "date rape," with roughly the same incidence of intoxication reported by perpetrator and victim alike.

Novello said she was "shocked" by a survey of high school students in which nearly one in five girls, and two in five boys, said it was "okay to force sex if the girl was drunk."

She cited research showing alcohol and/or drug use is the best predictor of early sexual activity, and is associated with more unplanned pregnancies, more sexually transmitted diseases and more HIV infection "than any other single causal factor."

In a related matter, a nonprofit foundation, the Carnegie Council on Adolescent Development, released a different report yesterday that characterized adolescents in America as "a kind of kind of battlefield, literally as well as figuratively," in which a quarter of the nation's teenagers are at high risk of engaging in health- and life-threatening activities.

The Carnegie report found that adolescents in the United States are 15 times more likely to die from homicide than their English counterparts. It found that suicide rates tripled among 10- to 14-year-olds and doubled among 15- to 19-year-olds between 1968 and 1985. And it found that between 1980 and 1986, reported physical abuse of children and adolescents rose by 58 percent and sexual abuse rose 214 percent.

The Carnegie report called for more school-based health clinics, fuller health insurance coverage for youths, tougher gun control laws and a reduction of sex and violence in television programs and in movies.

Festival Avoids Alcohol, Tobacco Support for the Good of the Community

WASHINGTON POST JULY 25, 1997, USA

FESTIVAL, From B1

over its two days last year, has been marred by violence, which police said was fueled in part by alcohol.

Last year, the festival was shut down early when three people were shot and wounded and two others were injured by broken bottles after several fights erupted among young men in the crowd. Festival organizers, community workers and police said, some of the violence was gang-related, aggravated in part by heavy drinking.

Afterward, festival organizers were blasted on the air by Elmer Huerta, a physician who is host of a popular local Spanish-language radio show on health issues. Huerta accused the organizers of selling out the community by relying so much on beer money.

The salvo led to meetings between Huerta and festival organizers. Per-domo said the festival's board of directors decided unanimously this year not to seek beer or tobacco sponsors.

The Marlboro cigarette company offered to be a sponsor, and organizers turned it down, Perdomo said. The festival has about $20,000 in sponsorship money lined up and is

company or foundation will help us," he said. "Right now, we don't know how we'll pay for" the festival.

During the last decade, alcoholic beverage and tobacco companies have poured millions of dollars into sponsoring minority events and publications. Some critics have said the corporate donations are a form of marketing to burgeoning consumer

currently running a $20,000 deficit, which could double by the end of the weekend, Perdomo said. "We hope a

groups—Latinos and blacks—who suffer disproportionately from alcoholism and diseases associated with smoking.

As word of the festival's decision spread through the Spanish-language press this week, Perdomo said, he received dozens of congratulatory phone calls, some from as far as Florida and New York.

Local health advocates and D.C. police joined in giving kudos to the festival's organizers.

LATINO FESTIVAL TO CLOSE STREETS

The 27th annual D.C. Latino Festival will be held from 11 a.m. to 7 p.m. tomorrow and Sunday on Pennsylvania Avenue from Ninth Street to 13th Street NW. The following streets will be closed from 9 p.m. today to 11 p.m. tomorrow and from 8 a.m. to 11 p.m. Sunday:

- 10th Street from E Street to Constitution Avenue NW.
- 11th Street from E Street to Pennsylvania Avenue NW.
- 12th Street from Constitution Avenue to E Street NW.
- 13th Street from E Street to Pennsylvania Avenue NW.
- Pennsylvania Avenue from Ninth Street to 14th Street NW.

SOURCE: D.C. Office of Emergency Preparedness

THE WASHINGTON POST

"They're very courageous should be commended for th stand in favor of public health in sr of the consequences," said Jeann Noltenius, executive director of t Latino Council on Alcohol and bacco, a nonprofit national gro that combats alcohol and toba problems among Latinos.

"This kind of action needs to taken in the Latino and black co munities. We applaud the Lat community for stepping up and s ing no to the seductive goodwill the alcohol and tobacco industrie said the Rev. Alpha Brown, chairm of the 'cause children count coaliti inc, a D.C. nonprofit group th fights underage drinking and sm ing.

Brown said he was so inspired, donated $100 to the festival from own pocket.

The festival will feature music at booths selling food, artwork, crat and educational material tomorro and Sunday on Pennsylvania Aven NW between Ninth and 13th street A parade will be held at 11 a. Sunday on Constitution Avenue N between Seventh and 14th stree NW.

Last Call: Alaska Town Trades the High Life for the Dry Life

By Hal Bernton
Special to The Washington Post

BARROW, Alaska—Jim Christensen's midnight police patrol used to be dominated by familiar, dreary tasks. He picked up binge drinkers who stumbled about—and occasionally died—in winter temperatures that sank below minus 40 F. He broke up domestic disputes of drunken men and women. He arrested tipsy drivers and cited beer-drinking youths.

Almost all of his work was somehow related to alcohol and its epidemic and often destructive abuse in America's northernmost town, an outpost nearly 300 miles inside the Arctic Circle.

But during the past few months, a remarkable quiet has settled over Christensen's work and that of Barrow's other public safety officers. On a recent patrol, he found no one stirring in a battered public housing apartment whose hallways used to serve as a hangout for chronic drinkers. The streets—once alive with vehicles ferrying drinkers from party to party—were almost empty, as was the jail. Even the detox center had beds to spare.

"I've been here 18 years and never seen it so quiet," Christensen said. "My biggest complaint is that it's boring—almost too boring."

Barrow has gone dry. Following an October election in which voters once again barred the sale of alcohol, the town that tolerated its importation and posses-

sion now bans booze completely. Possession of alcoholic beverages subjects offenders to fines of up to $1,000.

The ban, which went into effect Nov. 1, was approved by a narrow seven-vote margin, and prohibition in this town of about 3,500 is proving just about as controversial as it did in Chicago in the 1920s. Most of the town's residents are Inupiat, the Northern Eskimos; their leaders, largely drawn from the ranks of local whaling captains, lobbied hard to outlaw alcohol. They said they'd had enough of child abuse and neglect, suicides, murder and accidents

before the ban took hold. In the next four weeks, those visits dropped to 35.

"People are sober, and we have time now to sleep through the night," Peters said. "It's been a paradise."

Others argue that the ban may have curbed some drinkers but that others either have become more secretive or leave Barrow to binge in the bars of Fairbanks and Anchorage. Many non-natives, as well as some Inupiat, don't believe the government should dictate drinking habits, and they have petitioned for a new election that could bring alcohol back to town. "I've done nothing to

WASHINGTON POST MARCH 11, 1995, USA

Night life in Barrow, Alaska, has quieted down since the town approved prohibition in October.

ctime even more accessible as oil wealth turned Barrow into a far-

(B) ALCOHOL MENTAL AND PSYCHOLOGICAL EFFECTS:

Reporter LOUIS B HOMER
Photographer SHIRLEY BAHADUR

Drinking alcohol is destructive

TRINIDAD GUARDIAN April 29, 1995

SHOBA DUBAY

GAYTREE BEEPAT

REHANA ABRAHAM

JILL SITAHAL

RONNIE FARFAN

LENNON BORREL

SIMONE JEFFERS

DALIA CLIFFORDS

DAWN BOODRAM

PETER DAVE FAIRLEY

SHURLAND SINGH

LORNE ALLADIN

MOHAMMED HADID

JUSTIN HERNANDEZ

SHOBA DUBAY 17, Harris Village, San Fernando, self employed,

"I do not believe that young people should be drinking alcohol. The money that is used for buying it could be put to other uses, especially at a time when there is a shortage of money.

What upsets me about people who drink is the way they behave after they have had a few drinks. They want to touch and hug and make all sorts of advances."

GAYTREE BEEPAT 20, 11 Concord Street, La Romaine.

"I think that drinking alcohol is totally bad. Physically and mentally it causes damage to the person who indulges in it. People who drink have a limited number of friends because most people do not like to associate with them. They often cause a lot of problems to their families. When they drink they do not know how to behave. People who indulge in alcohol are always in financial troubles."

REHANA ABRAHAM 13, La Fortune Woodland

"A relative of mine drinks with other people and he behaves in such a way that I am ashamed of him. He sets a bad example. What I dislike about people who drink is that they like to touch and can't control themselves whenever they get drunk.

An occasional drink is not bad, but when it is overdone it becomes a real problem not only for those who drink but also for their family."

LENNON BORREL, 4 Market Street, Palo Seco

"I do not believe that teenagers should drink alcohol. Even at Carnival adults should

they consume.

Drinking leads to bad behaviour and many persons become violent after they have had a few drinks"

SIMONE JEFFERS 18, of St Joseph's Convent, San Fernando

"I do not approve of young people drinking alcohol. Although it makes them feel cool it retards their reflexes and they do things they will not normally do.

The law should be stricter on those proprietors who sell alcohol to young people. Excessive drinking has been the cause of domestic violence.

It also affects the mental behaviour of

on the sale of alcohol to prevent people from drinking excessively."

DALIA CLIFFORDS 16, Gulf View

"Young people are still drinking alcohol although there are laws preventing the sale to those under 18 years. Teenagers who attend concerts are allowed to drink freely.

Once a teenager starts to drink it is difficult for him or her to stop. When they receive a driver's licence another type of trouble begins.

We need to work on the causes why people drink and treat the problem from these.

SHURLAND SINGH 21, unemployed

"I used to drink but when I realised that it could have led me astray I stopped. Drinking alcohol is the fastest way to lead young people astray. Since I have stopped I am at a higher level of behaviour.

In many cases alcohol has been the cause of the breaking up of families. People should not be drinking at all."

LORNE ALLADIN 18, La Romaine

"I do not consume alcohol because it produces negative influences. I have seen too many relationships broken up because of drinking. What

is not of God should not be around".

MOHAMMED HADID 17, Claxton Bay

"Some people drink alcohol to take care of their problems. Alcohol is not a way out. It is a way to get inside of problems. Too many problems are caused by drinking."

JILL SITAHAL, 17

"Drinking is not good because it disrupts families. The way people behave after they drink is always terrible. Drinking causes financial problems and very often it is the children who suffer.

Those who drink will also suffer from kidney and lung problems. Peo-

ple at work are also affected by those who drink."

DAWN BOODRAM 17, Gasparillo

"Drinking alcohol is unhealthy and it causes a type of behaviour which is disliked by many persons. Drinking also causes many health and financial problems".

JUSTIN HERNANDEZ 22, Harris Street, San Fernando

"I don't have a problem with people drinking alcohol once they can handle the amount they drink. If I am liming I must have something to drink to make me feel real cool

RONNIE FARFAN 18, 67 Dow village, South Oropouche.

"When I am liming, I must have my drink. It makes me feel like a man. All I have to say though is that people should not overdo it"

PETER DAVE FAIRLEY 22, Piparo

"Drinking is good but it is not good to drink everyday. It should be occasional. Use it but don't abuse it"

Underage alcopop buyers beat store safety checks

by Paul Nuki and
Edin Hamzic

SUNDAY TIMES JUNE 22,1997,ENGLAND

CHILDREN as young as 15 are being illegally sold alcopops in supermarkets despite the stores' claims that tough new vetting procedures have eliminated underage buying.

A Sunday Times investigation has found that pupils can walk out of school and into a supermarket which will sell them the high-alcohol fruit drinks without challenge.

Ten days ago the big four supermarkets — Sainsbury, Tesco, Safeway and Asda — rejected a call by the Co-op to stop selling the drinks after The Sunday Times revealed that manufacturers were using alcopops, worth an estimated £375m in sales this year, to target underage drinkers.

Safeway, reflecting the line adopted by the big four, said rigorous security measures would prevent the drinks from being sold to those under 18. "We take a very responsible attitude to the selling of alcopop drinks," a spokesman said. "Our scanning technology in all stores provides a prompt to checkout operators to confirm that the purchaser of any alcohol is over 18."

Last week, however, a team of five underage teenagers had little problem buying alcopops in London, Manchester and Edinburgh. In total, 37 transactions were attempted at

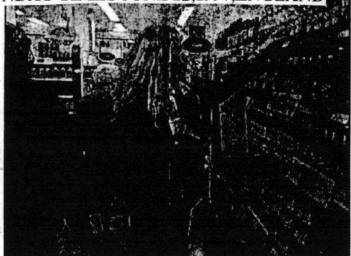

Buying a drink: Lisa Connor, 16, talked her way through

branches of 10 stores. In only four cases were the teenagers — aged 15 to 17 — challenged about their age. They were prevented from buying alcopops in only two stores.

Natalie Price, 15, from Kingston upon Thames, bought five bottles of alcopops, including Hooper's Hooch and Woody's Pink Grapefruit, from London branches of Sainsbury, Waitrose, Tesco, Asda and Somerfield in less than three hours. She was not challenged.

Lisa Connor, 16, from southwest London, was stopped at the checkout of Waitrose when she tried to buy two bottles of Hooch. "The cashier asked me if I had proof I was 18 and I said

no. Then she called her supervisor who asked how old I was. I said I was 21 and she waved me through," she said.

The only stores to refuse the teenagers alcopops were branches of Sainsbury in London and Manchester.

Last week all the stores approached by The Sunday Times's teenagers said they would investigate why their detection systems had failed.

George Howarth, the Home Office minister in charge of licensing, welcomed the Sunday Times survey. He said: "The government attaches great importance to the problem of alcopops and underage drinking."

Additional reporting: John Barratt

Why this beer is Strong

EXPRESS JANUARY 2, 1996

By DAVID CHASE

BRIAN LARA and Richard Clarke both attended Fatima College. Clarke remembers that he was "about two years ahead" of the world's greatest batsman at school. He is 27, one year older than Lara and also unmarried.

Like Lara, Clarke drinks beer.

He doesn't play cricket and doesn't even follow the game but, being a brewer, he makes the beer that the world's greatest batsman drinks... at least when he's in Trinidad and Tobago.

Three years ago, in 1992, Carib Brewery Ltd asked its Research and Development Department to come up with a beer of higher alcohol content than Carib.

Six weeks ago, Carib Strong was launched with much fanfare, giving beer-drinkers a stronger, more full-bodied and tastier product.

Main man behind the new beer was senior research and development technician and brewer, Richard Clarke.

Clarke, employed with Carib since 1992, told the Express in an interview on Friday that the new beer was 7.6 per cent alcohol, against the regular Carib's 5.2 per cent alcohol.

Carib Strong is slightly darker in colour, has more body than Carib and is more bitter; but that bitterness is offset by the beer also being sweeter, although the sweetness comes not from sugar but from what Clarke calls "esters", by-products of fermentation also known as "higher alcohols" and which he described as very flavourful.

ing out the light. Beer, Clarke explained, was photosensitive and deteriorated if exposed to light for long periods.

He didn't actually say it, but one got the impression that drinkers of regular Carib were "putting away" the product so quickly that the light was hardly getting to it. He did say, though, that Carib lovers preferred the flint bottle because it allowed them to see what the product looked like.

Carib, said Clarke, was one of a very few beers in the world which were marketed in flint bottles.

Clarke said that in the six weeks that Carib Strong had been on the market, the new beer had received "phenomenal acceptance. Demand has been greater than supply" and the product has been selling more than Stag and Heineken put together.

He was quick to note, however, that Carib would remain the brewery's main focus. But when you belly-up to the bar and call for a beer, have you ever wondered just what goes into its making?

The basic ingredients are malt, hops, yeast and treated water.

"Water," said Clarke, "is not the best in the world" and must be filtered and sanitised and have its hardness increased by the addition of calcium which improves taste and yeast performance in a process known as Burtonising, a name derived from Burton-on-Trent, the name of a town on the River Trent in England.

The malt, a malted barley imported from Europe, is gently heated and this produces sugar... by enzyme activity.

RICHARD CLARKE

NEWSDAY Saturday December 23, 1995

ALCOHOL NEWSDAY DECEMBER 23,1995 page 5

Caribs against Carib Strong

DESCENDANTS of the Carib people in Trinidad are strongly objecting to the new Carib Strong advertisements.

In a letter signed by Joseph Huracan and Susan Ayohalre, claiming to be descendants of the indigenous Caribs, the characters used in the commercials to promote the new popular beer was objected to. It stated:

"As descendants of original peoples, we must voice our disgust over the recent Carib Strong advertisments, in particular the television spot, which uses a Native American representation, seemingly of a North American tribe, to sell the alcoholic beverage.

"It is obscene, firstly, that the descendants of the people who first slaughtered, mutilated and culturally brutalised the original inhabitants of this country, should now call an alcoholic beverage by that name. The name must be removed. This is a dialogue that has been too long in coming.

"This is secondly all the more heinous when one considers that alcohol was one of the main weapons of the colonisers wherever they went, along with their guns and Christian religion.

"Even today in North America — the home of the tribes which the actor attempts to imitate — alcoholism is still one of the major scourges of Native Americans. These people are still oppressed and held on reservations — even suffering worse internal and external oppressions than black people in the USA. Alcohol is still being used today to cloud the minds of people from consciousness as it was used in slavery.

"It is therefore a crime against humanity, specifically indigenous Amerindians — the Caribs, Arawaks, Ciboney — who already are under-represented and misrepresented in our history and popular imagination, for the real owners and benefactors of "Carib" to use these people as objects even if one or two of them can be bought.

"The untruth of the historical stereotype of the Arawaks being passive and doll-like the Caribs, warlike cannibals, still persists in our history books. But the truth is a conscious Western policy of genocide has resulted in the extinction — no the murder of at least 100 nations/ tribes of living, breathing, beautiful peoples and the death of 20 million.

"Right now there are many protests internationally especially in the USA, against such ads and namings which objectify a people and commodify their heritage, sacred dances and sacred objects for the purpose of selling products.

"This is not the lie of Pocahontas, this is the truth of now. Amerindian peoples are not dead and have no intention to keep silent and/or die and we will not have our tribal nation, sacred dances, objects, songs, places desecrated — especially by the descendants of our attackers.

"This country was the home of a civilisation of peoples before the invasion by European powers. This is a call to all the now resident peoples, especially those with Amerindian ancestry to find out more about the harmonious and dynamic human culture that existed here before and for them to respect the living and dead presences.

"We call on the relevant parties to withdraw the campaign immediately and change the name. International indigenous people pressure groups are being contacted as regards this matter."

248

School dinner? Make mine a lager

GUARDIAN Newspaper June 21, 2001, ENGLAND

Andrew Osborn in Brussels

British schoolchildren caught swigging beer know they will be punished but in Belgium, where quaffing ale is a national sport, schools are to start supplying pupils with beer at lunchtime, believing it to be healthier than fizzy drinks.

In a scheme that makes Britain's now defunct milk promotion campaign look tame by comparison, a Flemish beer lovers' club has approached 30 schools and suggested that they substitute low-alcohol beer, called tafelbier, for sugary drinks such as lemonade and Coca-Cola.

Apparently unconcerned at the prospect of pupils falling asleep at their desks in the afternoon, at least two schools have already agreed, and one has launched a pilot scheme.

Almost 80% of children who took part in the pilot scheme in Belgium's Limburg province said they had enjoyed having beer instead of a soft drink and other schools are expected to follow suit when the new school year begins in September.

According to the chairman of De Limburgse Biervrienden, the beer club behind the scheme, pupils will be able to choose between lager and bitter, neither of which will be stronger than 2.5% alcohol.

"Beer is for the whole family," its chairman, Rony Lange-naeken, said. "And this scheme will be for children between the ages of three and 15."

Citing a Belgian study which shows that soft drinks and fruit juice can increase the risk of obesity and even cancer in children, Mr Langenaeken argues that beer is healthier because it contains less sugar. "It's good for their figure and very healthy as well."

He dismisses the idea that pupils may become too intoxicated to concentrate on their studies. "You'd have to drink five or six litres of the stuff to get drunk and these will just be 25cl or 33cl bottles. I used to drink it when I was just six years old and I still do every day."

TORONTO STAR JULY 18,1999,CANADA

'90s crowd guzzling hard lemonade

Sweet taste masks high alcohol content that young set seeks

BY VINAY MENON
POP CULTURE REPORTER

As the room spins and the vodka vice clenches mercilessly around your dehydrated internal organs, the last thing you taste is lemon.

And as a rush of saliva coats the back of your throat and you crumble awkwardly in front of the porcelain god, you find yourself damning Mike.

Or Joe. Or Vex. Or whatever brand of hard-spiked lemonade you consumed excessively that evening.

Because, despite more than two years of "it's just a fad" and "it'll never last" street-wise prognostications, the postmodern cooler — heavy doses of hard alcohol imbued with lemon — seems here to stay.

"Coolers were a fad in the '80s that came and went," says Bob Froese, executive vice-president with The Brainstorm Group, a Toronto ad agency. "A lot of people still perceive the cooler category as what they remembered from the '80s, when in fact it is quite different today."

Indeed. About a dozen lemon-flavoured beers and vodka or rum-based products now flood the Toronto market. And they're helping boost booze consumption for the first time in more than a decade.

Statistics Canada reports that Canadians purchased 138.3 million litres of spirits in 1997-'98, up 6.8 per cent from 1996-'97.

And here's the citrus rub: There

bites you on the ass. You never see it coming."

Adam Vowles, 19, who has been drinking for four years, says, "The stuff tastes so good that people drink it faster and then get drunk faster."

Lemonades now represent about

Alcohol worse than illegal drugs
says expert

ADMINISTRATIVE officer of the National Drug Council (NDC), Esther Best, says she would quicker adopt a child exposed to cocaine or heroin, than one who is opened to alcohol.

Best, who spoke about "Facing Life Acceptance" at a recent seminar organised by Rebirth House, told recovering addicts that legal substances are," much more detrimental to a child than an illegal drug.

"We often ostracise women who smoke cocaine.

"I am not saying that it is okay to take cocaine.

"All I am saying, is that legal substances are far more dangerous to a child than an illegal substance.

"It's an undisputed fact and I will take on anyone on that.

"Alcohol has the most debilitating effects on a foetus and it is much more damaging to kids," Best said with concern.

ESTHER BEST

She also stated that we have no concept of how much abuse occur when someone consumes alcohol.

Best, who went abroad to study social work and was placed in a juvenile detention facility, to help young boys, continued: "These boys knew more about life than I knew in my 28 years.

"We had children who were in there for parental neglect.

"There was even a 12-year-old boy who had shot a colleague outside of the school building."

She also spoke about one boy who was taken away from his alcoholic mother and placed under their care.

"Then one day she said she was coming to see him."

However, it turned out that the mother never showed up because she was too busy drinking with her friends, which left the lad devastated.

"She had put their meeting to another day.

"That night," Best related," the boy hung himself and when we went to tell her the tragic news she told us she will deal with her son's death later.

"She even went so far to say that she did nothing for him when he was alive, and so, she couldn't do anything now that he is dead."

A week later, the woman got a lawyer and sued the District of Columbia for the death of her son.

"Up to the last time I spoke to the social worker, she never accepted responsibility of not being there for her child, which pushed him over the edge.

"She didn't keep her promise," she continued, showing how things go wrong, when drugs come between families.

See ALCOHOL on Page 30

251

Maryland

DRIVER'S HANDBOOK

Maryland Department of Transportation
MOTOR VEHICLE ADMINISTRATION
6601 RITCHIE HIGHWAY, N.E.
GLEN BURNIE, MARYLAND 21062 USA

CHAPTER 4
ALCOHOL, DRUGS, AND DRIVING

In 1904, 400 persons died in auto accidents nationwide. During recent years, over 45,000 persons have died annually. Alcohol was a major factor in over half of these deaths. Whether drivers are social drinkers or heavy drinkers, all can be problem drivers once they are on the highway.

DRIVE TO SURVIVE

DON'T DRINK

THE PROBLEM

For the past several years, about half of all fatal motor vehicle crashes have alcohol as a cause. The numbers of potential accidents and near misses are unknown. Alcohol is responsible for more deaths on the highway than any other cause, drinking drivers and drinking pedestrians contributing directly to about half of all traffic deaths. Driving while under the influence of alcohol is one of the most irresponsible offenses you can commit. **A VEHICLE IN THE HANDS OF A PERSON INFLUENCED BY ALCOHOL IS A DEADLY WEAPON.**

THE EFFECTS OF ALCOHOL

When you drive, your brain is a computer, constantly receiving information through your senses and making decisions that help you keep your vehicle moving safely through traffic. Alcohol short-circuits the computer. It slows reflexes, impairs coordination, reduces visual acuity and dulls normal caution. The first driving ability affected by alcohol is judgment. Concentration becomes difficult. You can't think as clearly, as quickly or as rationally as you usually do and you can't act as fast.

But worse yet, you aren't aware of that. Along with everything else, alcohol short-circuits the red warning light in your computer. You don't know that you're impaired. You even develop a false sense of well-being and confidence. In short, you become a menace to yourself and everyone else on the highway.

It is difficult to convince a drinking person that small amounts of alcohol increase the possibility of becoming involved in accidents, particularly fatal ones. A person who has been drinking may:

- Drive too fast or too slow for prevailing conditions;
- Fail to dim lights for oncoming traffic;
- Pass improperly, leaving insufficient clearance, taking too long, or swerving too much;
- Make frequent lane changes;
- Fail to remain centered in the lane;
- Overshoot and/or disregard traffic signals;
- Lose alertness and adaptability in emergencies;
- Take too long to brake, longer than the normal person without a drink.

16

252
DRINKING AND DRIVING WILL RESULT IN
LOSS OF LICENSE

THE PHYSIOLOGY OF ALCOHOL

Alcohol is a drug. It's not a stimulant, even though its exhilarating effect makes people think it is. Actually, it's a depressant that affects your central nervous system. It acts much like an anesthetic to lower or depress the activity of your brain. You don't digest alcohol. It's absorbed directly into your blood stream where it is carried to all parts of the body, including the brain. And it's the concentration of alcohol in the blood that affects your judgment and your physical coordination. How fast alcohol builds up in the blood depends on several things:

- The amount of alcohol (number and strength of drinks consumed)
- Time elapsed since drinking began
- Body weight
- Quantity and kind of food in the stomach.

(Amount and kind of food only slows down the absorption process and extends the time it takes alcohol to enter the blood stream.)

DRINKING AND BLOOD ALCOHOL CONTENT

NOTE: Commercial drivers are not permitted to have any detectable alcohol in the blood or on the breath.

Blood alcohol content (BAC) is simply a precise way of stating the amount of alcohol in a quantity of blood. It is expressed in percent and is measured by chemical analysis.

For example, .05% (point-zero-five percent) stands for a specific percentage of alcohol in the bloodstream. At slightly above .05% BAC, the risk of causing a crash doubles. Some persons (especially inexperienced drinkers and inexperienced drivers) cannot drive safely even below .05%.

Immediately after an alcoholic beverage is swallowed, the alcohol starts to move from the stomach into the bloodstream. The rate of this movement and how much alcohol gets into the blood depends primarily on how much alcohol is in the drinks taken. The rate at which alcohol moves to the bloodstream is governed to a lesser extent by the amount of food in the stomach and the intestines. It depends only to a very limited extent upon how the drinks are mixed. Thus, two (2) ounces of pure alcohol taken into the stomach within a period of one hour will result in about the same blood alcohol content whether consumed as martinis, straight shots, highballs, wine, beer, or a mixture of these.

BAC is determined by the amount of alcohol consumed, the time required by the body to destroy alcohol, and the person's weight. The body eliminates alcohol at a constant rate that cannot be changed. A heavier person has more blood in his system to dilute alcohol. Therefore, a lighter person will be more affected if he drinks the same amount as the heavier person.

No two people react exactly the same to alcohol. Even your individual temperament and the mood you're in can affect the results of drinking to some degree.

The .05% to .10% range is critical. Somewhere in that range you've had too much to perform any activity that requires any degree of coordination or judgment. In particular, you are too intoxicated to drive.

If you think you might drink beyond .05%, let someone else drive, or take a cab or bus. It may be the most important thing you ever did.

If you drive or attempt to drive at a BAC level of under .05% there is legal presumption that you are not under the influence of alcohol. A BAC level of .07% but less than 0.10, is

17

253

CRIMINAL AND ADMINISTRATIVE PENALTIES FOR DRIVING WHILE INTOXICATED OR DRIVING UNDER THE INFLUENCE OF ALCOHOL, WHILE UNDER THE INFLUENCE OF DRUGS, OR A CONTROLLED DANGEROUS SUBSTANCE

1. Any person who drives or attempts to drive a motor vehicle on a highway or on any private property that is used by the public in general in this State is deemed to have consented to take a test if the person should be detained on suspicion of driving or attempting to drive:

- While intoxicated;
- While under the influence of alcohol;
- While so far under the influence of any drug, any combination of drugs, or a combination of one or more drugs and alcohol;
- While under the influence of a controlled dangerous substance;
- In violation of an alcohol restriction; or
- A commercial motor vehicle with any alcohol concentration.

A person may not be compelled to take a test, but upon receipt of a certified statement from a police officer that a test was refused, or that the results were an alcohol concentration of 0.10 or more, the Motor Vehicle Administration shall suspend the driver's license or driving privilege in Maryland as follows:

- A refusal: 120 days for a first offense and one year for a second or subsequent offense. In addition, if the person was operating a commercial motor vehicle, the commercial driver's license or commercial driving privilege will be disqualified for 1 year for a first offense, 3 years for a first offense while transporting hazardous materials required to be placarded, and disqualified for life for a second or subsequent offense while operating any commercial vehicle.

- Test Results of 0.10 Alcohol Concentration or More:
  45 days for a first offense and 90 days for a second or subsequent offense.

- Test results of 0.04 alcohol concentration or more when driving a commercial motor vehicle.

  A. Disqualified from driving a commercial motor vehicle for one year (three years if the vehicle was required to be placarded for HAZMAT) for the first offense.
  B. Disqualified for life for a second or subsequent offense.

The licensee has 30 days in which to request a hearing to show cause why the driver's license should not be suspended concerning the refusal to take a test for alcohol or for an alcohol concentration of 0.10 or more at the time of testing.

If the hearing is requested within 10 days from the issuance of the police officer's Order of Suspension, suspension will be stayed pending the hearing. Representation by an attorney is permitted at the hearing.

- Driving while intoxicated:

  A. First Conviction: Up to one year imprisonment and/or not more than $1,000 fine. While transporting a minor, up to two years imprisonment and/or not more than $2,000 fine.

  B. Second Conviction: Up to two years imprisonment and/or not more than $2,000 fine. While transporting a minor, up to three years imprisonment and/or not more than $3,000 fine. A conviction of this violation within three years after a prior conviction is also subject to a mandatory minimum penalty of imprisonment for not less than 48 consecutive hours, or community service for not less than 80 hours.

  C. Third or Subsequent Conviction: Up to three years imprisonment and/or not more than $3,000 fine. While transporting a minor, up to four years imprisonment and/or not more than $4,000 fine.

Driving privilege may be revoked for not less than 6 months.

In cases of a second revocation, the driving privilege may be revoked for not less than one year. In cases of a third revocation, the driving privilege may be revoked for not less than 18 months. In cases of a fourth or subsequent revocation, the driving privilege may be revoked for not less than 2 years.

20

254

The accompanying chart lists the penalties for OUI offenses occurring within a 10-year period.

Massachusetts

DRIVER'S MANUAL

U·S·A

Penalties for Operating a Motor Vehicle Under the Influence of Alcohol or Drugs			
Conviction (Within 10 Years)	Fine	Prison Term	License Suspension
First Offense	$500–$5,000	Maximum 2½ years	1 year
For your first offense, the court may allow you to complete an alcohol education course to reduce your license suspension period.			Over 21, 45–90 days Under 21, 210 days
Second Offense	$600–$10,000	Minimum 30 days Maximum 2½ years	2 years
Third Offense (Felony)	$1,000–$15,000	Minimum 150 days Maximum 5 years	8 years
Fourth Offense (Felony)	$1,500–$25,000	Minimum 1 year Maximum 5 years	10 years
Fifth Offense (Felony)	$2,000–$50,000	Minimum 2 years Maximum 5 years	Lifetime

Alcohol

Whether it's in the form of beer, wine, or hard liquor, alcohol is a depressant that **slows your reflexes, increases the time you need to react, and distorts your vision and judgment.** At the same time, alcohol often makes you *feel* more confident about your actions, and it can cause you to take chances while driving that you normally wouldn't take. This is a dangerous combination that often leads to serious motor vehicle accidents and tragic deaths.

were over 18 at the time of the offense) and will reduce to 180 days the 1-year suspension (if you were under 18 at the time of the offense), in addition to the suspension already imposed and any penalty assessed as a result of your court case or any other law. If you fail to complete the program, you will be subject to the full suspension period. A reinstatement fee will also apply.

Buying, Possessing or Transporting Alcohol

If you are under 21, it is illegal to...

- Buy alcohol or have someone buy it for you
- Possess, carry, or transport alcohol unless accompanied by a parent or guardian

Violating either of these laws requires a 90-day to 1-year license suspension and possible fines and other penalties. **The penalty for buying or attempting to buy alcoholic beverages by a person under 21 has increased to 180 days.**

Open Container Law

You may *not* drink alcohol while driving or have an open alcoholic beverage inside your vehicle. If you are convicted of this offense, you will be fined $100 to $500. If you are under 21, you can be arrested, fined, and have your license suspended.

False or Altered Licenses/ Identification Cards

It is against the law to use a false license or ID, to alter a license or ID, or to use another person's license or ID. It is also against the law to use false information to obtain a license or ID. In most cases illegal use of these is a felony and serious penalties may apply. These penalties are not limited to an attempt to purchase alcohol. *M.G.L.c.90,§22(e) allows the RMV to suspend your license or right to operate in Massachusetts for 6 months. A conviction is not required. If you are convicted of this offense, your license will be suspended for 1 year.*

256

HIGHWAY CODE

ENGLAND

Penalty table

| Offence | Maximum penalties | | | |

Offence	IMPRISONMENT	FINE	DISQUALIFICATION	PENALTY POINTS
*Causing death by dangerous driving	10 years	Unlimited	Obligatory–2 years minimum	3–11 (if exceptionally not disqualified)
*Dangerous driving	2 years	Unlimited	Obligatory	3–11 (if exceptionally not disqualified)
Causing death by careless driving under the influence of drink or drugs	10 years	Unlimited	Obligatory–2 years minimum	3–11 (if exceptionally not disqualified)
Careless or inconsiderate driving	-	£2,500	Discretionary	3–9
Driving while unfit through drink or drugs or with excess alcohol; or failing to provide a specimen for analysis	6 months	£5,000	Obligatory	3–11 (if exceptionally not disqualified)
Failing to stop after an accident or failing to report an accident	6 months	£5,000	Discretionary	5–10
Driving when disqualified	6 months (12 months in Scotland)	£5,000	Discretionary	6
Driving after refusal or revocation of licence on medical grounds	6 months	£5,000	Discretionary	3–6
Driving without insurance	-	£5,000	Discretionary	6–8
Driving otherwise than in accordance with a licence	-	£1,000	Discretionary	3–6
Speeding	-	£1,000 (£2,500 for motorway offences)	Discretionary	3–6 or 3 (fixed penalty)
Traffic light offences	-	£1,000	Discretionary	3
No MOT certificate	-	£1,000	-	-
Seat belt offences	-	£1,000	-	-
Dangerous cycling	-	£2,500	-	-
Careless cycling	-	£1,000	-	-
Cycling on pavement	-	£500	-	-
Failing to identify driver of a vehicle	-	£1,000	Discretionary	3

Alcohol

* Where a court disqualifies a person on conviction for one of these offences, it must order an extended retest. The courts also have discretion to order a retest for any other offence which carries penalty points: an extended retest where disqualification is obligatory, and an ordinary test where disqualification is not obligatory.

88

257

New drivers. Special rules apply to drivers within two years of the date of passing their driving test if they passed the test after 1 June 1997 and held nothing but a provisional (learner) licence before passing the test. If the number of penalty points on their licence reaches six or more as a result of offences they commit before the two years are over (including any they committed before they passed the test), their licence will be revoked. They must then reapply for a provisional licence and may drive only as learners until they pass a theory and practical driving test.
Law RT(ND)A

Note. This applies even if they pay by fixed penalty. Drivers who already have a full licence for one type of vehicle are not affected by this when they pass a test to drive another type.

Other consequences of offending
Where an offence is punishable by imprisonment then the vehicle used to commit the offence may be confiscated.

In addition to the penalties a court may decide to impose, the cost of insurance is likely to rise considerably following conviction for a serious driving offence. This is because insurance companies consider such drivers are more likely to have an accident.

Drivers disqualified for drinking and driving twice within 10 years, or once if they are over two and a half times the legal limit, or those who refused to give a specimen, also have to satisfy the Driver and Vehicle Licensing Agency's Medical Branch that they do not have an alcohol problem and are otherwise fit to drive before their licence is returned at the end of their period of disqualification. Persistent misuse of drugs or alcohol may lead to the withdrawal of a driving licence.

6. Vehicle maintenance, safety and security

Vehicle maintenance
Take special care that lights, brakes, steering, exhaust system, seat belts, demisters, wipers and washers are all working. Also
- lights, indicators, reflectors, and number plates **MUST** be kept clean and clear
- windscreens and windows **MUST** be kept clean and free from obstructions to vision

89

258

TORONTO STAR DECEMBER 13, 1993

Impaired driving charges up 39%

Higher-alcohol beer may be a factor, police say

BY CAL MILLAR
STAFF REPORTER

There's been a 39 per cent increase in the number of people charged so far this Christmas season with drinking and driving, Metro police say.

They are still trying to determine reasons for the increase over last year.

But one factor may be that more people are drinking home brew and new brands of beer on the market this winter with higher alcohol content, said Metro Constable Devin Kealey.

Many people may be getting into cars and driving without realizing they've gone over the limit, he said.

"Drivers have to be educated about what they're drinking," Kealey said.

"Right now they're going to parties and drinking what they think is a safe limit, but they may be getting quite a bit more alcohol.

As of Friday, the latest day for which figures are available, 39 people had been charged with impaired driving through the R.I.D.E. program (Reduce Impaired Driving Everywhere), compared with 28 for the same period last year.

Police have checked 96,121 vehicles so far during the month-long 1993 campaign, compared with 93,583 motorists stopped during the same time last year.

Despite the increase in impaired driving charges, Kealey said there haven't been any fatalities in Metro.

"Everyone must be encouraged not to drink and drive," he said.

"It's important for everyone to realize that impairment begins with the first drink."

236

259

Canada's worst crime is drunk driving: Judge

TORONTO STAR JANUARY 29,1995,CANADA

BY DAVID VIENNEAU
OTTAWA BUREAU CHIEF

OTTAWA — Drunk driving is the most horrific crime in Canada, causing injury, death and heartache for thousands of people, a Supreme Court of Canada judge has declared.

"Every year, drunk driving leaves a terrible trail of death, injury, heartbreak and destruction," Mr. Justice Peter Cory wrote in a judgment released Friday.

"In terms of deaths and serious injuries resulting in hospitalization, drunk driving is clearly the crime which causes the most significant social loss to the country."

Cory's concerns were expressed in a 9-0 decision in which the court restored the 1991 impaired driving conviction of Nathen Bernshaw of Victoria, B.C.

In so doing, it tinkered with the rules governing roadside ALERT breath tests. A majority of the court determined police could wait 15 minutes before asking a suspected impaired driver to provide a breath sample.

TOUGH STAND

Evidence shows that ALERT test results can be inaccurate if just prior to the test the individual has consumed alcohol, belched or vomited. Friday's decision marked the second time in as many days that the court has taken a tough stand on drinking and driving.

Thursday it warned bar owners they could be held liable if their soused patrons injure somebody after heading out on to the highway. It has previously upheld the constitutionality of ALERT roadside tests.

In Friday's decision, Cory referred to Statistics Canada figures that paint a shocking picture of carnage on Canadians roads and highways.

The agency reported that alcohol was a contributing factor in 43 per cent of motor vehicle accidents between 1983 and 1991, leading to 17,630 deaths and almost 1.1 million injuries.

Other Statistics Canada figures showed that in 1987, accidents in which alcohol was a factor were responsible for 327,660 days of in-hospital medical treatment and more than 5.1 million days of lost activity and employment.

"These figures are mute but shocking testimony demonstrating the tragic effects and devastating consequences of drinking and driving," Cory wrote.

"The social cost of the crime, great as it is, fades in comparison to the personal loss suffered by the victims of this crime through the death and injury of their loved ones."

Bernshaw was stopped by police after they noticed his car drifting back and forth on the road. He was asked to provide a sample of breath for the ALERT device and it recorded a "fail" mark.

Bernshaw's trial conviction was overturned when the B. C. Court of Appeal agreed with his lawyer that the police officer should have asked whether he had been drinking in the previous 15 minutes before the test.

The way police administer roadside tests is important because they must have reasonable and probable grounds to suspect someone is driving impaired before they can demand a formal breathalyser test for use in court.

Failure to pass an ALERT test has been considered reasonable grounds.

WAIT 15 MINUTES

While the court was unanimous in restoring Bernshaw's conviction, the judges reached their decision through three routes.

Four judges, led by John Sopinka, determined it was okay for police to wait 15 minutes to administer a roadside ALERT breath test if they had reason to believe an immediate test would skewer the accuracy of the results.

Sopinka wrote that in this instance, the weaving car had given police reasonable grounds to administer the test.

Three others, led by Cory, said the ALERT test should be administered immediately, regardless of whether the alleged drunk driver had only just imbibed, belched or regurgitated.

"The requirement to undergo the ALERT testing immediately should be regarded as one of the obligations that flow from the right to drive," Cory wrote.

"An impaired driver is a potentially lethal hazard that must be detected and removed from the road as quickly as possible."

Hundreds lose licences

...for drunk driving since Breathalyser

GLEANER JUNE 24,1997 JAMAICA

By Reginald Allen
Staff Reporter

NEARLY 500 MOTORISTS have lost the right to operate motor vehicles after being convicted for driving under the influence of alcohol since the Breathalyser test was introduced in November 1995. Some 772 evidence (fixed centre) tests have been done so far.

Those testing positive – numbering 711 – include three women and two police personnel who were driving private motor vehicles.

About 47 per cent, or 364, of these offenders figured in traffic accidents, according to the Police Information Centre (PIC).

Other than those involved in traffic accidents, for whom the Breathalyser test is mandatory, testing is done in circumstances where the police have "reasonable cause" to believe a motorist is driving under the influence of alcohol, for example, zigzag driving and alcohol on the breath.

Conviction for first time offenders carries a fine of $3,000 or up to six months in prison, with 14 demerit points. This almost guarantees automatic suspension of the offender's driving licence for a period to be determined by a Resident Magistrate. A second offence could attract a $5,000 fine or 12 months' imprisonment.

Former licensed driver Eric Xyminis of Golden Acres, Spanish Town, for example, felt the full weight of the Breathalyser Act last year when he pleaded guilty to driving under the influence of alcohol in the Old Harbour RM Court. After having failed to stop following his involvement in a traffic accident on the Mighty Gully bridge outside the St. Catherine town, Xyminis was slapped with a $3,000 fine for drunken driving, in addition to having his licence suspended for two years.

Police traffic Inspector B. Powell of Traffic Headquarters in Kingston said failure of the Breathalyser could land one in jail.

"It is an arrestable offence, so you would be taken into custody and brought before the court where, if you are convicted, your licence would most likely be seized there and then," Inspector Powell warned.

The resistant rate to the test continues to be low, the PIC indicated, pointing to only 50 persons (6.5 per cent) of those required to be tested refusing to do so. There were 31 cases of refusal in 1996. A refusal automatically attracts arrest.

Experts say it takes 35 milligrams of alcohol in 100 millilitres of breath, or 80 milligrams per 100 millitres of blood, to fail the Breathalyser test. This, on average, is said to be translated into three beers or two stronger drinks consumed within 60 to 90 minutes prior to the test.

Grieving Mom May Face Prison After Letting a Drunk Drive

Ex-Husband Took Daughters on Fatal Ride

WASHINGTON POST NOVEMBER 28,1994,USA

By Sue Anne Pressley
Washington Post Staff Writer

WIMBERLEY, Tex.—The last time Shirley Draper saw her ex-husband, Gregory Cook, and their two daughters alive was on a Sunday morning in late September as the trio climbed into Cook's 1992 automobile. They were headed to a restaurant in nearby San Marcos for breakfast.

The vehicle was a testament to Cook's chronic drinking and driving problems. Outfitted with a court-ordered system to measure blood-alcohol levels, the ignition would not start until Cook—or someone who was sober and willing to assist—breathed into the machine. On that Sunday, Sept. 25, Cook would not have been capable of starting the car; tests later showed he had a

blood-alcohol reading of 0.22, more than twice the legal limit for intoxication.

It would be three days before the car and its occupants were seen again, submerged in a pond at the bottom of a steep incline a few miles from Draper's home. Cook had plunged over the hill at high speed and into the 10-foot water. By then, Draper allegedly had told authorities she knew her ex-husband had been drinking heavily when he left her driveway with the children. Authorities say she also acknowledged she knew one of the young girls would have had to breathe into the machine for Cook to operate the car.

Now, in an unusual case that has divided this friendly central Texas community and is becoming a touchstone for the national movement against drunk driving, Draper, 34,

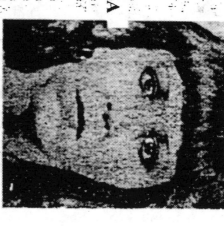

Shirley Draper's ex-husband had car with court-ordered breath analyzer.

has been indicted by a Hays County grand jury in the deaths of her daughters, Shauna Cook, 10, and Marissa, 8. Charged Nov. 10 with two counts of injury to a child and two counts of endangering a child, she faces the possibility of life in prison.

The case has the poignant elements of a tragedy that might have been averted, throwing open a window

See DRUNK,A1⁴, Col.4

CHAPTER 9. OBSCENITY, PONOGRAPHY, PROSTITUTES AND PIMPS, IS THIS WHAT YOU WANT YOUR DAUGHTERS AND SONS TO DO?

Drug lords or dealers in cocaine, other hard core drugs and other organised crime figures covertly disguise their illicit operations by utilising legitimate business places as fronts to throw off suspicion. Night clubs, discos liquor bars are some of these legal operations and places where women can be used in the sex trade. Monitoring on these business are police vice units and some raids often produce startling results.

EVENTS ARISING ON THE SUBJECT BETWEEN 1997-2002
  (a) "18 held for indecency" Express August 13,1997,page 3
  (b) "18 charged for dirty dancing,DJ to patrons: the more you pay, the more you see" Trinidad Guardian August 13, 1997, page 1
  (c) "12 held in club raid, women arrested for suggestive dancing" Trinidad Guardian August 22,1997, page 3
  (d) "16 held for indecent acts" Newsday August 13,1997
  (e) "Night clubs, police clash over lewd dancing laws" Newsday August 17, 1997, page 5
  (f) "10 charged with lewd acts in raids"Independent August 22,1997, page 5
  (g) "Lawyers ask cops to demonstrate lewd dancing" Express May 27, 1998, page 3
  (h) "Relatives weep for guilty nude dancer,14"Express November 20,2001
  (i) "Night club dancing mom escapes jail"Newsday June 21,2002

In 1998 after a year the issue came to the the forefront headlines as additional arrests were made by the police and defence lawyers for those arrested called for reform of the law. As a consequence, the Guardian Newspaper ran a commentary question:"Should dirty dancing be made legal" Trinidad Guardian August 29,1998,page 9.

During the interval between 1997 and 1998, there have been comments both pro and con the subject precipitated by eventful arrests which included fifteen women at the Santa Maria Hotel and bar. It was this case which created a stir because of the nature of the questions by the defence attorneys to the prosecuting police officers. Here are the comments in court asked by the defence attorney and responded to by the police "during the dance, I saw two defendants pull aside their underwear and exposed their vagina... I told the defendants that they were indecently attired and that they had indecently exposed their person."(quoted from the article "Lawyer ask cops to demonstrate lewd dancing" Express May 27,1998,page 3).

Another issue that is at the forefront is conformity to the laws that govern the use of "obscene language in public", in 1998 during a drama play by some leading actors/actresses at the Little Carib Theatre, the police had to warn the stage activists about the use of obscene language in the play "Jean and Dianh"

"Watch your contents police say"Express July 19,1998

"Controversy continues to surround Jean and Dinah" Express July 23, 1998.

In many countries there is a growing concern about the explicit sex and the expletive obscene language content in movies especially with cable programming. The US Government has challenged Holly wood to modify its programming policy and come up with remedies to curb exposure of children to excessive crime and sex displays. Other countries are too looking at levels of unsavoury shows and requiring family life quality programming. In the US the Federal Communications Commission(FCC) has already taken action including the sale of ponography at stores, New York City's mayor has zoned out such stores from the famous times square and others have followed suit.

LIBERTY ABSOLUTE, AND LIBERALISM ABSOLUTE HAVE BEEN CHALLENGED TO MODERATION BY DECENCY LIMITS.

TT MIRROR FEBRUARY 16, 2001

FRIDAY FEBRUARY 16, 2001

This is not a fete

This is madness!

WE know this picture is offensive.

We publish it to illustrate the "madness" now taking place at Carnival fetes across the country.

This is just one of several pictures of such vulgar poses brought back over the past few weeks by our photographers.

We apologise to readers who are offended by publication of this picture.

Picture by DERSON CHARLES.

EXPRESS FEBRUARY 16,1998, page 3
INDEPENDENT FEBRUARY 16,1998

THE MUSIC clearly went to the head of this woman as she lets it all hang out with a band of men around her during the Brass Festival fete at PSA grounds on Saturday night. The lady in question went on to strip off her pants and perform several lewd acts for her male admirers right in front of the cameras.

NOT ME, IS THE MUSIC

Photo: KENROY AMBRIS

young girl, whose behaviour created quite a stir.

among those who were cautioned by the police was this

266
Shameless behaviour
by some of our women
By WATCHDOG
BOMB JANUARY 23, 1998

AH DAMN fuming this week! How the hell show and dance organisers and police can allow dirty women to perform all sorts of shameless, disgraceful loud antics on a public forum and behave so vulgar at fetes and not do anything about it?

How can you have almost naked women wining, opening their legs wide to show of their G-Strings better and performing sexual acts on stage and nobody stops them?

It's disgusting and these women should be jailed. If they want to show off their "goods," then why don't they hold their own strip-tease shows privately? Look, we don't want more strippers and the authorities must do something immediately about that. Jail all of them for indecent exposure!

spending any money on protecting paying patrons from the slime who attend fetes to prey on innocent people enjoying themselves?

It appears not and probably that's why a brawl at the Carib fete in Champs Fleurs continued to get out of hand until a young man was stabbed.

People must stop attending these fetes if promoters can't look after their safety.

And have you heard the utter rubbish that Nizam Mohammed is talking? It seems everytime he opens his mouth these days, he puts his foot in it. And the TWO Opposition leaders are following in his footsteps. Manning was talking so much nonsense that the speaker was forced to shut him up! And Rowley is out to outshine the other PNM leader.

She was caught doing her vulgar thing at the Carib fete last Friday night - showing all for who want to see

'flesh trade' girls held

BOMB SEPTEMBER 5, 1997,

IMMIGRATION OFFICERS are trying to crack a ring involved in recruiting teenage girls from Guyana for prostitution in TT.

Over the weekend, Immigration officers from Port-of-Spain made a surprise raid on several nightclubs in the South and held 10 Guyanese girls, ages ranging from 18 to 22, and charged them with prostitution and some with being in the country illegally.

A source told The BOMB a number of Guyanese girls are coming to this country under the pretext as visitors and later end up as models parading in skimpy outfits and performing all kinds of lewd and suggestive dances.

They're also selling their bodies for high prices.

The source said the raid was planned dis-

crectly and only a few Immigration officers were told at the last minute for fear that word would have leaked out to the nightclub operators.

COPS LEFT OUT

The police were also left out of the raiding party.

The women appeared in court last Monday in South to answer the charges.

The BOMB was told years ago Guyanese

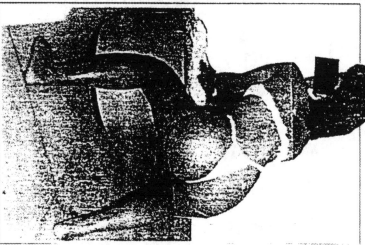

From modelling at fashion shows, the young girls turn to lewd dancing (above)

245

WIRE FRIDAY, OCTOBER 18, 2002

WireSpecial

FOUND under the many headlines of "massage girls wanted" and "escorts girls available", a new form of prostitution is growing.

Ever since its existence in local print media, the front put up by certain businessmen regarding these advertisments are a way of getting mostly "high-profile customers."

The young men and women employed with these agencies are not only involved in prostitution, but their employers use them in locally filmed "blue movies".

(15 years in jail... if you get caught!

UNDER the Sexual Offences Act of 1986, it is illegal for anyone to "procure another for prostitution, whether or not the person procured is already a prostitute, either in Trinidad and Tobago or elsewhere".

Relatives weep for guilty nude dancer, 14

EXPRESS NOVEMBER 20, 2001

By ALWYN DE COTEAU
South Bureau

A 14-YEAR-OLD GIRL yesterday pleaded guilty to dancing naked in a lewd and suggestive manner in a nightclub.

She was held when police raided the Prince Palace nightclub on Upper Hillside Street, San Fernando, shortly after midnight on Saturday. Four other women were also held and charged with dancing in a lewd and suggestive manner in a public place.

The case against the 14-year-old girl was held *in camera*.

The girl, who said she lived in Chaguanas, was remanded by Magistrate Melyn Daniel to the St Jude's Home for Girls, Belmont, until November 29, pending a probation officer's report.

The girl's father later told reporters she stayed with an aunt in Chaguanas and that he "never knew she was involved in nightclub dancing until he heard that she was arrested.

Other relatives of the girl were in tears at the end of the hearing in the San Fernando Fourth Court.

One of the dancers who was also charged, Cyanne Victor, 20, of Claxton Bay pleaded guilty and told Magistrate Daniel she became a nightclub dancer after her husband had left her with two children, aged two and three years, to look after.

Daniel then asked her: "When your children grow up and find out that their mother danced in a nightspot, how will you feel?"

CYANNE VICTOR, 20, sits in the back of a police jeep with other girls after the police raided Prince Palace nightclub on Upper Hillside Street, San Fernando, shortly after midnight last Saturday.

Photo: TREVOR WATSON

270

Lap dancing:
TORONTO STAR AUGUST 5, 1995, CANADA

DALE BRAZAO / TORONTO STAR

HIS STARS: Terry Koumoudouros of the House of Lancaster and four of his dancers. Koumoudouros says he doesn't allow any 'hanky-panky.'

☞ Continued from A1

Metro. Some call it dirty dancing. And it's legal.

It may not be what Ontario Court Judge Gordon Hachborn had in mind last year when he handed down his landmark decision legalizing the controversial dance that has turned some Metro strip bars into what critics say are virtual brothels.

But it's what those club owners have made of it, often over the vociferous protests of area residents, politicians — and many of the dancers themselves.

Lap dancing has created such a stir that Metro council will consider banning it at its Aug. 16 meeting, a month before an appeal of Hachborn's decision will be heard by the Ontario Court of Appeal.

"Anything goes at some of these clubs now," says Detective Terry Wark, lamenting how the Hachborn decision effectively handcuffed morality cops in their attempts to police the strip bars.

"Masturbation. Fondling. Fingering and sex," Wark says. "It's become legalized prostitution.

1) - The price of table dancing is $10.00 per dance. "YOU DO NOT HAVE TO DO ANYTHING EXTRA OR SPECIAL TO EARN YOUR MONEY!!!!

2) - Dancers will never allow a customer to touch their Breasts or their Genitals. Any Dancer caught allowing the customer to touch, lick or kiss their private parts will be dismissed immediately.

3) - It is totally forbidden for a dancer to be engaged in any sexually explicit activity within the club. Activities such as penetration, hand jobs or blow ____ ____ "ALSO, IT IS TOTA' ____ ORBIDDEN FOR ____

DALE BRAZAO / TORONTO STAR

DIRTY DANCING: Some dancers are asked to sign release forms like one at left.

NEWSDAY JULY 14, 2002

Taking a stand on lap dancing

Newsday July 14, 2002

LAS VEGAS: A gambling mecca also known as Sin City, is taking a stand for its infamous strip club performers — at least the ones who do lap dances.

A proposed ordinance would legalise lap dancing and then enact new regulations on the practice — despite the mayor's half-serious backing of the activity as a boon to business.

One proposed restriction, for instance, would ban the common custom of tipping dancers by stuffing dollar bills in their G-strings.

The new law would also prohibit any touching near the genital area and raise the minimum age for lap dancers to 21 from 18.

Clark County commissioner Yvonne Atkinson Gates, author of the proposal, said lap dancing is now illegal in the county, home to Las Vegas, but that the current law was vague and rarely enforced.

"What we're trying to do is do a better job of controlling it. According to our police department, there's a lot of prostitution in this kind of activity," she said.

Las Vegas Mayor Oscar Goodman last year urged constituents to go out and have a lap dance as way to support local business, which had slumped with the travel industry after the September 11 hijacking attacks.

Nightclub dancing mom escapes jail

NEWSDAY JUNE 21, 2002

By SUSAN BOODRAM

A 19-YEAR-OLD mother of one who pleaded guilty yesterday to lewd and suggestive dancing at a San Fernando night club, was given a second chance and some sound advice by a San Fernando magistrate.

Cradling her 14-month-old baby in her arms, Michelle Williams left the court with a pensive look on her face after she was reprimanded and discharged of the charge by Magistrate Sumnoneol Ramsaran.

"I don't think a fine or a custodial sentence is necessary in this case since you do not have to protect society from her, rather you need to protect her from society," Magistrate Ramsaran told Prosecutor Sgt Hansraj Morali, who said the defendant had no previous convictions or pending matters.

Williams had initially entered a not guilty plea when she was brought before the court last November, but yesterday she made an about turn and changed her plea to guilty.

The prosecution led evidence that around 11.30 pm on November 17, police officers carried out a police exercise at Prince Palace Recreation Club, Upper Hillside, San Fernando, where Williams, among others, was observed dancing in her underwear in a lewd and suggestive manner on a stage in the club. Williams was arrested and taken to the San Fernando CID where PC Ricardo Albert laid the charges. The court heard that the defendant was six months pregnant at the time of her arrest.

The girl told the magistrate that she had no family, and had limited secondary school education. Magistrate Ramsaran expressed his compassion to the teen: "Young ladies are under pressure in society. You need to make something of yourself.

"You still have a long time to settle in life and you are still very young...I hope you find maturity in life and make something of yourself. I am discharging you so that no conviction is against your name. Make the best of it," he advised.

Hinds: Cable TV spewing filth to youths

Page 14 NEWSDAY Thursday, March 28, 2002

By FRANCIS JOSEPH

GOVERNMENT Minister Fitzgerald Hinds said yesterday that cable television was spewing filth on the minds of the young people in this country.

He said Government spends $5 million annually on the Information Channel, but accepted the view that not many people would want to look at that station when it has to compete on a 24-hour basis with cable television, operated by the business community. The Minister was a guest at yesterday's Business Round Table discussion at the Hilton called to deal with the crime situation, among other things. Hinds' statement followed comments by William Latchman, public relations officer of DOMA who said that his organisation's thrust was to get the Government to do what it is supposed to do. Latchman said if the business community does what the Government is supposed to do,

then Government will sit idly by. He suggested that the Information Channel be used to prepare 250,000 children for the future.

"It is not that parents do not want to train their children, but they don't know how," Latchman told the business representatives and the media. Earlier, Vidya Lall, of the Centre of Criminology gave an outline of a survey conducted by her Centre aimed at dealing with the increase in school violence. Chief Secretary of the Tobago House of Assembly (THA) Orville London admitted that people will not look at the Information Channel. He advised that a programme aimed at dealing with improving the life of children be marketed aggressively.

CHAPTER 10. THE AUTOMOBILE AS A KILLING MACHINE. RISKING POLICE AND PEDESTRIANS LIVES IN CAR CHASES

I took up the "1995 STATISTICS OF ROAD TRAFFIC ACCIDENTS IN EUROPE AND NORTH AMERICA" PUBLISHED BY THE UNITED NATIONS. In this publication it gives a chronology of statistics from 1980 to 1993 arranged by country and under a number of subject headings such as: "Total Number of Persons Killed", "Total Number of Persons Injured", "Total Drivers Injured", "Road Traffic Accidents Involving One or More Persons Under the Influence of Alcohol."

I took the opportunity to look at the figures for a few popular countries and here is what the statistics provided:

1993 ROAD TRAFFIC ACCIDENTS
RUSSIAN FEDERATION
Total Persons killed--37,120 Total persons injured--192,802

UNITED KINGDOM
Total Persons Killed--3,814   Total Persons Injured-302,306

UNITED STATES OF AMERICA
Total Persons Killed--40,115 Total Persons Injured-3,125,000

I took up the publication "ANNUAL STATISTICAL DIGEST OF TRINIDAD AND TOBAGO 1993" published by the Central Statistical Office 1996, the details shown on page 146, No.40

Total Persons killed in Vehicular Accidents---161

Total Persons Injured ---3,532

While the above statistical figures do not decipher which deaths or injuries are from speeding, nevertheless the fact is that the compilation of such information on accidents indicates that the automobile is a potential death trap, Apart from drunk driving or intoxication by alcohol, "speed" is a major cause of vehicular accidents.

We must ask our selves these questions(1) why do countries establish by law speed limits? (2) why are speed humps lawful?

Habits are perpetuated, but when there has been a consistency of catastrophic danger to human life by a man-made invention called the automobile, we need to stop and take a re-visit to what is wrong with the automobile as manufactured or with the persons in conduction of the vehicle on our roadways. It is my opinion that both are at fault, the driver who breaks the speed limit and the manufacturer who provided the vehicle with capability to accelerate at speeds above required as safe.

For every vehicle that comes off an assembly line at a manufacturer's factory, the manufacturer must have some responsibility for the package built into the vehicle to be sold to a consumer. Speed is a manufacturer's inducement and an ingredient to entice the potential customer. Competition is the game among manufacturers and inputs of accessories and new innovations are splashed on the brochure pages of each new model as an end product.

The console dashboard with speedometer that shows 100 mph or more and its equivalent in metric are panacea for a heavy foot on a light accelerator pedal. The temptation to put the pedal down to the flooring and to test our ability against the speed of the vehicle is a temptation for many drivers and eventually it becomes the norm once the vehicle is out of home garage and on to the road. I ask the question why must a driver have to go at 75 miles an hour plus?

The faster the vehicle travels is the more blurred the vista ahead of the driver appears and the scenery on either side of his or her vision, not to even mention the braking condition and acute rapid response on the reflexes of the driver who is conducting the vehicle at the steering wheel.

Least we forget, that all vehicles are required by law to be insured, and have we stopped to think with the previous statistics of road vehicular accidents, injuries and fatalities what it cost in terms of payout by the insurance companies due to the negligence of speedsters? and the resulting rise in insurance.

Having made the previous statements it is urgent that countries find an alternative to combat the spate of onslaught let loose on lives by the methods of manufacturers' and their vehicular product.

The solution I wish to provide is to be found in some of the articles that I have put as supporting information to buttress my views in this chapter, however such views have not been implement by countries that make such suggestions, my views go beyond that by expansion. There is only one opinion so far that I have seen that parallels my solution and it is contained in a letter to the editor of a newspaper by a concerned individual.

My recommendation for this chapter to be applied to the recommendations at the end of this book is that(1) a United Nations Treaty or Convention be established providing a uniform speed code for all countries(2) that manufacturers be required to place speed capping devices that will govern the speed of vehicles no more than ten miles per hour above the uniform speed code limit(3) Only vehicles ordered by governments for ambulances, fire tenders, police, prisons and such emergency and security bodies be imported beyond the required law., and it these vehicles are to be auctioned or sold at a later date, it is incumbent upon the government to see that speed capping devices be placed on such traded vehicles upon sale. (4) Police officers lives are endangered when drawn into pursuit speed chases by un-yielding criminals or suspects who refuse to stop. Even the lives of other drivers and innocents are in danger.

The law should murder and life imprisonment where death of a police officer or innocent occur and where injury occur the penalty should be no less than fifty years in prison.

The three recommendations above be included in any UN Treaty and the fourth recommendation be left to national judicial systems to consider the severity. Time for a radical change if change is to become a reality for the better on our roadways.

277

NEWSDAY MARCH 3,1997

SPEED CAPPING/GOVERNING DEVICE

Speed limit chaos on Tanzanian roads

DAR ES SALAAM: Bus services throughout Tanzania were in chaos as traffic police enforced a new road safety order, local newspapers reported yesterday.

Under an order that took effect on Saturday buses must be fitted with devices to limit speed to 80 km (47 miles) per hour. But many bus operators ignored the order designed to cut road accidents, police officials said.

The semi-official Sunday News said bus services in many areas were crippled as police ordered buses off the road.

Dar es Salaam regional police commander Alfred Gewe was quoted as saying that only 202 out of 385 buses inspected complied with the new rule.

The government is trying to reduce road accidents which claimed over 1,000 lives last year.

(REUTER)

278

Brussels seeks 62mph car limit

SPEED CAPPING/GOVERNING DEVICE

SUNADY TIMES APRIL 6,1997, ENGLAND

by Peter Conradi
Brussels

SPEED limits on motorways across Europe could be cut to 62mph (100km/h) and all modern cars forced to run on unleaded petrol under proposals being drawn up by the EU to reduce air pollution.

The measures, likely to be passed by the European parliament this week, will require manufacturers to fit new cars with devices to restrict top speeds as well as eliminate leaded petrol by the turn of the century.

Car makers will also have to ensure that vehicles average 57 miles per gallon by 2005 — a go of their vehicles, which would make them slower.

also plans to reform the way cars are taxed to penalise vehicles that are the heaviest polluters.

Ken Collins, a Labour MEP and chairman of the parliament's environment committee, said tougher speed limits were needed as part of a package of measures to reduce exhaust emissions. Besides fitting speed governors, car makers would also be urged to reduce the power-to-weight ra-

in the pollution-conscious United States.

The European commission

"We all drive too fast and there is no doubt that a fast-moving vehicle emits more pollution than a slow-moving one. For that reason we are in favour of speed limits," he said.

Europe-wide curbs are certain to be resisted by Germany, which has no speed limit on much of its Autobahn network. Britain is also lukewarm about the idea. The issue, however, will be decided by majority voting. Sweden, Finland and the

Netherlands are the most sympathetic to change.

Car makers warn that the measures will cost £40 billion to implement over 15 years, which they say will be catastrophic for the motor industry and expensive for motorists.

Roger King, of the Society of Motor Manufacturers and Traders, said there would be little environmental gain from reducing the speed limit. "A 62mph speed limit would be a total frustration, we would all become law-breakers."

At the heart of the proposals is the planned curb on fuel consumption, seen by MEPs as

a first stage towards a target of 95 miles per gallon (mpg) by 2010. According to car makers, average consumption is currently about 40mpg.

Equally controversial is the proposal, endorsed by the commission, to sell only unleaded fuel by 2000. While demand for leaded fuel has dropped dramatically since catalytic converters became obligatory on new cars in 1992, it still accounts for about a third of sales in Britain.

John Dawson, the AA's policy director, said: "We would be seeking exemptions for older vehicles if there was no

proven alternative fuel available."

The final package will be subject to qualified majority voting in the council of ministers. If three big nations object, they can block particular elements of the plans. It is likely a compromise, binding on member states, will emerge reducing speed limits.

The maximum speed allowed in other countries is either 130km/h (81mph), as in France, or 130km/h (75mph), as in Belgium and the Netherlands. A ban on leaded petrol is certain to go through with temporary exemptions.

Watercraft builders set speed caps

TORONTO STAR NOVEMBER 17, 1999, CANADA

SPEED CAPPING/GOVERNING DEVICE

BY HAMIDA GHAFOUR
STAFF REPORTER

Those personal watercrafts that whiz by at breakneck speeds on quiet cottage lakes won't be going any faster.

Two of the biggest manufacturers of the machines have agreed informally to cap the maximum speed that their products can reach at 104 km/h (65 m.p.h).

"Some of the higher end watercrafts were reaching up to 60 to 64 miles an hour (96 km/h to 103 km/h)," said Mark Lacroix, a spokesperson for Que-

bec-based Bombardier Recreational Products, which makes the popular Sea-Doo brand.

"What we wanted was to stop a speed war between manufacturers."

The speed cap is a voluntary pledge that Bombardier and Minnesota-based Polaris will honour, he said.

Although the agreement was made in the United States, the cap will also affect personal watercraft by both companies sell in Canada.

The speed cap is effective immediately on new watercraft

but will not affect those used for racing.

Bill Ariss, boating safety officer with the Canadian Coast Guard, said the change is a positive one, although watercraft accidents make up a "very, very small" proportion of fatal boating accidents because most operators wear life jackets.

A speed cap may also be cost-effective.

One executive said adding an extra mile per hour to a model costs an additional $1 million.

THE SUNDAY TIMES · 9 JANUARY 2000

SPEED CAPPING'GOVERNING DEVICE

Don't look, but Big Brother just got into your car

We newspaper columnists are self-centred egotists, so I doubt that my colleague Jeremy Clarkson will have read this far; he will have checked his own column on page 15 and then gone off to the pub.

Which is just as well. He is not going to like what I am about to say. Unless I have made a grievous misjudgment — in which case, since he is considerably larger than me, I offer a craven apology — Jeremy is one of those testosterone-fuelled men who regards it as his inalienable right to drive his absurdly powerful cars the way he chooses.

The average male motorist is a sucker for those advertisements that promise you a car that will accelerate faster than a nuclear particle and leave the more puny specimens in its lead-free wake. We pay lip service to notions of safety and reliability, but we are brilliant drivers and all that safety stuff is really for wimps who do not know how to handle half a ton of metal and rubber. Have you ever heard a man admit to being not very good behind the wheel? Precisely. Here is why Jeremy and his pals are about to blow several gaskets.

We learnt last week that, within 10 years, electronic gadgets may be fitted to all cars that would prevent the driver exceeding the legal speed limit. We are not talking about the crude speed limiter that has been fitted to lorries and buses for years. This is infinitely more sophisticated.

There would be a satellite navigation system to pinpoint exactly where your car is and a computer built into the car would be loaded with a digital road map encoded with the speed limits for each street and road in Britain. Push your foot too hard on the accelerator and the gizmo will cut off your fuel supply. Apparently it works. For three years they have been trying it out and the findings will be presented to John Prescott next month.

Road safety campaigners love the idea. They say it would reduce the number of people injured in accidents every year by a third. Two thirds of the 3,500 deaths on the roads would be prevented. Surely nobody can argue with that. Are you kidding?

some of the ways in which our freedoms to escape Big Brother have been eroded in recent years, he just might.

A few weeks ago a senior executive from Peugeot impressed me with a demonstration of a gadget to be installed in its latest car. It is a tiny mobile phone fitted to the dashboard; when you shout "Traffic" at it, a voice comes out of a speaker telling you what lies ahead.

It could not do that unless somebody, somewhere, knew where you were at that precise moment, as well as knowing how much traffic there was ahead of you. The way they know is that you are being photographed by cameras fitted to motorway gantries and little blue lampposts on A roads. But don't worry, they say; the cameras can photograph only the middle of your number plate and not the whole number.

That may well be true, but I shall bet a Box Brownie to a digital camera that if, one day, "they" decided it made better sense to snap the whole number, they would have no problem. And if they want to take a picture of your front-seat passenger and feed it to a central police computer . . . well, why not?

Another company, Global Telematics, has a system called Orchid that does everything except make the tea and find you a new companion for life. If your car is stolen, the

inbuilt computer tells a satellite where it is to within 10 yards anywhere in Europe. If the thief tries to drive off, it can shut down the fuel supply. If you are driving a delivery van and stop for a cup of tea, the boss will know. The van's computer can report back every five minutes if that is what is wanted. Wherever you are on the main roads of Britain somebody, somewhere, is keeping an eye on you. It is the same if you leave the car and try hoofing it. By last spring the number of closed-circuit television cameras (CCTV) installed in our fair land had passed the 1m mark and has been shooting up ever since. If you wander around any big city centre, it is reckoned that you will be filmed about 300 times in a day.

Switch on your mobile phone and that tells another computer precisely where you are. Use your loyalty card in a supermarket and you have told another computer more about your personal habits than you might wish your best friend to know. Or your boss.

That's another thing. In the modern office, bearing in mind the amount of time you are being photographed by one surveillance camera or other, you might as well wear full television make-up and have done with it. The computer will also know how long you spend at the keyboard or in the loo, what

phone calls you have made and if you have sent an e mail to your secret lover at the next desk.

Strange, is it not, that people allegedly so concerned with their personal freedoms should allow themselves to have become so spied upon. Do you remember being asked whether you minded? No, neither do I.

We have allowed it to happen, I suspect, for three reasons. First, it has been gradual. The earliest CCTV cameras started appearing in shops — the private property of the owners — and we all enjoyed a good giggle when we were caught on camera and our pictures were displayed on fuzzy monitors. Then they invaded our public spaces and the monitors were tucked away, watched by solitary security men.

Second, each little advance in the onward march of Big Brother has been sold to us with a promise of great benefits. We may not care for the notion of being photographed on the open road, but what joy to be able to dodge the traffic jam three miles ahead. Not that we will have succeeded in dodging it for long if every other driver seeks the same escape route.

We may not like being ogled by security cameras the moment we leave our front gates, but if it means the streets are safer to walk, well, that must be a price worth paying. Assuming, again, that the crime is not merely being displaced elsewhere. Not to worry, there is a solution to that, too: more cameras in even more places.

We may be a tad uneasy about every Tom, Dick and Tesco knowing our most intimate shopping details, but we console ourselves with all those bonus points and discounts. We tend not to question how much cheaper the food could be if the shops were not spending so much money on operating the schemes in the first place.

Mostly, however, I believe we have allowed the great surveillance society to develop because we never were too concerned about our personal privacy in the first place. We tend not to question how much cheaper the food could be if the shops were not spending so much money on operating the schemes in the first place.

Mostly, however, I believe we have allowed the great surveillance society to develop because we never were too concerned about our personal privacy in the first place. Politicians have spotted that, which is why they have been compliant and pay only lip service to defending our freedom from intrusion. That, plus the fact that it suits the interests of the state. Politicians in power love information: the more the better.

John Humphrys

In control: Prescott has new ways of making you drive more slowly

LETTERS

SPEED CAPPING/GOVERNING DEVICE

HOW TO STOP ROAD DEATHS

THE EDITOR: It will be wise for the Ministry of Transport and the Licencing Department to observe our highway laws and apply them properly.

Ninety-nine percent of our road deaths occur on our major highways. The speed limit on our highways is 50 mph or 80 kph. But vehicles are being licensed for reaching 120 mph and more.

Why not govern-down (by laws) all vehicles not to exceed the speed limit? The only vehicles which should not be governed-down should be the police, ambulance, army and emergency vehicles. This measure will save hundreds of innocent police on our roads.

lives and will help to curb other crimes. The crooks and the criminals will not be able to out-run the

Vehicles travelling at such terrific speed become a "bomb" similar to the airplanes which struck the World Trade Centre in New York and Washington. Why licence a vehicle to go beyond the lawful speed limit? If a maniac wants to kill himself, he or she should not use our highways to do so. They should hang themselves in the seclusion of their house or go into the safety of the forest to do so.

Not on the highways where innocent human beings lives are endangered. Why should a vehicle travel beyond 50 mph or 80 kph when the law says you should not?

The Ministry and Licencing Authority should be held responsible for this oversight.

DR HARRY RAMNATH
Marabella

90 km/h limit eyed for trucks

TORONTO STAR FEBRUARY 27,1997,CANADA

Safety bottom line: Minister

■ Day 2 of the blitz, A34

By CAROLINE MALLAN
QUEEN'S PARK BUREAU

Trucks may be forced to reduce their speed on Ontario highways to 90 kilometres an hour in an effort to clean up the industry's safety record, Transportation Minister Al Palladini said yesterday.

"Speed limits are on the table and I think that we would get support from industry," Palladini told reporters yesterday, adding that Ontarians can expect more tough safety measures to be announced in the coming months.

The minister, who this week introduced legislation that would impose a fine of up to $50,000 on the owner or operator of a truck that loses a wheel, said public safety has to be the bottom line.

"What I think and what industry and what Ontarians will think might be totally different," he said. "But safety has to be practised and I think the rigs should be travelling at a safe speed, where that vehicle can stop in the case of an emergency."

Palladini said a safe speed might be 90 km/h, rather than the current 100 km/h limit.

He said the lower limits might be introduced along with stricter rules to keep trucks out of the passing lane.

"One thing for sure that does

☞ Please see 90 km/h, A34

New device puts brake on speeders

CANADA

SHARP EYE: Constable Robert Frison, of Metro's traffic services, points a laser speed measuring device at vehicles on Eglinton Ave. W. in Etobicoke. Police say these new units are more accurate than radar systems and make it easier to nab speeders.

TORONTO STAR AUGUST 30,1996,CANADA

PETER POWER / TORONTO STAR

TORONTO STAR AUGUST 20,1999,CANADA

Police chase rules studied

Tsubouchi wants life sentence for loss of life

BY CAROLINE MALLAN
QUEEN'S PARK BUREAU

Ontario's solicitor-general called yesterday for a sentence of life in jail for anyone who kills someone while fleeing police.

David Tsubouchi told a meeting of the Police Association of Ontario, the police unions' umbrella organization, that he is pushing the federal Liberals to drastically increase the penalties for fleeing and for killing or injuring someone while trying to outrun the police.

"I am pressing the federal government to make changes to the Criminal Code that will toughen the penalties for such drivers and that should mean the possibility of a life sentence," he said.

The solicitor-general also said he thinks anyone whose driving while fleeing police results in a loss of life should face a lifetime driving ban. He said he is working with the Ministry of Transportation to up the penalty from the current maximum suspension of two years.

Tsubouchi's speech follows a series of tragedies where both innocent bystanders and police officers were killed as the result of a police chase.

Stolen car in police pursuit going 160 km/h, sources say

TORONTO SATR MARCH 24, 1999, CANADA

Vehicle's owner warned off chase, 911 tapes show

■ Chase rules coming soon, B5

> **'I was following the car, I was not chasing it.'**
>
> — RENÉ ROBICHAUD
> CAR OWNER'S FRIEND

By JOHN DUNCANSON
POLICE ISSUES REPORTER

A stolen car flew by a police radar trap on Kingston Rd. at an estimated 160 kilometres an hour just 33 seconds before the crash that killed a Macedonian priest, police sources say.

Constable Dwayne King was on radar patrol on Kingston Rd. near Morningside Ave. when the stolen Buick raced by abaçç

9 p.m. Sunday, according to sources.

A 911 tape of conversations between a police dispatcher, two civilians who were following the stolen car and other officers at the scene has become the critical piece of evidence under review by the province's special investigations unit.

Police sources who know the contents of the tape say it shows what happened in the frantic few minutes before the crash which killed Father Ilice Miovski, 50, a leader in Toron-

to's Macedonian community.

The father of two grown children died instantly when the stolen car sheared off a utility pole and spun wildly out of control on Kingston Rd., near Manse Rd.

One of the key issues emerging in the tragedy is the role of two civilians whose voices are heard on the tape: Edmond Pallot, the owner of the stolen ve-

hicle, and René Robichaud, the friend who was helping him follow it.

Pallot had left his 1996 Buick Regal idling in Robichaud's driveway on Homestead Rd. and noticed it missing about 9 p.m. Sunday.

The two got into Robichaud's van to look for the car and spotted it a short while later on a nearby residential street.

As they followed the car, Pallot called police on a cellular phone.

Pallot told reporters Monday that he lost the car about two

☞ Please see Stolen, back page

NEWSDAY JULY 7,1998, page 3

Mom killed in police chase

Newsday July 7, 1998, page 3

By RICHARD CHARAN

DHARMATIE MOONASAR repeatedly begged for her life, while she, and four passengers of a run-away PH taxi were taken on a high-speed chase through the streets of Chaguanas, as the crazed driver attempted to elude police, and three motorists whose cars he had just hit.

However, the 38-year-old mother of one, of Boysie Trace, Kelly Village, was virtually held hostage by the driver who refused to stop the vehicle. She died instantly, when the car, a yellow Ford Laser motorcar, crashed into a tree, a wall, and the garage of a home.

The PH driver was last night in critical condition at the Port-of-Spain General Hospital, and should he survive, police say, a charge of manslaughter as well as a number of traffic violations, will be preferred against him.

The four other passengers of the car, Parbatie Ramkaran, Sita Ramoutar, and Serena Mahabir,

JOSEPH, aged nine, son of Dharmatie Moonasar.

PHOTO BY AZLAN MOHAMMED.

friends of the dead woman, and an unnamed male, were all treated for minor injuries and discharged. *Newsday* spoke to lucky survivor, Parbatie, who recalled that at around 9.30 p.m. on Sunday, the group of women left a chutney show held at the Rienzi Complex, Couva, and Parbatie, who was in the front,

seat passenger, said that the driver put his hand around her neck to prevent her from getting hold of the steering wheel.

After speeding through several back streets, the driver ended up in a dead end road where the car crashed into a tree, a wall, and the garage of a house before coming to a stop.

Police believe that the dead woman met her death when the car struck the tree.

The driver was thrown from the vehicle on impact, and was found under the collapsed shed sometime later. "That man take my sister's life," was all that her brother, Micheal could say.

Dharmatie's only child, nine-year-old Joseph was inconsolable, as he related how he last saw his mother on Sunday afternoon. "The last thing she told me was to eat all my food", a meal of chicken, peas and rice.

Dharmatie was one of ten children. She lived with common law husband, Richard.

Cpl Sookdeo is investigating.

In search of a ride home. She said that the driver called out to them saying that he was heading to Chaguanas.

During the trip the four women negotiated with the driver to drop them at Kelly Village for $40. "All of us got in with another man, and we pass on the (Solomon Hochoy) Highway."

But when the driver took the off ramp at the Chaguanas flyover, all hell broke loose, Parbatie said. In attempting to make an illegal right turn onto the Montrose Main Road, the "PH" car collided with another vehicle. But instead of stopping, the driver sped from the scene, driving the wrong way along a one-way thoroughfare.

In a scene of absolute mayhem, the car struck two other vehicles, while other motorists barely escaped by pulling onto the pavement. "We kept begging the man to stop and let us out, but he tell us to shut up."

CHAPTER 11. CRIMES AGAINST HUMANITY--THE ROMAN CATHOLIC CHURCH'S INVOLVEMENT IN MURDERS/GENOCIDE: MAKING ORGANISATIONS PAY FOR THE CRIMES OF THEIR POSTHUMOUS LEADERS, SINCE NO STATUTE OF LIMITATION SHOULD APPLY IN INTERNATIONAL LAW AS SHOULD APPLY IN A CHARTER OF AN INTERNATIONAL CRIMINAL COURT--WE HAVE NOT FORGOTTEN THE

Pope Says Church to Ask Forgiveness

Washington Post September 2, 1999

VATICAN CITY—Pope John Paul II said the Catholic Church would start a new page of its history in 2000 by publicly seeking forgiveness for the errors, injustices and human rights offenses it committed.

Speaking at his weekly general audience, the pope did not specifically list the church's errors but previous Vatican documents have spoken of seeking forgiveness for its treatment of Jews, the Inquisition and human rights abuses.

"As the church looks to the great jubilee of the year 2000, she is aware of her continual need of purification and penance," he said. "She therefore wishes to ask pardon for the sins and weaknesses of her children down the ages."

Why the Pope is sorry

SAVING FAITH *John Paul's condemnation of religious intolerance highlighted the church's great assault on human rights: the Spanish Inquisition.*

A14　The Globe and Mail, Thursday, January 12, 1995　CANADA

BY ERNA PARIS
Special to The Globe and Mail

I N November, the Pope issued a remarkable statement in anticipation of the 2,000th anniversary of Christianity. The church, he wrote, has an obligation to express "profound regret" for the weaknesses of her sons and daughters who sullied her face over the centuries. "Members of the church, he went on to say, have practiced "intolerance and even the use of violence in the service of truth."

It is widely believed that the Pope was referring to the church's involvement in two of history's most inhuman episodes: the Spanish Inquisition and the Nazi regime.

The papal announcement was both startling and, from a theological point of view, revolutionary. The church, the Pope was suggesting, cannot concentrate on saving souls while ignoring the world of heretics. On ridding the world of heretics served to purify the true faith. The literal meaning of the phrase used to describe the death sentence meted out by the Inquisition . . . "act of faith."

Time magazine's Man of the Year, the author of a book that has stood atop bestseller lists around the world, Pope John Paul II is very much a man of the moment. Today, he arrives in the Philippines to begin an 11-day Asian tour that will see him rally the faithful in the name of the Catholic Church. But while the Pope is responsible for administering the day-to-day workings of religion, he also addresses faith's larger ramifications. Recently, as a way of preparing a clean slate for the church's 2,000th anniversary, he looked back at the church's way belief can sometimes go terribly wrong.

which as Protestants, homosexuals and "witches."

Hannah Arendt coined the phrase "the banality of evil" in reference to the Holocaust, but she might have been talking about the day-to-day business of the Inquisition. The charges brought against the convert class were strikingly commonplace. A heretic might be someone who was wearing clean clothes on Friday, the Jewish sabbath, or a father who placed his hands on the head of his child without making the sign of the cross as a blessing. One woman was sent to the stake for seeming to smile when she heard the name of the Virgin Mary. People who escaped were "burned" in their absence — in effigy. Even the deceased were accused. Their bones were dug up and put on trial.

Family bonds disintegrated, and fear was rife since even small children might unwittingly reveal Jewish practices that had taken place in their home. Incriminating conversations of years earlier, from easier, pre-Inquisition days, were remembered and reported.

And like the Nazi bureaucracy that provided a solid framework for the Holocaust, the Spanish Inquisition was superbly organized. In 1483, Ferdinand and Isabella created a special body, called the council with responsibility for all matters connected with heresy. The Suprema, as it was called, established a formal hierarchy of command. The Inquisitor-General, appointed by the monarchs and responsible to them, was at the top, assisted by everyday workers, including Inquisitors. The Inquisitors everywhere in Spain knew better than to cross the powerful Inquisitor-General. In one case, he angrily ordered a group of his underlings to burn a prisoner

In Pedro Berruguete's 15th-century painting, the church's inquisitors lord it over the condemned.

Why the Pope is sorry

A14   The Globe and Mail, Thursday, January 12, 1995

> The Inquisition's practices — and it is surely this that troubles the Pope — are painfully familiar to the modern observer: spies, torture, isolation cells, secret trials and a network of informers

For an astonishingly long time — from 1481 until 1834 — the Spanish Inquisition (officially known as the Holy Office of the Inquisition Against Depraved Heresy) exercised firm control in Spain. The Holy Office was established by King Ferdinand and Queen Isabella, with the permission of Pope Sixtus IV, to purify the Catholic faith.

In 1391, many were suddenly faced with a choice between death or forced conversion. Thousands converted, of course, and some turned into sincere believers. But not all became devout Christians. Baptism consisted merely of a few drops of holy water and was not accompanied by instruction in the new religion. By the middle of the 15th century, some "old Christians" — as distinguished

The Spanish Inquisition was created to punish baptized converts and their descendants, and not (contrary to common belief) to persecute unconverted Jews;

The practices of the Holy Office in Spain — and it is surely this that troubles Pope John Paul II — carry with them a painful familiarity for the 20th-century observer attuned to abuses of human rights. The authorities made use of spies, torture, isola-

At the heart of the *auto da fe* was a clever semanticism that would disturb a Pope as sensitive to language and politics as John Paul. Since the official business of the Holy Office was to purify the faith and save souls, a euphemism had to be invented to mask the reality of execution. In the parlance of the Inquisition, prisoners condemned to death were immediately "released to

The Inquisition's frenzied attack on the *conversos*, as they were called, lasted about 40 years, until virtually all the most likely victims had been flushed out and sent to trial. (One inquisitor was heard to complain loudly that there were no more "Jews" to prosecute.) Only then did the Inquisition begin to turn its attention to other minorities

(In spite of the stern reputation that has followed him through the centuries, Tomas de Torquemada is not reviled in all quarters. Just last November, I interviewed a Spanish priest who spoke respectfully of "Father Torquemada" throughout our conversation.)

In the museum of the Prado, in Madrid, there hangs a famous painting by the 15th-century master Pedro Berruguete of St. Dominic presiding over an *auto da fe*. It was commissioned by Torquemada himself

The painting ostensibly depicts the so-called "papal" inquisition that was established in the 12th century to root out the Albigensian heresy in southern France.

Beneath them in the lower right corner of the canvas are the condemned. Two men are shackled to the stake, consumed by flames; others wait their turn. Unlike the inquisitors, these are stick figures without importance. The loss of their insignificant lives is irrelevant to the somnolent men seated above them. Berruguete has depicted the essence of tyranny: the desensitization of the perpetrator and the diminished human status of the victim.

THE SUNDAY TIMES · 29 NOVEMBER 1998   LONDON, ENGLAND .

Martyr to the cause: Cranmer paid the ultimate price for his faith when Mary restored England to Catholicism.

Now Catholic bishops are planning to apologise for her excesses

Catholics to say sorry for Bloody Mary's terror reign

THE SUNDAY TIMES · 29 NOVEMBER 1998

by Christopher Morgan
Religious Affairs Correspondent

THE Roman Catholic Church is drafting an apology for the religiously inspired excesses of Bloody Mary, one of England's most brutal monarchs.

The Catholic bishops of England and Wales have identified the five-year reign of Queen Mary, daughter of Henry VIII and elder sister of Elizabeth I, as one of the most savage eras in the history of the 2,000-year-old church.

The 28 bishops are deciding whether to make their formal apology next week as a contribution towards Human Rights Day and as part of the church's campaign in the run-up to the new millennium to reconcile its modern claim to the moral high ground with its often violent past.

Queen Mary's reign between 1553 and 1558 marked the high point of the counter-reformation, when the Papacy attempted to reclaim countries lost to the Protestant reformers earlier in the century. Nearly 300 Protestant leaders were burnt at the stake in England.

The most prominent martyr was Thomas Cranmer, Archbishop of Canterbury and author of the Book of Common Prayer. Facing death in Oxford, he signed six "recantations", saying that all Protestants should obey the queen and follow her faith, but at his last sermon in St Mary's Church he regained his nerve and declared: "As for the Pope, I refuse him as Christ's enemy."

He then ran to the stake shouting "This hand has offended" and thrust it into the fire so that the fingers that signed his original recantation were burnt first. He was then consumed in flames.

Mary was the daughter of Catherine of Aragon, whose marriage annulment from King Henry was the catalyst for the Rome, breaking away from Rome. Mary saw it as her personal crusade to re-establish the link, and married Philip II of Spain in a vain attempt to bring England back into the Catholic sphere. Her policy was deeply influenced by friars sent directly from Rome to keep her on message.

Church leaders are unwilling to accept blame. British bishops and the Secretariat are still discussing the final form of words and a decision may not be taken in time for Human Rights Day. There is, however, believed to be a consensus among the bishops that Bloody Mary is a stain on their forebears.

The steps towards an apology were set in train in 1998 when Pope John Paul issued a plea to his followers to prepare for the millennium by atoning for the past. In his Apostolic Letter, Tertio Millennio Adveniente, he urged Catholics "to return with a spirit of repentance" to periods of intolerance and violence, such as the Holocaust and the Inquisition.

Holocaust and the Inquisition results will be published before Ash Wednesday 2000, which the Pope has set aside as a day of repentance. Catholics in Britain, and all over the world, will hold a ceremony in the afternoon asking forgiveness for the sins of church members throughout history.

In the Guy Fawkes's night celebrations at Lewes in East Sussex, prayers are said in commemoration of the 17 Protestants burnt outside the Star inn during Mary's reign. Local Catholics are, however, offended that an effigy of the Pope is still burnt as retaliation in the festivities.

Pope Urges Indians to Forget Church's Past Mistakes

Washington Post September 15, 1987

By David Maraniss
and Loren Jenkins
Washington Post Staff Writers

PHOENIX, Sept. 14—Pope John Paul II urged Indian leaders to forget his church's past "mistakes and wrongs" and look to its current efforts for Indians' rights. But a spokeswoman for Indian Roman Catholics told him there was still much to be done in his church, and in America.

Addressing a three-day conference of about 1,600 Indian leaders from around the United States, the pope described the initial encounter between Europeans and American natives as a "painful reality" for the natives' descendants.

"The cultural oppression, the injustices, the disruption of your life and your traditional societies must be acknowledged," he said, while specifically praising Friar Junipero Serra, the early Franciscan missionary who embodies, for Indians, all the ancient abuses of the church.

"Unfortunately, not all the members of the church lived up to their Christian responsibilities," he said. "But let us not dwell excessively on mistakes and wrongs, even as we commit ourselves to overcoming their present effects."

The unfortunate past to which the pope referred involved the zealotry of many Roman Catholic priests who accompanied the Spanish conquistadors colonizing the West in the 17th and 18th centuries, proselytizing among the Indians they encountered and, often, killing those who would not convert.

"The church still has much to answer for to us," said Sacheen Little-Feather, an Apache delegate to the Indian conference here. "It is a matter of the church's cultural genocide against the Indians that must still be addressed by the missions."

To the Indians, the chief representative of that dark era of Spanish-Catholic colonization is Serra, a Spaniard who helped found the Catholic missions of California.

Catholic history records him as a staunch defender of the Indians, whom he worked zealously to convert. Indian history remembers him for the deaths of Indians who resisted his efforts.

Pope John Paul II had been expected to honor Friar Serra's missionary labors in the 18th century by beatifying him, a church step toward proclaiming him a saint. But the protests of native Americans forced the pope to reconsider.

Nonetheless, in his address today, the pope praised Serra, a church martyr known as the "Apostle of the Californias" for his evangelizing mission.

Jeannette Henry Costo of the Eastern Cherokee Tribe and spokeswoman for the Indian Conference said: "I'm sorry, I'm terribly sorry he said that. I think it's disgusting. We have presented evidence here that Serra committed atrocities at his California missions against Indian peoples. The pope talked about perpetuating our language, but praised a man who tried to destroy it."

Staff writer Laura Sessions Stepp contributed to this report from Tempe, Ariz.

WORLD HISTORY
MADE SIMPLE

BY

JACK C. ESTRIN, M.A.

Chairman, Social Studies,
Richmond Hill High School, N.Y.C.

MADE SIMPLE BOOKS
DOUBLEDAY & COMPANY, INC.
GARDEN CITY, NEW YORK

97

The penalty was to be banishment and confiscation of property. This was a relatively humane punishment since the common people were putting heretics to the torch.

Frederick II ordered in 1224 that heretics were to be punished by fire and mutilation; this barbarous practice was then endorsed by Pope Gregory IX. Pope Innocent IV then legalized the use of torture to secure recantations. In the thirteenth century the Inquisition was turned over to two new organizations, the Franciscan and Dominican Friars. They gave to it an orderly procedure. The primary object of the Inquisition was to save the soul of the heretic. For this purpose he was confronted with the accusation (not the accuser), asked to confess and to do penance. If the heretic recanted, he was punished by temporary imprisonment, banishment, property loss, or he was forced to go on a pilgrimage. If he was stubborn, he was then subjected to torture of the cruelest kind to force a confession from him. This failing, he was turned over to the secular arm for burning or mutilation, torture to enforce conformity, death for free thinking.

If the heresy persisted, then the Church could apprehend the heretics, jail them and submit them to a Holy Inquisition.

The Albigensian heresy was exterminated by the Inquisition. During the course of the heresy, the Pope and the Emperor Frederick Barbarossa had ordered the clergy to proceed to the infected areas and to conduct inquests. If they found any who would not be "instructed" by them, they were to turn them over to the secular authorities for punishment.

Widespread heresy could be met by the ultimate weapon only—the crusade. When Innocent III took papal office, the Albigensian and Waldensian heresies were rife in Toulouse, in the southern part of France. He tried persuasion through dispatch of preachers into the region, but to no avail. Raymond VI, count of Toulouse, was tolerant of these heretics (while formally a Catholic) and refused to use force against them. He was therefore excommunicated. Raymond ignored the excommunication. Innocent had no choice but to preach a crusade against Toulouse. He did so and in 1209 Philip Augustus of Paris (who was more interested in Raymond's land than his faith) led an army southward. Frightful slaughter was inflicted upon the inhabitants of Toulouse, both the heretics and the innocent. The battle cry was, "Kill all . . . for God will know his own." The heretics were in this manner exterminated.

OFFICE OF THE PRIME MINISTER
TRINIDAD AND TOBAGO
PUBLIC RELATIONS DIVISION.
PRESS RELEASE

WHITE HALL,
ST. CLAIR,
PORT-OF-SPAIN.

PRESS/RELEASE NO: 625   8th November, 1974.

RELIGION, SCIENCE, UNIVERSITY AND RACISM
CONVOCATION ADDRESS DELIVERED BY DR. ERIC WILLIAMS,
PRIME MINISTER TO ANDREWS UNIVERSITY, BERRIEN SPRINGS,
MICHIGAN, ON 27TH OCTOBER, 1974.

The distinguished Caribbean psychiatrist, Frentz Fanon of Martinique,
who placed his services at the disposal of the Algerians in their War of
Independence, whose classic, The Wretched of the Earth, was almost compulsory
reading for university dissentors up to a few years ago, raised one of the
most crucial questions facing the world today in his equally well-known work,
Black Skin, White Masks, the sub-title of which is "The Experiences of a
Black Man in a White World".

I am a student particularly concerned at the moment with the New World
experience in the field of race relations. I am also a representative of
a small Caribbean country with which your Church has established a harmonious
relationship. Your President has kindly invited me to participate, from the
standpoint of the academic discipline of history, in your Convocation, the
theme of which is "Seeking Understanding of God's Creation". You are also
today dedicating a new science complex. Against this background I have
selected as my subject "Religion, Science, University and Racism". I trust
that you will not consider this an impropriety or a subject inappropriate
African slavery was the foundation of church power in the new world.

The church that was brought to America by the European invader, whether
catholic or puritan, was a militant church, engaged in an internecine civil War
over religion. The blood of heretics was the seed of the church: whether the
Inquisition, or Calvin's persecution of Servetus, or the savage sentence of
Zwingli that the anabaptists should be "drowned without mercy". As Milton
testified, new presbytar was but old priest writ large.

PENTECOSTAL ASSEMBLIES OF CANADA

AN EXAMPLE OF A CHURCH BY CONTRAST THAT IS NOT KNOWN FOR ANY OVERT HUMAN RIGHTS VIOLATIONS

PENTECOSTALS: WHO THEY ARE AND WHAT THEY BELIEVE   27

PAOC General Superintendents

George A. Chambers
1919-1934

James Swanson
1935-1936

Daniel N. Buntain
1937-1944

Campbell B. Smith
1945-1952

Walter E. McAlister
1953-1962

Tom Johnstone
1963-1968

Robert W. Taitinger
1969-1982

James M. MacKnight
1983-1996

William D. Morrow
1997-

AME Church Bicentennial

EARLY BLACK FOUNDED CHURCHES WHICH HAVE FOUGHT AGAINST RACISM AND SLAVERY IN THE CHURCH IN U.S.A

NEW PITTSBURGH COURIER, MAY 2, 1987

CELEBRATION—Rt. Rev. Richard Allen Hildebrand, Presiding Bishop of the Third Episcopal District, is shown addressing the congregation during the Third District Bicentennial Celebration held at St. James AME Church, Pittsburgh.

RECOMMENDATIONS

(1) STATE RIGHTS OVER INDIVIDUAL RIGHTS: Individual rights granted by a constitution are not absolute but are subject to abrogation. Democracy does not always mean that the voice of the majority is right, this is one of the drawbacks of absolute democracy.

Protectors of civil liberties may at times impede that which is good for the collective will of the state. Therefore any constitutional reform must establish that the rights of the state for the good of all must take precedence over individual rights.

(2) MERGE ARMY AND POLICE INTO ONE NATIONAL SECURITY FORCE: Trinidad and Tobago does not need an army, Costa Rica and Lichtenstein disbanded their armies long ago and established a single National Security Force that polices and defend their territorial sovereignty against crime, internal insurrection and external aggression.

Exigencies and training of former army personnel into methods of policing can easily be worked out since joint army/police patrols have been on-going for a long time, existing salaried manpower will be actually doubled limiting annual recruitment of personnel and limiting the augmentation of addition salaries from the national budget.

(3) FIREARM POLICY AND AIR GUN LAW OUTDATED: The cutlass, machete is a more vicious weapon and always ready it needs no accessory. A new semi-automatic handgun can cost $US 300.00 and in Trinidad from $TT3000.00(see displays, prices pages included in that chapter). A house,lot of land or car cost far more than a handgun so how do you compare the process of relative valuation? A gun is useless as a weapon without the installation of ammunition. The mystique of how a firearm operates has been dealt with in that chapter. The rifling of a handgun's barrel is merely the grooving of the inside of barrel in spiral turns allowing more accuracy and distance(see description in chapter) so it makes little difference in a smooth bore FPS.Backward values policy.

Time to allow law-abiding adults the use of rifled airguns. Time to empower the longstanding,stable family,law-abiding citizens who own their home and a lot of land, with financial assets the right to own .22 semi-automatic pistols(no higher calibers) and remove their vulnerability to armed criminals. This will include junior police officers of proven character the right to a lease .22 caliber(not higher)firearms especially provided for at their assigned station. Retired senior police officers will be allowed .22 caliber(not higher) handgun ownership since they have re-entered the civilian ranks. Guards of security firms be allowed .22 caliber automatic handguns. Only the National Security forces be allowed higher caliber automatic weapons. The firearm policy become a state law a one man's arbitrary domain of who he feels deserve a firearm.Wild West?

(4) YOUTH CURFEW LAW NEEDED: In the chapter, I provided the reader with several newspaper reports of youths 16 years and younger raped murdered or in trouble while out late at night and into the early dawn of morning. It is a wide spread habit which has become pervasive.

With high crime rate, violence and drug trafficking in schools, there is need to preserve younger generations for a better future. In the USA, England and a few countries youth curfews have been implemented, we need to put such laws in place.

Youths or juveniles 16 years and younger should not be allowed on streets by law between the hours of 9.30pm and 6.00am daily unless accompanied by an approved parent or approved adult guardian, or travelling with approval. Failure to comply will render such youths to be picked up by the police and provide officers with identification as to their age, parent/guardian, address before being turned over to such adults with a warning.Further infractions of the law by both parent and youth will bring penalty according to the law.

(5) POPULATION GROWTH CREATING POVERTY, URBAN SPRAWL AND CRIME: The reader has only to read the number of poverty cases I have included in this chapter to see the effects of physical and mental demands. Government can no longer play god father/mother, substitute parent for children the government did not make.Taxpayers money each year are absorbed in provisions to feed, clothe, educate, transport, medicate, employ the down-trodden, while parents-single or not keep ad infinitum supplying the poverty sexual reproduction factory of society with babies.

Government must legislate/mandate a two child policy per family! The tax system must be re-orientated to give incentives to those who try hard to maintain good, stable family structure with two children. The more children one makes the more you pay or provide alternatives to the state.

Many birth certificates of children have the mother's name alone, but every child must have a father(unless test tube).Therefore by law every birth certificate must carry the name and address of both parents unless in cases of rape, medically proven test tube or paternity challenge. Too many men are escaping their responsibility. There must be a law that upon pregnancy, both mother and father(she must know who he is) be required to register their names and address, place of employment,address and submit to a medical at the doctor's office who will retain such record. Failure to comply will require the police to investigate if there is a paternity challenge.

To counter any paternity challenge there must be by law established a National DNA Database of every individual including children. This forensic system will be useful for any criminal challenges of identification need by the police and coroner/pathologist.

Too many homes squatting on the hills and plains unchecked without any individual home identification (street and house number). Government must limit the number of houses per each new housing development settlement(allowing greater management control by police station precinct of residences and home identity). The Municipal, Borough or Regional Corporations must enforce under their law Act No. 21 of 1990 article 140.

Abandoned buildings and lots left by absentee owners and used as havens for criminal activity are now being successfully cleaned by the Community Environmental and Enhancement Programme workers. Act No. 21 of 1990 articles 177, 188 demolition of abandoned buildings must be enforced and charges of expense passed on to house/land owners.

Loitering can be a nuisance and the right to peaceful assembly only applies to non-nuisances and non-congregating for unlawful purposes. Rights to the quietude and non-hawkers on pavement immediately in front of a residential home or commercial must follow the law on loitering which must be enforce. Amend chapter 11.02 of 1980 Laws.

On domestic violence, the only way to curb violence in the home is for girls and women to make wise choices in their selection of male friends, background check is important or we will continue to see deaths at the hands of boyfriend or spouse. Even with a strengthen domestic violence law.signs of temper must be looked for early. Men too must be careful in the type of women they choose lest they take up unsavoury women. Good character is a virtue. Maybe a shame policy of putting the pictures,names,addresses of abusers in public places such as post offices, bus terminals etc may be useful.

(6) LEGALIZE ABORTION AND EUTHANASIA: A law must be established that a embryo is not a human being. Late term abortion as established medically beyond the third month is illegal with exception to the endangerment of the mother's life abortion for rape, incest, and severe deformities are legal grounds.

Euthanasia should be legal where over lengthy period, establish by law a brain dead, comatose or vegetable state exist. Where terminal illness, or extreme pain persist,hopeless is end. 1 Samuel 15 verses 1--3, Numbers 31 verses 1--18.

(7) A PUNITIVE LAW TO DEAL WITH DELINQUENT PARENTS OF JUVENILE DELINQUENTS: If as a responsible parent you have tried to give proper guidance to your child, but your child has followed bad company and has become lawless and un-manageable; then any proposed law will require such a parent to report to the police the child for warning and counselling, this is to absolve blame from the parent by investigating the home environment and may question neighbours to get a clear picture of the problem. When such a child under 18 years breaks the law, then he or she will face the court.

This law proposed is to deal with parents who have been ir-responsible in their control of their child and has encourage or allow their child to engage in anti-social behaviour resulting in breaking the law. Such parent must pay for the crime of their child by methods which such a law will require. I have included in this chapter a number of reading information on this area as other countries seek to grapple with this problem of the delinquent parent and the delinquent child.Amend Cpt 46.01,Act 19,1994.

(8) MAKE ILLEGAL, ABUSE MANUFACTURE AND TRADE OF HIGHER ALCOHOL ABOVE (2 % ALC) BY UNITED NATIONS TREATY AND DOMESTIC LAW. ALCOHOL IS A CASUAL FACTOR IN CRIME: In this chapter I defined alcohol from the Oxford Dictionary, it is the ingredient that intoxicates. It has an addicting effect and alteration on the behaviour of the imbibe of alcoholic beverages by its stupefying effect. It is more dangerous than marijuana and is compatible with cocaine, heroin and other hard drugs. It is the only drink that is included with a warning in motor vehicle driver manuals and the only drink that the blood level and breath is tested by police. Where is the breathalyser law? Amend Chapter 48:50

There is need for a UN Treaty on narcotic drugs and psychotropic substances classing alcohol above (2 % alc) as a dangerous substance and therefore illegal for production and international trade.

(9) EXISTING LAW BANNING OBSCENE LITERATURE, STRIP DANCERS, PROSTITUTES AND PIMPS MUST

(a) include cable television programming (b) confiscation of the proceeds and property of those involved in the sex trade(as in the proceeds of crime in drugs etc) (c) zone night clubs, recreation gambling clubs, alcohol establishments, discos, entertainment establishments outside of residential areas (d) Strengthen the

environmental police mobile fleet and noise decibel testing apparatus into a national network attached to county police stations.

(10) UNITED NATIONS TREATY AND DOMESTIC LAW A REQUSITE FOR VEHICLE MANUFACTURERS TO INSTALL SPEED CAP DEVICE CURBS WITHIN ROADWAY SPEED LIMIT LAWS.(a) Only emergency vehicles, ambulance,fire ,police,military vehicles allowed above the speed limit law (b)death or injury from police high speed chase require stiff jail penalty.

WE HAVE NOT FORGOTTEN

(11) CRIMES AGAINST HUMANITY-MURDERS/GENOCIDE: MAKING ORGANISATIONS PAY FOR THE CRIMES OF *THE*IR POSTHUMOUS LEADERS, SINCE NO STATUTE OF LIMITATION SHOULD APPLY IN INTERNATIONAL LAW AS SHOULD APPLY IN A CHARTER OF AN INTERNATIONAL CRIMINAL COURT-CONVENTION ON THE NON-APPLICABILITY OF STATOTORY LIMITATIONS TO WAR CRIMES AND CRIMES AGAINST HUMANITY

Adopted by the General Assembly of the Onlted Nations on 26 November 196B* United Nations, **Treaty Series,,** *vni.* **754, p. 73>**

Convention on the Non-Applicability of Statutory Limitations to War Crimes and Crimes against Humanity, 1968

The Convention, in article 1, provides that no statutory limitation shall be applied to the following crimes, irrespective of their date of commission:

(a) War crimes as they are defined in the Charter of the International Military Tribunal, Nürenberg, of 8 August 1945 and confirmed by resolutions " % *

(b) Crimes against humanity whether committed in time of war or in time of peace .

(12) On January 14,20001 provided a research paper "POLICING THE NATION OF TRINIDAD AND TOBAGO" I suggested and with documentations the need for a law that will allow the police via the courts to be allowed to intercept mail and tap/bug phones/ cell phone eavesdropping of suspected and known criminals as part of police intelligence gathering and information surveillance co-ordination(pages 1,2,11 and 12).

In police communications/observance systems I suggested the use of thermal imaging zoom cameras used in the under-belly of surveillance aircrafts,heat scanning devices with heat sensing equipment(pages 3,6,13,15)

Vehicular traffic video cameras scanners on selected streets and police cars; and station close circuit television monitors of selected streets (pages 5, 6, 16, 18).

In police identification systems, I suggested the use of integrated multifunction computers fitting of police cars with computer consoles capable of bringing-up the photo or mug-shot and criminal record of legal name and address of owner or anyone stopped by the police.

Look up car number plates stolen or otherwise, voice activated allowing police officers to speak into computers without having to drive back to the station precincts, and hooked up also to Transport Licensing Department.

Computer database on fingerprints, with cross-checking, criminal records history, missing persons, illegal aliens and deported persons, stolen firearms/firearms records and portable finger print equipment of a small reader on which a suspect's fingers are placed on a small reader while the computer automatically relay back to police station precinct from the police car(pages 4,5).

High density mapping of "crime hot spots and methods of control (pages 7, 8, 20, 21, 23).